EMDR for the Next Generation: Healing Children and Families

By

Joanne Morris-Smith and Michel Silvestre

EMDR for the Next Generation: Healing Children and Families.

First edition, December 2013
Second Edition, June 2014

Disclaimer: While every effort has been made by the editor, authors and the publishers to ensure that all the material in this book is accurate and correct at the time of going to press, any error made by readers as a result of any of the material, formulae or other information in this book is the sole responsibility of the reader. Readers should be aware that the URLs quoted in the book may change or be damaged by malware between the time of publishing and accessing by readers.

ISBN printed soft cover: 978-1-910309-20-9
ISBN printed hard cover: 978-1-910309-21-6
ISBN ePub: 978-1-910309-22-3
ISBN Kindle: 978-1-910309-23-0

Printed by Lightning Source UK Ltd..

Published by: Academic Publishing International Limited, Reading, RG4 9SJ, United Kingdom, info@academic-publishing.org

Available from www.academic-bookshop.com

We would like to thank our spouses Thérèse and John
for all their support.

Note about the children's drawings.

The children's drawings in this book have been reproduced without any enhancements or touching up. As a result the visual quality of their reproduction is variable

About the authors

 ***Joanne Morris-Smith*** is a Consultant Chartered Psychologist who has been working in clinical child psychology for the last 33 years and has worked in a number of British teaching hospitals. She is an EMDR Europe Accredited Child & Adolescent Trainer, an EMDR Europe Consultant and also an EMDR Institute Facilitator. She chairs the EMDR Europe Child & Adolescent Section Committee. In 1995, Joanne founded and continues to run a child trauma clinic in Surrey. She also has a private practise and works as an expert witness with children exposed to physical/emotional/sexual abuse, domestic violence and murder.

 ***Michel Silvestre*** is a clinical psychologist and a family therapist who has been in private practise since 1999. He is an accredited EMDR Institute Facilitator, former Chair of the EMDR France Association and an EMDR Europe Accredited Child & Adolescent Trainer for France. He is a graduate of the Mental Research Institute, Palo Alto, California and a Lecturer at the University of Psychology in Aix-en-Provence. He also trains and lectures extensively in France, Belgium and Quebec in Canada. He is a member of both the American Family Therapy Association and the European Family Therapy Association.

Both Joanne and Michel have been awarded prizes for their work in EMDR research from the University of Lorraine in Metz – Michel for his work in developing EMDR in France and Joanne for applying EMDR with children and adolescents in Europe.

Contents

i

Contents

Contents

Contents

Foreword

It is very exciting when two esteemed colleagues collaborate on a book on EMDR and family therapy. It is even more exciting when the book exceeds expectations. Such is the case with Joanne Morris-Smith and Michel Silvestre, who have written *The Next Generation: EMDR for healing children and their families*. As you will see in their opening to the book, both have many years of clinical experience with children and families. Joanne had excellent training in attachment theory and therapy in the UK and with autistic spectrum children. Michel trained at the renowned Mental Research Institute in Palo Alto, California in addition to his graduate work in France. In addition, both have been highly involved in training other child therapists in EMDR throughout England, France and Europe. What they have learned as therapists training other clinicians also informs their book. From their accounts, they both were looking for better therapeutic methods for working with children and their families, parents and/or caregivers. The present book is testimony to their clinical skills, their dedication to improving therapy, their excellence as teachers, and their organizational skills.

Let me say a word about their organizational abilities: because of their vision of having EMDR child trainers organize the training in their own countries, they (along with others), made it happen. EMDR child training leaders in each country are now trained to the same standards across the UK and Europe, acting as training heads in their own countries, due to their greater knowledge of their own country, the culture, the language, the professions and the laws. Further, child training leaders are required to submit videos of their own work with children in four different age groups (0-2; 3-4; 5-7 and 8-12) to actually demonstrate their own proficiency. Due to this rigorous standard, Europe is now ahead of the US in the basics of actual practice of EMDR with children, as the US has no such behavioural standards of competence. Such clear standards are helpful, not only to the practitioner, but also to researchers. No other therapeutic approach has such a consistent treatment package. Even cognitive-behavioural approaches have components that vary from study to study, making it difficult to compare results.

The sense of history of EMDR in the UK and Europe with children that Joanne and Michel convey in their introduction is wonderful, as they are able to document its beginnings in Bergen, Norway in 1996, and carry it forward, as it spread from country to country. Joanne, in particular, made sure that training occurred every few years in London, so that child therapists, trained in Parts I and II, could obtain the credentials to become child training leaders for children in their own countries.

I hope the above comments establish that there could be no better qualified EMDR practitioners and experts to write *EMDR for the Next Generation: Healing Children and Families.* And because of their complementary areas of knowledge and experience, it is definitely a case of two heads being better than one.

On the first reading of *EMDR for the Next Generation* I was impressed with its integration of family therapy with EMDR and the insights derived from such. However, on second reading, I am even more impressed with the way these two clinicians interweave knowledge of research, developmental psychology, family therapy, neuroscience, and clinical cases into a tapestry of understanding that illuminates the field of EMDR therapy. Every five to ten years I have been fortunate enough to find a book that is so progressive and integrative of thought in psychology and psychotherapy that I recommend it to everybody. Outside of seminal books in EMDR (thanks to Francine Shapiro), they have been such books as Daniel Goleman's *Emotional Intelligence*, The Developing Brain, by Daniel Siegal, and *The Brain that Changes Itself* by Norman Doidge. *The Next Generation* is now one of those books for me. I will be recommending it heartily to my consultees; to all EMDR therapists; to non-EMDR therapists who wish to learn about EMDR with children and families; to parents of children in EMDR, or contemplating it; and to lay persons.

Readers may note that I have had a professional relationship with these authors, who have learned from Sandra A. Tinker-Wilson and myself (among others) with our work with children and EMDR, and used the knowledge as building blocks in a way that is additive: honouring the past and turning it into something creative, new and better. Only extremely knowledgeable and experienced clinicians, learned in multiple disciplines could have written this book. It is an honour to write a foreword to it. That there is only one other book integrating EMDR and family therapy (*Handbook of EMDR and Family Therapy Processes* edited by Shapiro, F., Kaslow, F.W. and Masfield, L., 2007) is perhaps silent testimony to the complexity and difficulty of the task.

The Next Generation is a very thoughtful and emotional book. The research cited is well-selected and fascinating. It provides a background for the cases described in the book; allowing for each case to be intellectually stimulating as well as relevant. In addition, the cases are emotionally evocative. They might bring a lump to your throat, or a sense of awe, or might even be startling. Successful cases that might be considered highly rare in their resolution, appear so frequently in the book that you might get the sense that they are more common than in other forms of therapy. I was a CBT, marital, family and interactional therapist for a number of years before being an early adopter of EMDR. I remember being astonished at the outcomes I started seeing with EMDR. I still get astonished at times, and this book adds to that sense of wonder. The final chapter is a description of child and family cases that range from simple, to highly complex and involved, taking place over a period of years. These cases illustrate the diversity of application possible with EMDR, as it gets successfully applied to anorexia nervosa, Autistic Spectrum Disorders (ASD); intergenerational domestic violence; traumatic bereavement of an eight-year-old girl's father, where the girl has a diagnosis of Asperger's; to suggest something of the range of application.

In fact, one of the most interesting chapters is the chapter on children with Autistic Spectrum Disorders (ASD). It provides many specifics on using EMDR with such children. While I have worked with therapists or consultees who have used EMDR with ASD, this is the first time I have seen anything in print. It will be a boon to EMDR therapists who might have ASD children in their caseload and might be apprehensive about where to start. There are enough cases, and enough conceptual aspects provided to be of great help to such a clinician. It reminds me of how we all started with EMDR: we tried something and it worked. So we tried it again with another child and it worked again. It's good to remember that the first, single observation is the beginning point of science. Where we go from there is validation and clarification. This chapter lucidly shows how EMDR provides the therapist and the parents of the ASD child an understanding and a resolution of the symptom. Having consulted with an Autism Program for ten years (before EMDR), I wish I had had this chapter back then to deal with some of the symptoms that I saw on a frequent basis. The behavioural approaches we used back then provided no such understanding and no such resolution.

EMDR for the Next Generation integrates child development, the neuroscience of trauma, and the practice of EMDR in a way that no other book in the field does. The understanding of the case deepens as these different aspects are explored. The format goes something like this: a child becomes traumatized and the family seeks therapy; the family context is explored; and different members of the family are treated, based on the dynamics of psychosocial situation. Research that is relevant to the age of the child and the child's development, as well as pertinent research in neuroscience become part of the case study. A particular case might be examined repeatedly in different chapters, deepening our understanding in additional ways. In fact, when one looks at the chapter headings in this book, it is as if the authors have taken almost every current topic of importance related to EMDR and psychotherapy and applied it to working with traumatized children and families; whether it is neuroscience, developmental psychology, resilience, dissociation and integration, attachment theory, attunement, preverbal memory, the concept of the window of tolerance, and/or trauma diagnosis and how it relates to DSM and ICD diagnoses. This is not an overly simplistic approach, and the authors have done EMDR and the field a real service by being willing to look at the complexities of EMDR, children, and family therapy. Thus, clinical cases are looked at like diamonds, where many facets are examined, not just one or two. This is accomplished with clear writing, and an eye to what is helpful to the practitioner. The chapter on case histories is a good example of that. In fact, this book does what a good book on EMDR should do: it covers the basics, such as how to apply the eight phases of EMDR treatment to children of different ages and their families or caregivers. It also explores the more complex topics, such as the manifestations of dissociation in children, or the importance of attunement.

One of the implications of this book is that the best EMDR and family therapists are trained in working with children, adolescents, adults and families: certainly no easy task, and not accomplished overnight. We are fortunate to have authors who have accomplished this themselves, along with their excellent selection of research, pertinent to the topics at hand. Their book is up-to-date on the literature, but also honours earlier research that has been groundbreaking. A wealth of useful resources is included for the interested practitioner to use in assessment, child development and related topics.

Overall, this is an exciting and truly integrative work, aimed at helping the next generation of children. However, it is also integrative enough and state-of-the-art enough to be aimed at being of great value to the next generation of EMDR therapists.

In gratitude,

Robert H. Tinker

Preface

How it all began

Joanne Morris-Smith

The second eldest of four children born to two social scientists with rather liberal and considered slightly left wing parents, I grew up with a great degree of freedom of choice and opportunity. The only main requirement my parents stipulated was that none of us consider ourselves finished with our education until we had been to University. My first degree in psychology was gained from the University of Zimbabwe, which at the time was still a part of University College London. Zimbabwe, then called Rhodesia, was a troubled land with conflicting politics and interest. I did not realise at the time how traumatised the land was becoming as I was growing up in it. It was whilst I was studying for my Masters in Child Psychology at the University of Nottingham in 1977 with Professors John and Elizabeth Newson that I began to become more aware of how the troubled adult world in Rhodesia was impacting on its children.

It all began when during the course I mentioned that at home children made their own toys. At the time, the commercial production of 'imitation' wire toys for export had not yet begun. Thus what I was saying was quite surprising to the course members and I decided that the best way to demonstrate these to them would be to collect some of them and bring them over. I initially approached the psychology department at my old University with this idea. They were rather disconcerted and did not feel it was something that they would want to participate in. Thus my father and a colleague, who were working in the townships at the time as social workers, organised a competition at a local school. They arranged for the children to be given books as prizes for their work. They were told just to bring in a toy they had made. The children were delighted to get books as prizes as these were treasured and costly and also thrilled to know that their toys were going abroad so others could see them; it made them feel famous and valued.

I ought to explain that the children were financially impoverished, but resource rich and very creative as all children can be when given the opportunity. The culture of making toys is a phenomenon which exists up and down Africa and seems to be a part of the 'child culture' as children are taught how to make toys by other children not by their adults. They commonly make their own toys from available resources to hand, clay, wood, maize cobs, tins, bottle tops, lengths of wire, bits of rubber, rags, cardboard and plastic. From these they would fashion their own miniatures of the world around them as they experienced it. Wire cars with long extended steering wheels that they could then push around as they walked on dusty paths were a favourite as well as maize cob dolls. The joy of these toys was that they could be created at any time and changed in any way according to the child's spontaneous imaginative whim.

The competition gained a wonderful collection of completely original and unique toys, which were then shipped over to Nottingham. The toys were subsequently exhibited at the Bethnal Green Toy Museum and are now housed long term in a Toy museum in the Peak District. The toys included a variety of wire cars, maize dolls, household implements and furniture in clay, wood and wire. There was also a helicopter made out of wire covered with scraps of stockings and then painted in camouflage green and brown with a toy soldier peering out of it. Gunship helicopters were by then beginning to make regular appearances in the skies as the political troubles grew and provided sights that were becoming a part of the children's daily world view.

My clinical life has been spent working in different teaching hospitals in the British National Health Service and I have been fortunate to encounter many wonderful and gifted therapists and other leading specialists who have helped me to develop. Whilst I gained a very broad experience of most of the kinds of problems children and adolescents and their families encounter I also continued to develop a greater expertise in understanding the Autistic spectrum disorders and helping these children, as knowledge of them was a particular aspect of the Nottingham University's Masters Course. The children were troubled by daily living and trying to understand a world in which they could not fully communicate nor fully understand. Their idiosyncratic thinking and encounters with daily life led to the development of multiple fears and coping strategies that were often maladaptive and in time produced greater problems for them and their families.

After 15 years of working with these children in particular and also others I felt it was time to learn something new and I was given the wonderful opportunity of working with Dr Dora Black and her team at the Royal Free Hospital learning about traumatic bereavement and trauma in children in the Children's Trauma Clinic. The clinic saw children who had been exposed to the most devastating trauma of all; the loss of one parent at the hands of another; which effectively meant that they lost both parents one dead and the other incarcerated. There were also children suffering from traumas as a result of domestic violence in lesser forms, abuse and traumas from other man-made causes. The work involved identifying their needs and working with them and the systems around them to try to achieve positive futures for them, including the legal system. It was a very steep learning curve and I learned that if one did have to hear, digest and study very traumatic material that the good thing about being able to do this was that the child was then no longer 'alone' in their devastation. I also soon realised that in fact most of the therapy that I was doing was exactly the same sort of therapy I had been doing with autistic children; the difference being that the autistic spectrum children were traumatised by everyday life, including things like haircuts when in their eyes this literally meant pieces of themselves being chopped off; and the others being traumatised by man's incredible inhumanity and carelessness towards his fellow men. There was a sense of achievement in being able to relieve some of all these children's pain and suffering and helping them and their carers back onto the path of a happier and more spontaneous childhood, though we were constantly looking for better methods to achieve this.

It was in the course of this work that I came to hear of a very strange new treatment for trauma and decided that I would need to learn more about it. I was highly sceptical when I heard that waving fingers in the face of a patient could bring about significant healing. I undertook my level I Eye Movement Desensitisation and Reprocessing (EMDR) training in Bergen with Dr Roger Solomon, an EMDR Institute Trainer in 1996. I remained very sceptical during this and thought that the videos that were being shown had been done so by using actors rather than authentic clinical sessions. I could not see how to apply the adult techniques to children and felt that they would not tolerate nor understand the complexity of much of the process.

I consoled myself that there was one day to climb one of the mountains around Bergen before a further two-day workshop given on EMDR with children given by Dr Bob Tinker and Dr Sandra Wilson. I anticipated a further two days of implausibility and assumed if there were videos these too would probably be acted by child actors! I must have been a very difficult trainee as I continually challenged and questioned both the clinical knowledge and the ideas being put forward. I am eternally grateful to Bob and Sandra for persisting with me rather than asking me to leave. Their patient, clear and insightful answers and their obvious genuine commitment to treating children with empathy and respect together with their wonderful clinical skills and numerous video tapes and case examples convinced me that I should abandon my scepticism and learn all I could from them. There were so many excellent examples with such a variety of children and problems using child-friendly terminology and adapted protocols to different developmental levels with obviously genuine cases and in all of which significant spontaneous and incredible changes in their affect and belief systems occurred. I became fascinated and curious. How could all this therapeutic change be achieved in such a relatively brief period of time and in such an in-depth and spectacular fashion? I became determined to learn to do this therapy properly myself and actually try it out. At the time I doubted if I too could affect such changes and was in awe of Bob's gifted therapeutic skills.

I discovered that there was a United Kingdom & Ireland EMDR association and joined it. I began to attend the London meetings and try to find some supervision for the work that I was doing. This was a lonely period because although every meeting had a good attendance no one else there was working with children. With the help of Dr John Spector a small group of like-minded professionals began to collect. Then with the support of Professor Bill Yule we started an interest group at the Association of Child and Adolescent Psychology and Psychiatry in London (now known as the Association for Child and Adolescent Mental Health ACAMH). This was at first to share ideas and experiences of our use of EMDR and then the notion of developing a conference developed.

I met Bob and Sandra again at EMDR International Association conferences in the States and regularly pestered them for advice and impromptu supervision of my work. I also asked them if they would be prepared to come and give a similar workshop in England. They helped me to think out how such a workshop could be run and I went home full of plans. At the time I had little money and the whole thing could have been disastrous. I could not believe that you could just ask people to come and do this; and that they would trust you and commit to it; and then just come on a wing and a prayer. To my amazement they did in 1999 and the first workshop was attended by over 30 highly enthusiastic people. The ball had started rolling and Bob and Sandra gave two further child workshops in United Kingdom over the next couple of years and also gave an advanced workshop on troubleshooting in more difficult and complex cases in 2002.

In the meantime I was invited to join the UK & Ireland Board and had also began my EMDR Institute facilitator training and at Dr John Spector's request was giving speciality presentations on EMDR with children within the level II training. John has been a most wonderful mentor and supporter of the Child and Adolescent Sections both in UK & Ireland and in Europe even though this is not his area of clinical expertise.

By now I had begun the painful, revealing task of making videos of my work to learn from and from which to teach at Bob Tinker's suggestion. It was the children themselves who have taught me and continue to teach me the most about using EMDR with them and I began to discover just how incredible the child's capacity to heal themselves really was when the therapist could stay out of the way of the processing and enable it by using the protocol properly. I also discovered just how robust the process is, even when the therapist in the process of learning made mistakes. I learned in a series of steps how to trust the process and adapt it to meet very complex needy cases.

Michel Silvestre

My work as a psychologist specialised in family therapy has presented me with so many different clinical situations over the years. I had become interested in the work with families during the last two years of my psychological studies. Working with families always appeared to me the right thing to do. I had been fortunate to grow up in a very stable and protective environment that gave me a strong faith in family resources and made me appreciate the importance of attachment qualities in the making up of oneself.

My initial training as a family therapist has taught me the ability to work with all the different members of a family in order to help them develop their capacity to change when faced with difficulties. This co-construction of coping skills, in an interactive way, allows the mobilization of the family resources in the face of the multiple consequences of a traumatic situation. Nevertheless in many situations this family therapy work did not seem sufficient to erase the traumatic recurrent manifestations existing as traumatic flashbacks in their everyday life. Something was missing in the treatment offered that was needed in the healing process.

My first encounter with EMDR therapy was in 1994, during the first training organised in France in Aix-en-Provence by a psychiatrist François Bonnel. I realised that there was in this new therapy something that could be a response to some of the difficult situations I was dealing with, as a director of a counselling centre working primarily with domestic violence situations. The family therapy work seemed sometimes to have reached its limit when the recurrent fears or emotional hyper-arousal seemed to appear again even though the family and the couple work had been very satisfactory. The treatment of domestic violence has been the starting point of my interest in EMDR.

How to keep helping the victims and the perpetrator to go beyond the traumatic consequences of the violent behaviour when the family work does not help any further? How could I help the children, the passive victims of this violence, to carry on with living, growing and especially not to repeat in their own futures this dysfunctional pattern of relationships and behaviour? How could I help these children without asking them to constantly recount the traumatic events, but rather help them to focus on what happened and think and draw just what was relevant to them about the incidents?

EMDR Therapy, through its application and practise and the questions that arise as a result of this, aroused my curiosity and excitement. Looking back, I can say now that I experienced two major crossroads in my professional development. The first one was my training as a family therapist at the end of my university studies in psychology, when I went to the Mental Research Institute to undertake my clinical internship at Palo Alto, California. My practise as a family therapist was enriched by different experiences with a wide ranging population from psychiatric hospitals to non-profit organisations and private practise. The second major crossroad was in 1994 during this first EMDR training of two days. The consequences of this were multiple and enriched my professional life. My interest rapidly grew in how to integrate EMDR therapy and family therapy in particular in the work with children. This integrative approach seems to be very pertinent because we know that children, through their symptoms, express their suffering and also can express the family's suffering.

My first training in EMDR with children was in Paris, with Drs Bob Tinker and Sandra Wilson in the year 1999/2000. I was amazed by how this particular clinical work was being done. It gave me so much hope to heal the children and end the suffering and so much hope for them as future adults. Then I was taught and supervised by Dr Joan Lovett who demonstrated so much creativity in her work with children. I was later invited by Joanne to join the exciting European group of EMDR child and adolescent therapists. Years later I became a child and adolescent trainer.

In order to bring out the richness and complexity of EMDR, we have written this book with two hands intertwining our professional experiences. This book will talk about the specific use of EMDR with children, adolescents and also family work.

The Development of the European Model

Michel and I first met in Utrecht at the first EMDR Europe conference in 2000 where a child paper was presented by Carlijn de Roos and Renee Beer. At the end of the conference I was invited to join the EMDR Europe Board as a representative for Children and Adolescents. On the board giving great encouragement and support to the development of the Child Section over the years were Arne Hofmann, Ad de Jong and John Spector to whom we all in the Europe Child and Adolescent Section owe our thanks. In a chance encounter on the railway platform when leaving the conference I also met Margareta Friberg from Sweden. We recognised each other as both having been to the same workshops. I told her of the brief I had just been given, I was nervous and uncertain; Margareta was very enthusiastic and supportive and thus the first Country recruit, Sweden, to the EMDR Europe Child Section was historically made on a railway platform. We began the process of collecting names of child and adolescent clinicians who could become representatives for the Child Section of the European Board. We began to network and I invited everyone to give papers to the conference that the ACPP (now ACAMH) special interest group was planning to hold. We now had people who could give papers of case examples and we invited Bob Tinker and Ricky Greenwald to be the plenary speakers. Dr John Spector was invited as the EMDR Institute Sponsor in Britain and Chair of the UK & Ireland Association to provide the opening introduction. The conference had magically taken form.

Whilst most were able to come, unfortunately Michel was unable to commit to the conference as he was undertaking the painful task of closing down the Domestic Violence Clinic, one of the first its kind in France, due to budget cuts.

The conference held in October 2000 was attended by around 300 people and was held at the Church House in Westminster (Morris-Smith, 2002). This was particularly historic as it was in this building that in 1945 the first meetings of the United Nations Preparatory Commission and Security Council were held. It was a very thrilling conference, not only was it very controversial at the time, but none of us knew what the others had done and the papers were enthralling, as we each realised what was being contributed and what we could achieve collectively with the knowledge.

At the dinner after the conference the European Child and Adolescent (C&A) group was formed and it began to meet regularly every six months. The first country members were UK, Sweden, Netherlands and Denmark. And then the following countries joined over the next 10 years: Finland, France, Germany, Greece, Israel, Italy, Norway, Switzerland and Turkey. There are to date 17 Country members and more joining. The aim of the C&A Committee was to establish gold standards for training of EMDR with children and to develop a European model of understanding the developmental needs of children adolescents and their families in the context of EMDR. Our goal was to achieve consistent standards across Europe, with trainers for each European Country able to offer the training in their own language and with their own children so that the cultural aspects could be fully respected. Further to develop a Child & Adolescent Stream for the EMDR Europe Conferences and to promote research and knowledge in this domain and additionally to develop Child & Adolescent Streams for our national conferences and to form national sections in the national associations. If we could establish a consistent model of child training then we would be able in the future to compare cases and research between the countries (Morris-Smith, 2006).

The training for working with children and adolescents is not a replacement for the generic Level I and Level II or Parts 1, 2, & 3 EMDR training. The generic training sequentially precede the specialised training for clinicians in Child and Adolescents EMDR Therapy.

There were several models of working with children and adolescents using EMDR in the USA developed by Bob Tinker, Ricky Greenwald, Joan Lovett and Carol York. By this time most of them had also presented a workshop or a paper in some part of Europe and their work was known from those of the group who were also able to go to the EMDRIA conferences in the USA and their published papers. Ricky Greenwald, Joan Lovett and Bob and Sandra Tinker-Wilson also published their books in 1999 which had by this time also reached and spread across Europe.

The C&A section decided to follow the model of working with children and adolescents developed by Bob Tinker and Sandra Wilson and also informed by additional information from the work of Ricky Greenwald and Joan Lovett, whom by invitation had also given workshops in London.

The C&A Section further decided in 2001 that it needed to develop their own trainers and invited Bob and Sandra Tinker-Wilson to give the first trainers training and this was held in Colorado Springs in 2001. Five of the group who were EMDR Institute facilitators were able to attend it. It was followed by two further training sessions in 2003 and 2005 in Farnborough, UK. By 2003, Child and Adolescent Level I training were accredited by the EMDR Europe Association. Also by 2003, child training was already being given to clinicians in Spain, Sweden, UK, Germany, Netherlands, Israel and Italy; and a short form was also given as a part of Humanitarian Assistance Programme (HAP) work in Turkey following the earthquakes there. There are Child & Adolescent EMDR Europe Accredited Trainers in Denmark, France, Germany, Israel, Italy, the Netherlands, Sweden, and the United Kingdom.

In 2007, at the EMDR Europe Conference in Paris, Bob Tinker was a keynote speaker and received a standing ovation from 800 people for his wonderful work with children and adolescents. It was suggested by Bob and Sandra Tinker Wilson at this conference that we take on the next C&A European training of trainers. Thus in 2010 with the agreement of the EMDR Europe Child and Adolescents Trainers and the approval of the EMDR Europe Child Section Committee, the first ever all European C&A Trainers training was held in Farnborough and three more C&A trainers from Germany, Italy and Spain have been accredited.

The Child and Adolescent trainers soon realised that there was a need to develop a Level II training to work with complex traumatised cases. It is a part of the evolving process and individual prototypes were already tried in Finland, Germany, and Italy. The trainers group were beginning the process of delineating what should be included in this Level. The first intensive 4-day brainstorming of this advanced training was held in 2007. A European accredited level II training is now being given in Belgium, France, Germany, Netherlands, Finland, Switzerland and UK. To date, more than 3000 people have been trained across Europe to the same consistent standards.

We began to work together at the first EMDR Europe Accredited C&A Level I training in Paris in 2004. This proved an interesting and enriching learning experience. This book is our way of trying to integrate the complexity of the work with children and adolescents and their families. We hope to present EMDR therapy techniques for children in a broader developmental context aimed at creating a more holistic practise for children, adolescents and their families.

Chapter 1

EMDR: History and the Developmental Protocol

1.1. Introduction

Our work as psychologists has put us in contact with major and minor life events which have disturbed the functioning of the individual child or the family. One family was getting ready to settle to their evening meal when their world was shattered when a saucepan full of oil fell onto a little boy's chest; another family was traumatically bereaved when the eldest son died alone on a road on the way back from school; in yet another family, their dog bit the child when the parents were out at the local supermarket; in another case three children under the age of 5 years lost both parents and the world as they knew it, after having involuntarily witnessed domestic violence which culminated in their mother being dealt a fatal wound by their father.

How to help these families poses complex and challenging questions for the therapist and many different psychotherapeutic approaches may be thought of to intervene in such situations. What is unique about EMDR therapy is that it is a synergistic therapy which integrates many aspects of these different psychotherapeutic approaches (Servan-Schreiber, 2003). Briefly, it shares in common with psychoanalysis the concept that the current symptoms are a consequence of past experiences and it also utilizes free association. From the Cognitive Behavioural Therapy (CBT) perspective it works with cognitions and beliefs and in the processing it creates desensitisation to specific targets. In common with the Ericksonian perspective is the concept of dual attention to past and present and the altered state of consciousness. When considering the systemic family therapy perspective, it shares the "*here and now*" interactional processes with past experiences. From the transactional analytic perspective it shares the recall and transformation of significant life-event childhood memories into adult understandings. Finally, from Janet (1889) EMDR shares the hypothesis that in the aftermath of a trauma the memory is

1

stored in a fragmented way in which cognition, emotion and sensation are not integrated.

1.2. EMDR and Adaptive Information Processing system

EMDR therapy was discovered by Dr Francine Shapiro in a serendipitous way in 1987 (Shapiro, 1989a & 1989b). The first usage of EMDR therapy was within the adult population with military personnel suffering from PTSD. It consists of eight phases of treatment: History, Preparation, Assessment, Desensitisation, Installation, Body Scan, Closure and Re-evaluation. The core concept of the EMDR therapy is founded on Shapiro's Adaptive Information Processing model (AIP) (Shapiro, 1995 and second edition 2001).

The AIP model is based on the theory that the memory networks are the basis of perception, attitude and behaviour. It postulates that within each person is a physiological information processing system. Through this, new experiences and information are normally processed to an adaptive state. This physiological information processing system, like the body, is geared towards healing and health. Information is stored in memory networks containing related thoughts, emotions and sensations. With overwhelming trauma the physiological response interferes with adaptive processing. Traumatic memory is encoded in a state-specific way and does not get processed, it becomes *"frozen"*. It is stored as it was perceived at the time, in pictures, emotions and sensations and gives rise to dysfunctional reactions. Individuals who suffered traumatisation can develop a whole series of problems including nightmares, flashbacks, new fears and avoidance strategies. The information processing theory postulates that this blocked information processing is facilitated by alternating bilateral stimulation (ABLS) using eye movements, sounds or taps whilst the individual is mindful of the present and also their negative cognition, emotional response and sensation about the frozen memory. The client's attention is divided between internal memory networks and external stimulation.

This dual attention then enables information processing of the blocked, frozen information and thus enables traumatic memories to be metabolised or digested by the information system to healthy resolutions. This process facilitates adaptive information and enables the individual to forge new associations within and between memory networks. As a result of the metabolism of these blocks the individual develops new spontaneous insights and changes in their emotional and physiological responses which then lead to changes in their behaviour and adaptive healthy interaction with their environment. The AIP model hypothesises that EMDR therapy may be facilitating the natural healing processes that the brain is capable of achieving (Shapiro, 2005).

1.3.   How EMDR may be working

There are many fascinating theories and controversial hypotheses about how EMDR might be working, but to detail all these is outside of the scope of this book. To mention a few: It has been hypothesized that the dual alternating bilateral stimulation itself might be stimulating an orienting response. Neuro-imaging studies suggest that activity in the thalamus may be particularly important in this process by acting as a neural relay station (Lanius, 2008).

EMDR has also been hypothesized as a left/right hemisphere processing with the eye movements inducing a REM-like state in the awake state (Stickgold, 2002).It has also been hypothesized that bilateral stimulation may be kindling the brain stem (Solomon and Shapiro, 2008). Physiological alterations in the heart rate and heart rate coherence during the processing have also been put forward as significant components (Servan-Schreiber, 2003, Sack et al., 2008).

However, some of the most important recent research in this area in our opinion is the groundbreaking research from Pagani et al., (2012). They used EEG to fully monitor neuronal activation throughout EMDR sessions. Ten patients with major psychological trauma were monitored during their first and final sessions and compared to 10 controls. Their study was ground-breaking because of the methodology used which enabled them for the first time to image the specific activations associated with the therapeutic actions typical of the EMDR protocol. Their findings point to a highly significant activation shift following EMDR therapy from limbic regions with high emotional valence to cortical regions with higher cognitive and associative valence. This suggests that traumatic events are processed at a cognitive level following successful EMDR therapy, thus supporting the evidence of distinct neurobiological patterns of brain activations during BS (bilateral ocular stimulation) associated with significant relief from negative emotional experiences.

1.4.   Research findings for children and adolescents

What is beyond doubt is the number of validating studies of the treatment efficacy in adults in the literature, with EMDR therapy being seen as good as or faster and more effective than CBT. With children and adolescents the research literature is still very limited. A meta-analysis was undertaken in which the efficacy of EMDR in children with PTSD symptoms was meta-analysed from the perspective of incremental efficacy. The overall post treatment effect size for EMDR therapy was medium and significant. The results indicated the efficacy of EMDR therapy when the effect sizes are based on comparisons between EMDR and non-established trauma treatment or no-treatment control groups (Rodenburg et al., 2009). There are few validating studies in children to date. A recent study described a randomized comparison of CBT and EMDR in disaster exposed children. Both treatments showed significant reduction on all measures and results were retained at 3 months follow-up. The treatment gains in EMDR were achieved in fewer sessions (de Roos et al., 2011). A review of randomized control trials of EMDR with children and adolescents was undertaken by Greyber et al., (2012). A number of other articles and books on EMDR with children have been written including: Oras et al., (2004), Jaberghaderi et al., (2004), Ahmad et al., (2008), Zaghrout-Hodali et al., (2008), Adler-Tapia and Settle (2008, 2009), Bronner et al., (2009), Hensel (2009), Kemp et al., (2010), Ribchester et al., (2010) and Beer et al., (2010).

1.5. The history of EMDR for children and adolescents

Whilst we do not know all the history of the work undertaken in the early stages of the development of EMDR therapy for children and adolescents in the USA, a key piece of research was undertaken in 1992 with school-aged children who suffered from Hurricane Iniki in Hawaii (Chemtob et al., 2002). Some of the early pioneers in this field who have had a significant impact on the development of EMDR for children and adolescents in Europe with their books and teachings on the subject are Greenwald (1999), Lovett (1999), and Tinker and Wilson (1999). These are three key reference books that everyone reading this book should also read as their work helped to shape our work. We owe them a great deal and thank them for having provided the foundations, on which we could build the European developmental model of child and family EMDR therapy.

1.6. The developmental perspective

As EMDR developed first as a therapy for adults the different and developmental needs of children and adolescents seems to have only slowly been recognised in the training and little is taught about this on generic EMDR training. Thus the development of specialised training in EMDR with children and adolescents became a priority in Europe. The brief information on how to work with children and adolescents in generic training does not provide any family context for them. The work with adults is usually done individually and without taking much account of the family context or the developmental aspects of childhood and adolescence.

One of the misconceptions that seems to be arising is that a child will understand concepts in an adult way, when even in the early 20th century Piaget (1952) and others were developing theories of cognitive development which indicated just how different children's conceptualising capacity was at different stages of development. Whilst Piaget has been examined, criticised and elaborated on at great length over time, current neuro-developmental psychology literature continues to define evolutionary developmental processes and limitations at differing developmental stages (Gogtay et al., 2004). Children's cognitive development grows over time as they acquire greater neurological sophistication and knowledge. Their conceptualising capacity is dependent on their particular stage of development. Within each child is a complex bio-psycho-social developmental system which is unique to that child and is being shaped by genetic and temperamental characteristics, environmental exposure, family attachments and life events.

1.7.   EMDR within the context of the family

We cannot think about children and adolescents in isolation from the context of their family dynamics. Every child is being cared for, dependent upon and shaped in their personality development, interests, affect regulation and world view by their parents and carers. No child exists alone. Generally adults do not need other adults to regulate themselves emotionally and behaviourally; but children and adolescents do. Children do not have the same everyday knowledge of the world and may also need to be given educative information in order to develop insights and realistic understandings.

1.7.1.   Sarah – The importance of educational information

When seen, Sarah aged 10 years, felt herself to blame for the death of her mother and baby sibling in the house fire that resulted when aged just 3 years old, she had played with matches. She was stuck in her processing and unable to resolve this until an educational interweave was made. She was asked if she would give a 3 year old child a bottle of bleach to play with. This then helped her to access information about the duties and responsibilities of older children and adults towards very young children.

She was then able to process that it had been irresponsible and dangerous for the adults to have left matches around which such a young child could find and play with.

As entities, children are fluid, adaptable and malleable, and are shaped and reshaped over the years in their interactions with their social environment, primarily within their family but also within their schools and other settings. The quality of the family dynamics is reflective of the quality of the family's attachment patterns. And the quality of attachment that the child is able to achieve with their caretakers is going to greatly influence their development of resilience, coping strategies and resources. A child cannot, in the context of EMDR therapy, simply be considered to be a 'small adult'. They think differently at different developmental stages and they do not have the complex network of associations that adults have access to because these are still developing and taking form as they grow up. For the purposes of EMDR therapy, the child in our opinion must always be viewed within its family and developmental context.

Conceptualising and doing EMDR therapy with children and their families is a complex, multi-faceted and stimulating process. It is the knitting together of strands of many elements including consideration of paediatric neurobiology, elements of child and family dynamics, developmental aspects and attachment theory. Furthermore, we have to include the complexity and duration of what has proved to be traumatic to the child and its family context, taking into account the history of past events. All these aspects need to be considered in a dynamic evolving process to conceptualise and elaborate a treatment plan for each individual case. Thus the standard generic protocol does not by itself reach such a level of complexity of interweaving strands; nor is it able to meet the developmental needs of different stages of childhood. This book hopes to intertwine these points and integrate them together with the concept of the developmental protocol to meet the differing developmental needs.

1.8. The developmental protocol

The Piagetian model as a developmental model does, however, give a guideline to the thinking behind the adaptation of the standard generic protocol of EMDR to use with children at different stages in their development. Children understand concepts and reason differently at different stages using processes of assimilation and accommodation. Piaget's stages were as follows: 0-2 years sensory-motor period; 2-6 years preoperational and intuitive period; 7-11 years concrete-operational period;

and 11/12 years onwards formal operational period. These evolve like building blocks with development to each of the periods being dependent upon successful completion of each of the earlier periods. When using EMDR with children one has to take account of the developmental stage of the child's cognitive and emotional maturity.

To the best of our knowledge the reduction of the protocol to different developmental levels was originally conceptualised and developed by Bob Tinker. The content and length of the EMDR sessions reduces according to developmental levels and as more aspects of the standard generic protocol become irrelevant, they are discarded.

Essentially EMDR with children follows the same eight phases that the standard generic protocol does. It differs within the content of each phase to match the right developmental level of the child. We do not intend to re-write what is already written, in particular in Tinker & Wilson's book (p. 57), where the EMDR protocol phases are described. The developmental protocol is the adaptation of elements of the eight phase standard generic protocol to children's developmental and cognitive needs using the principle of 'minimal creativity'. The standard generic protocol used with adults and older adolescents is composed of the negative cognition represented as the NC, the positive cognition represented as the PC, the validity of the positive cognition represented as the VOC[1], the emotion, the subjective units of distress represented as SUDS[2] and the sensation. Alternating bilateral stimulation is achieved using eye movement represented as EM, or taps or sounds. Figure 1.1 illustrates how the Developmental Protocol works by dropping just those elements which the children cannot achieve because of their stage of development though one may try to get them as some children may be more advanced than others.

The elements of the protocol in brackets, for example the PC and NC, are ones that we may not be able to obtain at a given developmental level, but we should try to see if we can as some children can surprise us. However, we should not be at all pressurising about this. Time contracts as the standard generic protocol requirements become less meaningful at younger levels and the associational channels are shorter and fewer.

---

[1] The VOC is a self-report scale that runs from 1–7, where 1 represents totally unbelievable and 7 totally believable.
[2] Subjective Units of Disturbance Scale, SUDS, a 0-10 scale where 0 represents no disturbance and 10 the worst disturbance, was developed by Joseph Wolpe.

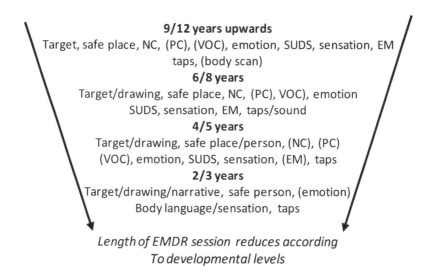

9/12 years upwards
Target, safe place, NC, (PC), (VOC), emotion, SUDS, sensation, EM
taps, (body scan)
6/8 years
Target/drawing, safe place, NC, (PC), VOC), emotion
SUDS, sensation, EM, taps/sound
4/5 years
Target/drawing, safe place/person, (NC), (PC)
(VOC), emotion, SUDS, sensation, (EM), taps
2/3 years
Target/drawing/narrative, safe person, (emotion)
Body language/sensation, taps

*Length of EMDR session reduces according
To developmental levels*

Figure 1.1: The Developmental protocol

Elements of the EMDR developmental protocol reduce in complexity the younger the child is, when the more difficult conceptualisations, including the VOC are not comprehensible or meaningful. Even with adolescents the meaning and understanding of the future may not be the same as that of an adult as they find it hard to realistically project into the future. Similarly, adolescents find it hard to give an accurate estimate of the extent of their feelings both positive and negative and may either considerably over or underestimate their strength.

We often observe with adolescents and children that a measure of 3 on the SUDS may not represent the same as an adult's SUDS of 3 would and that these scales can be up to or down to 100 or even up "*as high as the sky*" or "*down into the middle of the earth*". Thus the Developmental Protocol for children and adolescents is a protocol, which is changed only of necessity in order to meet the developmental needs of the child and to avoid making adult assumptions.

1.9.   Summary

In this chapter we have tried to give a brief introduction to EMDR, some of the history and research and its application to children and adolescents. We have also introduced the notion that this therapy occurs within the context of their families. We have introduced and outlined how the generic standard protocol is modified developmentally. We go on to discuss the above in more detail in later chapters.

Chapter 2

Aspects of Trauma, Neurobiology, Pre-verbal Memory and Sleep

2.1.   Trauma

In everyday life following a simple trauma we usually go through several phases to resolve the disturbing memories. Firstly we think about the disturbing event, we talk about it, we dream about it and this process repeats itself until the emotional disturbance is resolved leading to an adaptive resolution of the event. Trauma in Greek means a wound in the spirit, the body and the soul. The notion of personal invulnerability is destroyed and the spiritual beliefs are shattered.

A shocking event is traumatising when it has a long-term negative effect and creates long-term psychological damage. The shock shatters the spirit and the emotions. Carlson & Dalenberg (2000) define a traumatic incident as an event that was uncontrollable, extremely negative, unforeseen and sudden.

Knowledge about post-traumatic stress and its effects on children and adolescents developed through the 1980's and 1990's and numerous books and articles have now been written and some that have helped to shape our earlier thinking include: Terr, (1991), Harris-Hendriks et al., (1993), Pynoos (1995), Black et al., (1996) and Yule et al., (1999).

In our experience using EMDR therapy we have discovered that for children many things in their world can provoke traumatic responses not only for large "T" events such as a tsunami, a road traffic accident, an earth quake or abuse; but also small "t" events, for example being bullied at school, being shamed by accidentally wetting their beds, being made to feel stupid in a classrooms in front of their peers, being made to feel different because they have red hair or their parents cannot afford the latest 'in' gadget that all the other children have, being upset and embarrassed when their parents are not doing what the others' parents are doing, or feeling helpless and abandoned starting nursery school amongst many other events. These days it is more helpful to conceptualise traumatic incidents in terms of disturbing life events (Shapiro, 2009).

2.2. Neurobiology

This book cannot cover the full breadth of neurobiological research and readers can obtain further information in the bibliography and following the references to the literature. In trying to understand how the neurological processes are working, we have found the following helpful in shaping our thinking about trauma in children and we hope may be helpful to the reader. Neurobiology brings us fundamental knowledge about the development of the body, brain and memory in childhood.

Firstly, McLean (1985) hypothesized a model of the brain based on its evolutionary development. He suggests that the human brain is made up of three brains. Each of the brains or layers, developed successively in response to evolutionary needs. The first to develop was the reptilian brain followed by limbic system (emotional brain) and then the neocortex (the thinking brain). Each brain is geared towards separate functions, but all three interact. The reptilian brain consists of the brain stem and cerebellum. The brain stem governs survival and maintenance of the body including breathing, digestion, circulation, the reproductive drives and the "*fight, flight* or *freeze*" arousal response to life threatening events. The behaviours which are governed in the reptilian brain are automatic and resistant to change.

The limbic brain was the second to evolve and is found in all mammals and surrounds the reptilian brain. It consists of the amygdala and the hippocampus and is concerned with emotion, memory, some social behaviour and learning (Cozolino, 2002). It is related to expression and mediation of feelings including attachment. Last to develop was the neo cortex (cerebral cortex), which enables self-awareness including language, speech, reading, writing and conscious thought and enables future planning and abstract verbal and non-verbal logical processing. It includes large portions of the corpus callosum, which bridges the right and left hemisphere of the brain and also has areas for voluntary movement and processing sensory information.

Each of the three levels of the brain has its own perception of the environment and responds accordingly. A particular level may override the others depending on the environmental conditions. Even when one level supersedes the others, the three levels of the brain (sensori-motor, emotional and cognitive) are functionally mutually dependent and intertwined (Damasio, 1991, LeDoux, 1996 and Schore, 1994). The three levels of the brain and the corresponding information processing interact and affect each other simultaneously, functioning as a cohesive whole. The degree of integration of each level of processing affects the efficacy of other levels.

To simplify it, one may consider that the neuro-physiological reaction of the individual to a traumatic incident occurs in three stages. First, a threat once it is perceived it is relayed by the sensory cortex, through the thalamus to the brain stem firing the neurons in the locus ceruleus and this activates the sympathetic nervous system acting on the heart, blood vessels, respiratory centres and other areas creating physiological changes and the amygdala, which is the centre of the reptilian emotional brain and responsible for the fear response, is activated. Secondly, the visual cortex is activated creating flashback memories and thirdly there is a deactivation of Broca's area, the area of the brain responsible for mediating speech acts. These three elements characterise what we could call a post-traumatic stress disorder (PTSD) neurological signature (Servan-Schreiber, 2007.)

2.3. Developmental neurobiology

When thinking about children one has always to remember that the brain is still developing and differentiating. The standard generic EMDR protocol was developed for adults and it is assumed that their neurological and biological development is complete. With children such assumptions are not possible as they are evolving and have not yet developed the clear brain structures seen in adulthood.

2.3.1. Cortical development in healthy children

A longitudinal MRI study of cortical development in healthy children was undertaken by Gogtay et al., (2004) and shows how the brain progresses from 5 to 20 years of age. They illustrate how the grey matter wanes in a back to front wave as it develops and neural connections are pruned. The pre-frontal cortex emerged late in evolution and is among the last to mature. The young brain matures over time with more basic functions maturing earlier and higher-order functions maturing later, as Piaget and others predicted. This cortical development helps us to understand why the cognitive abilities of children at specific developmental stages are different.

Grey matter consists of neuronal cell bodies, dendrites and both un-myelinated axons and myelinated axons, glial cells and capillaries. White matter consists mostly of bundles of myelinated nerve cell processes (axons) which connect various grey matter areas to each other and carry nerve impulses between the neurons. As the child develops, more of the grey matter is pruned and greater myelination occurs, leading to greater specialisation. To put this simply, the white matter may be likened to roads which are continually developing in the child's brain and expanding and mapping routes to different towns and villages (grey matter). As the roads are being built (myelination) the speed of information processing increases as greater highways are built along the same routes.

As the child develops they tend to lose general flexibility and develop more specialized responses. Thus, for example, whilst young children have a greater capacity to learn all languages this capacity reduces over time as they become older and more specialised in their own language, by continually patterning it, learning it and practicing it.

The above helps us to understand why younger children are not able to regulate their inner emotional worlds, nor conceptualise and integrate them because they have not yet developed the cognitive structures to do this. Thus children remain dependent upon external higher-order executive functioning of parents and teachers to regulate them. We can learn from this how important it is that an assessment of the parent's effectiveness in being able to regulate a child's emotions and behaviours is in treatment planning. When a parent is themself triggered by unresolved internal childhood traumas they become less able to function as parents and may indeed regress to children themselves rendering their parenting ability ineffective.

2.3.2. *Michael – The effects of his trauma on mother*

Michael aged 5 years was referred by his paediatrician because he had developed a terror of doctors following a series of intensive medical procedures required to address a serious medical condition. He was refusing to allow anyone to examine his abdomen and became hysterical when anyone tried to do this. His mother became frantic herself at these times, unable to soothe him and would have to leave the examination room. It emerged in the treatment planning phase that his mother felt helpless and dreaded the hospital visits because she could not tolerate his screaming and distress. Her distress was overwhelming her capacity to soothe him. She had never told anyone before, but she had been chronically abused for several years as a very young child. Michael's screams were evoking her unregulated inner child and the flashbacks of what had happened to her. She needed extensive EMDR therapy in her own right and her therapy lasted 2 years. Early on in her own therapy she learned to discriminate her own past experiences from her child's and her parenting skills became more appropriate as she became capable of soothing him.

2.3.3. Behavioural adaptation to trauma

Perry et al., (1995) defined two continuums of behavioural adaptation in coping with trauma in young children with different neurobiological roots: the hyper-arousal (adrenergic) continuum and the dissociative (serotonergic) continuum. The hyper-arousal continuum is characterised by hyperactivity, distractibility and poor concentration. The dissociative continuum is characterised by passive avoidance, denial, surrender and freezing. What Perry et al., found was that children admitted to Accident and Emergency departments after traumatic events presented in two ways.

They either had heightened heart responses (hyper-arousal) or their heart rate responses which were initially high dropped to lowered heart rate responses (dissociative). He hypothesized that persisting fear and adaptation to the threat present in chronically traumatic situations over time, would alter the development of the young child's brain and would result in changes in physical, emotional, behavioural, cognitive and social functioning.

The persisting response over time would create neural 'super highways' in the immature brain and thus the child's information processing responses would tend to trigger the same defensive mechanism, time after time regardless of the context and how maladaptive it might become. Thus altering the child's developmental trajectory as they would be unable to use the full repertoire of their responses of flight, fight and freeze as only one of these would be likely to be kindled first.

Children who are chronically traumatized by domestic violence in early infancy may have no alternative but to respond with a freezing response and over time this may become their characteristic way of responding to threat, however maladaptive to the circumstances this may be, as this is the response which has been most conditioned. Interestingly, we have noticed clinically that children suffering from chronic traumatisation at different early developmental stages develop different responses. For example, children who were chronically traumatized around the ages of 2 to 3 years seem most likely to respond with biting, hitting, kicking and other demonstrations of the fight response, whereas those chronically traumatized in infancy seem to respond with the freeze response.

2.3.4. Cerebral volume changes after chronic PTSD

De Bellis et al., (1999) were able to show that some changes occurred in the hypothalamic-pituitary-adrenal axis and in the catecholamine excretion in severely sexually abused girls. He compared the MRI scans of 44 abused children with PTSD with 61 healthy control children. They found that children with PTSD have 7% smaller cerebral volumes. They found the brain volume was correlated positively with the age of onset of PTSD, thus the younger the child was at the time of chronic traumatisation, the smaller the brain volume was likely to be in comparison with the controls. He found that the brain volume was negatively correlated with the duration of the abuse, thus the longer the duration of the abuse, the smaller the brain volume. These findings may be related to higher cortisol levels and increased catecholamine concentrations found in PTSD. He also added a precautionary note that impoverished environments and lack of mental stimulation in early lives of the children were also likely to be contributory.

These findings are particularly concerning to the long term coping capacity of such young children. They also raise questions about whether successful EMDR therapy given early on could alter this prognosis in some way. Clinically we have found that some children who have been chronically neglected and abused and may be considered as 'failure to thrive' children, after being removed from these environments and placed in stable family homes and after EMDR therapy for the traumas that they have undergone, positively thrive and make amazing developmental catch-up.

It seems the combination of healthy positive parenting, nutrition and EMDR therapy to heal the emotional pain may be effective and this is a very important avenue for future research. We advise all those therapists who may work with this young chronically traumatised group to measure their head circumference, weight and height at the outset of treatment and then again 3 months, 6 months and a year later as in our clinical experience young children physically, emotionally, socially and cognitively seem to go through a growth spurt once the trauma has been treated.

2.3.5. Loss of startle response after PTSD

Ornitz and Pynoos (1989) demonstrated the loss of the normal inhibitory modulation of the startle response in small sample of children with PTSD. Clinically, we have noticed that traumatised children, who startle more easily to extraneous unexpected sounds during the sessions, learn to re-inhibit these after EMDR therapy. This suggests that this symptom of their PTSD may have resolved. If this were found to be the case through rigorous research, then there would be indications of EMDR working at a deeper level in neurobiological terms by helping to reset an autonomic early-warning regulation system. If this is occurring, which clinical observations suggest, then it is an indicator of the child regaining greater ability to internally re-regulate themselves and thus to focus and to learn.

2.3.6. Changes in evoked potentials after chronic traumatisation

Pollak et al., (1997) used event-related potentials to compare responses of maltreated and "normal" children to facial expressions. He found differences between the children when they were shown angry faces. In particular, maltreated children showed greater amplitude responses to angry faces. They didn't observe any differences in responses to happy and sad faces. Clinically, the implications of this are that the maltreated children may be more triggered by angry faces as a result of their life experiences. Thus they are more likely to respond to these more intensively and impulsively without discriminating them within their social contexts in the same way as other children might do. In turn this sensitised responsiveness may make them more vulnerable and arouse more containing and perhaps even stern or angry responses in others.

Along the same lines Cyrulnik (2006) described how a child, neglected, maltreated or who lived with a depressed and sad mother during his early neural development would learn to channel the information towards cerebral areas that will most likely trigger inner sadness within the child.

2.3.7. Abnormal cortical development in abused children

Teicher et al., (1997) showed evidence of abnormal cortical development in abused children. He found an increased prevalence of left-sided (predominantly fronto-temporal) EEG abnormalities in the abused children. He did this by using EEG coherence measures of 15 child psychiatric inpatients and compared them with controls. The abused children had a diminished left-hemisphere differentiation compared to controls. This suggests that the abused children were not developing or using as many different neural pathways. He suggests significant neuro-developmental changes have occurred.

Referring back to Gogtay's cortical development model this may indicate that they are not progressing and learning, or their grey matter is not being pruned or waning in the same way as other children and is suggestive of lesser sophistication and refinement in neural pathways. Clinically it suggests that they may be remaining more immature in their neurobiological development in some areas.

2.3.8. Neural integration in therapy

Siegel (1999) hypothesises that in therapy, with the focus on the multiple layers in the brain representing the trauma (in terms of the images, emotions, body sensations, linguistic statements and perceptions) that the child is helped to develop new configurations and new associational matrix of information for processing these. In clinical terms he is suggesting that therapy, by focussing all the components of the trauma, is helping the child to learn to think about the traumatic event in new ways. In this way the child is learning to change and develop new associational links to self-regulate and integrate their perceptions and experiences of the world.

Similarly, Shapiro's (2001) adaptive information processing model also postulates, that within each person is a physiological information processing system, through which new experiences and information are processed (integrated) to an adaptive state normally. This physiological information processing system, like the body, is geared towards healing and health, which in children is evolving and developing.

Siegel states that integration is a dynamic central self-organising mechanism that links the many internal and interpersonal processes into a coherent functional whole. Within a coherent integrated process, adaptive and flexible states are achieved. In healthy individuals coherent narratives and flexible self-regulation exist within the individual. They are able to flow between regularity and predictability to novelty and spontaneity and in this transitional process new self-organisational forms can be constructed for adaptive action. They are able to focus attention on both the here and now and on the integration of the past, the present and the future in both implicit and explicit memory. This promotes a deep sense of coherent self-knowledge.

In trauma, rigidities to the flow of energy and information have developed as adaptations that can lead to various difficulties as the mind flows to the extremes of either order (rigidity) or chaos. In our clinical experience children who are traumatised display such rigidity and chaos in their play, their social interactions and other behaviours and are not able to joyfully explore the world spontaneously. The child and the family's narratives of the trauma are fragmented and as a result what are passed on are the traumas and not the story of the trauma to the next generation. This is discussed later in the book.

2.4. Developmental aspects of memory and trauma

When considering traumatic memory we know from the literature on adults that traumatic memory does not decay over time, it remains as vivid and intense as it was at the time of the trauma and is frozen in exactly the same way as it was when it was recorded (Janet, 1889, van der Kolk, 1994.) It is stored in implicit memory which encodes the visual images, sounds, smells, sensations and movements and does not have a time context; it exists in the present. Unlike declarative memory which is verbally accessible, this implicit memory in the form of flashbacks and intrusive thoughts is only triggered by cues which evoke them in the present, it is situationally accessed memory (SAM) (Brewin, 2001).

2.4.1. Effects of trauma on the developing child

Perry, (2008) states that when trauma occurs during infancy, it is the lower areas of the brain, the brain stem and the diencephalon are affected. These areas regulate body functions and arousal and are incapable of conscious perception.

During the toddler years and early childhood the limbic system with its emotional reactivity and attachment patterning is most affected by trauma. The majority of the brain organisation Perry (2008) states takes place during the first 4 years of life. It seems then that the brain development in the first 4 years sets blueprints for the psychological immune system and for attachment.

During childhood and then adolescence the cortical areas of the brain become more active and are more directly impacted. Higher cortical areas enter their final developmental process in early adulthood.

For a long time a common assumption was that very young children would not recall disturbing and traumatic events because they would not have the capacity to understand them as they had not yet developed their semantic abilities and were thus unable to conceive of them.

2.4.2. *Alan – Early traumatisation*

In 1996, an elderly driver died at the wheel of his car, which then swerved up onto the pavement and carried a mother and baby in its pram down an embankment before crushing them against a wall. A 19 month old boy, Alan, was found later, crying and wandering around on his own on the pavement and taken to the hospital. Alan was physically well and returned home with his father. Everyone felt thankful that he had survived unhurt and thus he was not felt to be a cause for concern at the time and no psychological referral made. It was too shocking to the adults to conceive that he might retain these dreadful memories in any form. We shall return to his story later.

By then behaviourally identifiable symptoms of PTSD in younger children under the age of 48 months of age were detailed Scheeringa et al., (1995a & 1995b), but these were not widely known. A standardised semi-structured interview for assessing PTSD symptoms in infants and young children has since been developed (Scheeringa et al., 2003). More recently a screening tool has been developed to identify mental health problems in very young children in primary settings (Gleason et al., 2010).

However, despite the advances made in understanding young children's traumatisation, in our clinical experience with very young children, there remains a tendency to minimize or deny the impact of their trauma. Many children's mental health services in Europe are geared towards the treatment of school-aged children. There is still little focus on preschool children and infants apart from a few specialist services. It is our view that it is important that early intervention for traumatised pre-school children be addressed as soon as possible to prevent the skewing of their longer term developmental trajectories.

Following the terrorist attacks of 9/11 in the United States it became evident that whilst there was a vast body of knowledge from the VA programs about treating adult PTSD the knowledge about treating children was less developed and less integrated. The Federal Government established the National Child Trauma Stress Network (NCTSN) to address this and that brought together many centres of excellence in the field of child traumatology scattered across the States. The pooling and collection of all their different areas of expertise and resources led to a huge body of knowledge about trauma, its effects and treatment in children being collated and published, including younger children to mention just a few: Osofsky, (1994), Boris et al., (2005) and Liebermann et al., (2005). The NCTSN website is a very useful source of information (see Annex).

2.4.3. Pre-verbal memory

Just how old an infant is before they are able to register and retain implicit somato-sensory memories of traumatic events becomes a significant question for those working with children using EMDR. Further does the age and developmental stage at which the memory is stored affect how it is stored and how it may be treated; and a further question is whether the pre-verbal memory accessed by EMDR is a developmental precursor to the implicit memory seen in older children and adults or whether it is the same.

The human brain follows its own specific genetic blueprint in a series of developmental stages in utero and beyond. The brain is composed of billions of neurons and glial cells that divide, move, specialise, connect, interact and organise until they have formed a hierarchical group of functional structures that then are pruned and refined, or wan over time throughout childhood. It is a dynamic structure constantly pruning and changing and evolving in complexity. The brain organises from the bottom upwards with the lower parts developing first and from the inside outwards.

2.4.4. Memory development and sleep cycles

How and when somato-sensory memory develops in utero is a fascinating question and may well be related to the development of sleep as the circadian sleep cycles and memory consolidation seem to be intricately entwined.

There are many theories about why we need sleep and Maski et al., (2011) report that in addition to functional restoration and energy conservation, sleep provides the brain plasticity needed for learning and memory development. They describe sleep as a maturational process with its own sleep architecture and cycling which changes over the course of infancy and childhood.

They define sleep as distinguishable from wakefulness on the basis of behavioural and EEG observation and that it is present in the foetus by 26 – 28 weeks in utero. By 30 – 32 weeks there is a clear differentiation of sleep into 'quiet' sleep (NREM) and REM sleep with REM sleep accounting for 80% and NREM just 20% of total sleep. The REM sleep is said to be rudimentary at this stage with irregular and mixed frequencies. By 40 weeks the REM sleep has declined to 50% of total sleep. Sleep in the new born infant usually begins with REM sleep and may exceed 50 % of their sleep and they hypothesise that it may be important for the maturation of the brain and synaptic plasticity.

Circadian rhythm in cortisol levels emerges in the infant between 3-6 months and more defined waking stages become evident around 3 months. During the first year of life an association between the circadian rhythm and melatonin also becomes evident. Between 3-5 years day time napping tends to die off and REM sleep decreases to about 30-25% of sleep. They also note that slow wave sleep is maximal in young children and that it decreases with age by nearly 40% in adolescence and that slow wave sleep may be completely absent by 75 years of age.

Maski et al., (2011), report that adult-type dreaming emerges between the ages of 5-8 years. It is hypothesised that the function of dreaming is entwined with the 'off-line' memory processing, learning and consolidation which occurs during sleep. By middle childhood all stages of sleep are easily discernible and it becomes very similar to an adult's. This is to us a fascinating finding as it could help us understand why by the age of 8 years most children can more or less use the standard protocol's demands of negative cognitions, emotions and sensations in a concrete way, but have yet to develop a real sense of the future, as higher cortical development is not completed until early adulthood.

We think it is also important to note that Maski et al., (2011) report that during NREM sleep there is a shift from sympathetic to parasympathetic system and a reduced firing of the reticular activating system. Further that the cerebral metabolic rate for glucose consumption increases in REM sleep. REM sleep is defined as a state with an electrical appearance and metabolic rate similar to wakefulness. Similarly EMDR therapy whilst stimulating with ABLS in each set is engaging the sympathetic nervous system and by having the breaks between sets is also engaging the parasympathetic nervous system. Interestingly, in our experience children often report feeling hungry at the end of EMDR therapy sessions and this may be related to the above.

We suggest that sleep development is a major determinant of how somato-sensory or preverbal memory develops in utero and in early childhood and in the development of implicit memory in older children and adults.

2.4.5. In utero developmental aspects of memory

One of the earliest senses to develop in utero is that of smell and within a few hours of their birth the infant is able to respond to smells in an adult-like way. In the last trimester the foetus has been shown to detect and differentiate different sounds. Of particular note is the finding of de Casper and Spence (1991) who demonstrated that new born infants could recognise the prosodic characteristics of a passage of prose heard in the last trimester of their prenatal life.

The above research indicates that even infants in their last three months in utero were able to remember patterns of sounds. This suggests to us that if they can remember these they are likely to be able to remember other sound patterns, for example, those of chronic domestic violence. This may be particularly potentially damaging as the mother carrying the foetus would be likely to be in a very aroused state and cortisol may cross the placenta during these traumatic life events, potentially predisposing the child to future vulnerability (Yehuda and Bierer, 2008). Another study has shown that foetal heart rates are significantly increased when the mothers are experiencing stress (Wadwha, 1998).

Scaer (2005), reports that the ability of the foetus to process information from the major senses is relatively intact by the third trimester and possibly much earlier. He quotes work by Giannakoulopoulos et al., (1994) who found that after taking blood from foetuses there were dramatic elevations of plasma cortisol and endorphins that actually persisted after the traumatic event longer than one would expect in a child or an adult.

Thus, it seems that somato-sensory or pre-verbal memory starts to develop in utero and further evidence of the development of early memory in infants is in a number of studies including: (Gaensbauer and Hiatt, 1984; Perris et al., 1990; Meltzoff and Moore, 1994; Meltzoff, 1995 and Bauer, 1997).

2.5.   Case examples

Below are two case examples where we have used EMDR therapy and which have helped to shape our understandings of pre-verbal memory and what may be happening for very young children who have experienced traumatic life events.

2.5.1.   *James – Early traumatisation persisting*

In the first case James aged 17 months and his family were in a ferry disaster in which the ferry sank because the bow doors had been left open. The whole family suffered from post-traumatic stress disorder as a result. The father was injured trying to rescue his wife. The twins then aged 3 years were rescued from the water and placed on a shelf above the water level. James was then wrenched from his buggy by his frantic mother regardless of him being strapped in and was also placed on the ledge.

The whole family went to family therapy with a multi-disciplinary Child and Family Consultation team when James was around 3 years old. The first session was videotaped and looking at the video several years later, in hindsight, it was discovered that James had kept by the sink playing with water in a very mechanistic way until he was prevented from doing this, whilst his parents, siblings and therapists were talking. Feelings expressed were complex and related to mother's own traumatisation and James' anger and aggression towards her. The therapist together with mother developed a narrative of what happened. James was clearly alerted at various points during the narrative, however at that time no link was made between his repetitive play and the narrative. Thus the child's behaviour at the time, the symptom, was not contextualised and the narrative story did not include the child's perspective as he did not talk about the trauma, but was only able to demonstrate it by his actions. James' actions highlighted the way in which the traumatic memory was stored in his brain in a pre-verbal form and observable in his repetitive play. As we know now, for a narrative to heal a family, it has to take into account the different expressions of the trauma memory respecting the developmental level of each member.

In a state of shock, perceptual details overwhelm the child's capacity to selectively sort and attend to meanings of what is happening when they have never experienced anything like it before. Without such associations processing the memory, making sense of it, understanding it becomes impossible. Attaching words of the narrative to anchor the memory for meaning helps to give coherence to the child's unprocessed somatic-sensory fragments. It helps to glue them together and sets a frame for the reduction of confusion and also the separation of fact and fantasy around the event. Often children do not know the words describing the horrors they experience as we do not teach young children this form of traumatic vocabulary.

James' parents subsequently underwent counselling for themselves individually with adult counsellors, but remained traumatised by the event. The twins also received psychotherapy, but retained some traumatic memories which were successfully treated individually with EMDR when they were 15 years old. James, whose behaviour had become very difficult, underwent a series of different therapies with little apparent change.

By the age of 13 years he was displaying conduct disorder, oppositional defiance disorder, severe attachment difficulties and a complete lack of self-esteem. He was also throwing severe tantrums in which he would chaotically destroy his own beloved possessions and those of others. He displayed the same difficult defiant behaviours at school, at home and in other social settings.

The therapist was asked to see him and try what was, for them, still a new therapy, EMDR therapy, to see if this could help. With some trepidation the therapist saw him. When asked to describe his memory or experience of the ferry disaster he was completely unable to do this. When asked if he could draw it, he picked out a green wax crayon and holding it in a whole-hand infantile grasp, he made primitive scribbles on the page. Fearing that this was a typical adolescent signal of rebellion and non-cooperation it was a difficult moment in the session. Should the therapist challenge the boy or should they proceed? Bearing in mind the wise words of Bob Tinker "*to trust in the process*" and go with what is given, the therapist decided to go with the scribble.

At first the processing seemed to yield little result, with him saying nothing. However, during each set, considerable distress and physiological disturbance were observed. When asked what this sensation was, he was completely unable to speak about it. In a state of near-panic the therapist asked him if he could not say it to just show them, at which he put his arms and hands straight out in front of him and tilted them to one side. Making a clinical intuitive guess the therapist suggested that this might have been the sensation created when the ferry floundered. He was able to nod and then the processing became faster, he still had few words but started to tell the therapist he was feeling better.

When the therapist asked James to just show his feelings he was enabled to access his somatic-sensory memory and he was able to respond in a non-verbal way. When the therapist suggested that it might be the sensation of the ferry tilting he was able to hook the traumatic implicit memory to language for the first time. This intuitive guess worked as an educative cognitive interweave. Thus he was showing the therapist by his actions that he did have a traumatic memory but that it had up until that point remained unconnected to his verbal processing and communication abilities despite him then being 13 years old.

At the end of the above session with James, the therapist met with his mother who had not been present during the session to discuss how things had gone. The clinical decision was not to include mother in the sessions with James as she too was still to some extent traumatised by the event. She was asked what she thought of the scribble and she immediately recognised it as the colour of the seawater with the emergency lighting shining through it. James' very primitive scribble indicated that the traumatic memory was stuck at the age and stage of development that he had been at the time it occurred and he had not been able to transform it in any way since then.

2.5.2. *Alex – Premature birth and early memories*

In the second case, Alex aged 4 years was referred for help by his general practitioner at his parents' request. Alex had been born at 26 weeks and was a very precious child as previous pregnancies had unfortunately ended in miscarriages. He was very ill for the first 6 months of his life and had remained in the special care baby unit for that period of time. He was referred because he had chronic nightmares, day-time fears, tantrums and self-isolating behaviours. He constantly feared changes in routines, liked repetitive play and his nightmares were all of monsters with very long sharp pointy teeth, claws and horns.

Given his early life experiences, the therapist decided to target these first (following the EMDR therapy protocol of treating the past first) using the early narrative version of the developmental protocol. Alex's father was abroad on business. With his mother, and without Alex, the bones of a narrative were developed. In the next session Alex was told the narrative whilst being tapped by the therapist during its narration. The story went like this *"One day there was a mother called Jennifer and a father called Noel and they were very excited because they were expecting a baby. However the baby, Alex, came as a big surprise to them because he came early. They were not quite ready for him because they did not expect to see him so early. He too was not quite ready to be born and he needed to be placed in a special cot to protect him"*.

At this point Alex said, *"Oh yes I remember that."* The therapist was so surprised by this that they said *"You do?"* To which Alex replied *"Yes I do – you mean the one with the hands coming in"*. Alex was giving a description of an incubator from the perspective of the baby inside it experiencing the hands of the medical staff coming in. Alex was asked if he could remember seeing people or faces. He responded that he did and when asked what they looked like his reply was *"plasticky"*. At this point he was just asked to notice that and the tapping started again. At the end of this short piece of work Alex smiled and seemed a bit more relaxed.

His mother reported at the next session that he was happier and not as fearful all the time.

In subsequent sessions his nightmares were targeted using his drawings of them as targets (all of Alex's drawings showed long pointy needle-like features) and he took a lot of pleasure in thinking of ways of containing and destroying the monsters, putting them in boxes, stabbing them, shooting them, freezing them and turning them into water before finally rubbing them out. He became an easier-going child who began to participate more socially and his play repertoire expanded to more creative and imaginative themes.

2.6. Summary

In this chapter we have tried to draw together information and hypothesise from developmental neurology to help to understand some of the underlying systems and mechanisms which are interplaying within the child as we work with them, particularly in regard to the development of memory and traumatic events. We question as therapists just how many children may be stuck with pre-verbal traumatic memories without therapists knowing enough about this phenomenon to think to ask questions about this. In our opinion the work with Alex may not have been so successful if it had just targeted his nightmares without dealing with the earlier traumatic experiences in the Special Care Baby Unit. A very careful history taking needs to be made of the child's prenatal, birth and very early life experiences.

What we have learned is that echoes of traumas occurring very early in life may continue to affect the child somatically and behaviourally even in a safe setting leading them to respond, but not consciously, to early cues of potential threat (Perry, 2008). It has become apparent from the cases above and others clinical reports that somato-sensory or pre-verbal memory exists in children and adolescents who have been traumatised very early in life (Morris-Smith, 2002).

Chapter 3

Conceptualising Trauma Diagnosis and EMDR Treatment Considerations

3.1. Diagnostic tree

One of the puzzling aspects of using a trauma-focussed lens is that one starts to recognise trauma in many other DSM IV and ICD 10 diagnostic conditions other than in just PTSD. The question is how to connect trauma-focussed lens to the diagnostic system. In 1999 Bob Tinker developed the model of the "Diagnostic Tree" connecting the root causes of psychiatric and psychological conditions with the clusters of symptoms described in ICD 10 and DSM IV.

As we see in Figure 3.1, he identified four roots causes of dysregulated systems. These are teratogenic, constitutional, genetic and traumatic. Teratogenic causes include a wide range of different chemicals and environmental factors which disturb the growth and development of an embryo. These include lead poisoning and alcohol that creates foetal alcohol syndrome. Constitutional factors are those that are inherent to an individual that make him more or less resilient to life experiences. Genetic factors are caused by a spontaneous genetic error or transmitted through a genetic mutation and include amongst others Down's syndrome and Prader-Willi Syndrome. The fourth root is traumatic and there are many traumas that are manmade or caused by natural disasters, including road traffic accidents, rape, domestic violence, earthquakes and tsunamis.

Within the traumatic root category on the diagram, there are two types of traumatisation "T1" representing simple trauma and "T2" representing complex and multiple traumatisation. Within complex and multiple traumatisation, two further subcategories are defined, "R" and "NR". "R" is for individuals with resources including good attachments; and "NR" for

27

those without resources including insecure or disorganised attachments. The trunk of the tree represents the neuro-physiological system.

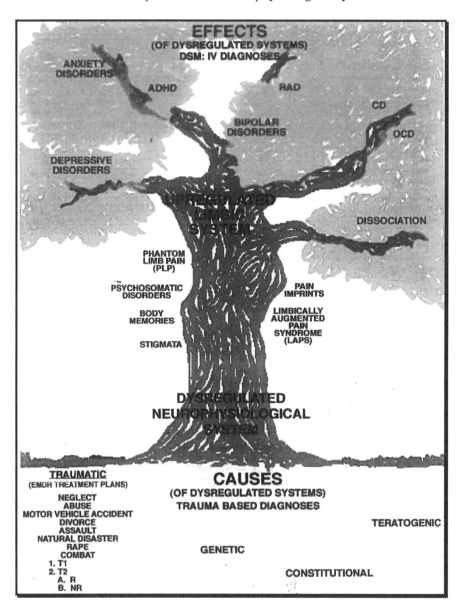

©Tinker, R. 1999

Figure 3.1: The diagnostic tree

At the base of the trunk is the neuro-physiological system which is being dysregulated by the traumatic roots. This leads to the development of sensory-motor and psychosomatic type disorders including body memories, pain imprints and phantom limb pains. As the traumatic roots dysregulate the neuro-physiological system, the limbic system also becomes disrupted and becomes hyper-aroused as a result. In the branches of the tree are the clusters of symptoms, which are created by the dysregulated neuro-physiological system and the up-regulated limbic system that are defined by the DSM IV and ICD as disorders. These clusters of symptoms include depression, reactive attachment disorder (RAD), dissociative disorders, anxiety disorders, attention deficit hyperactivity disorder (ADHD), bipolar disorders, obsessive compulsive disorders and conduct disorders.

3.1.1. *John – Clinical depression*

John aged 14 years was diagnosed with depression and suicidal ideation. The root cause of this was the death of his best friend who hung himself after breaking up with his girlfriend. He was treated with anti-depressant medication for six months, but his depression did not respond and it was not until he underwent EMDR therapy that this lifted. John blamed himself for not being there for his friend and felt that he should die and join him too, his target was his image of seeing his friend hanging in the woods. During the treatment his processing was looping around the following "*...he told me about what he felt for his girlfriend but he did not tell me what he was feeling inside. The bit that hurts the most is that I am not going to see him again and it makes me think what is the point of going on?*"

A cognitive interweave was offered by the therapist "*...I don't understand what would your friend say to you about what he did if he could say it?*" This then released the block and he answered after a short set of ABLS, "*He was always joking around and he would tell me that he made a mistake and life is precious.*" His final resolution of what happened was "*... I think you just have to make the best out of it. I think Bob would have wanted me to live. If his energy is around now he'll probably hear this. He'd probably be having a laugh now. He'd probably be quite happy about it, he'd probably want me to live my life, he probably didn't mean to do what he did, so he probably wants the people that he left to live life for him, he might want us to live it with him, because he is still around. I feel better I'd rather live life having known him than not know-*

ing him..." His depression was resolved within just three EMDR therapy sessions.

Relating to the AIP model to this diagnostic tree, it is clear to see how the symptoms defined in DSM-IV and ICD 10 could be related to underlying unresolved traumatic memories and experiences, which can become targets for EMDR therapy. The advent of the new DSM V classificatory system incorporates a new diagnostic category, complex posttraumatic stress disorder (C-PTSD). Rather disappointingly from the perspective of the child clinician, it does not have the desired and long-awaited diagnostic category of developmental trauma disorder (van der Kolk, 2005), which to our minds specifically identifies many of the children that we and other clinicians regularly see in their clinic. C-PTSD is defined as: "*... a psychological injury that results from protracted exposure to prolonged social and/or interpersonal trauma with lack or loss of control and disempowerment and in the context of either captivity or entrapment i.e. the lack of a viable escape route for the victim, either actual or perceived. It involves complex and reciprocal interactions between multiple bio-psycho-social systems. It includes sexual abuse particularly child sexual abuse, physical abuse, emotional abuse, domestic violence and torture. The core characteristics include: captivity, psychological fragmentation, loss of sense of safety, loss of trust, loss of self-worth, a tendency to be re-victimised and loss of coherent sense of self and attachment disorders particularly pervasive insecure or disorganised attachment...*" It will be interesting to see how the ICD – 11 due out in 2015 handles the root causes of disturbances and the clusters of symptoms.

From our neuro-developmental perspective with EMDR therapy in mind we focus on the root causes of the child's psychological disturbance which are to be found embedded in the child's developmental bio-psycho-social world and can cause dysregulation in any aspect of the child's functioning.

3.2. Diagnostic puzzle

One of the common complaints by clinicians coming to supervision soon after training, is that they are unable to find children with simple traumatic events to treat with most of their cases being multiple and complex. Research carried out by the USA (NCTSN, 2003) of Child and Adolescent clinicians working with traumatized cases, indicated that only 19.2% of some 2200 clients had simple PTSD. Most (77.6%) of the children were suffering from multiple or complex traumatisation. They did not have enough information to categorise a few children (3.3%).Over 1/3 sample was adolescent. However, most of the clinicians surveyed (98.6%) reported that the average age of onset was under 11 years of age. Over 90% of the children were abused or maltreated by a parent (81%), or other family member (10.6%). The diagnostic category of PTSD did not fit with the main symptoms of these children who were victims of interpersonal violence as their symptoms were more complex and multiple.

Thus, it is not surprising that we too in Europe are finding that many of the children presenting in clinics do not fit the PTSD diagnosis. Indeed many of these children will have complex, chronic and multiple traumatisation in their histories and they come in with a variety of presenting symptoms. Their clusters of symptoms are then diagnosed by the DSM V or the ICD 10 criteria. Yet underlying these diagnoses may be traumatic roots that may be amenable to treatment using EMDR therapy. Thus a child diagnosed with ADHD may perhaps not have an underlying organic condition, but may indeed be a child who remains in a hyper-aroused and agitated state from unidentified trauma in the past, or indeed the two conditions may co-exist as ADHD children often find themselves in potentially traumatising situations.

Children who suffer from multiple or chronic traumatisation may present at clinics at different stages in their development and be given different diagnostic labels, as different facets of their disturbance emerge or take precedence over time. Thus these children can present us with dilemmas in terms of diagnosis or in other words as a diagnostic puzzle.

Figure 3.2 illustrates how multiple and complex traumatisation may present with different symptom manifestations over time including conduct disorders, ADHD, eating disorders etc. How this traumatisation manifests itself may be a result of many different factors including how what happened impacted on the individual child, other environmental aspects and also family factors. At any one given time one or other of these facets of disturbance may be presenting symptoms and they will need to be addressed as they arise by which ever psychotherapeutic process may be most appropriate.

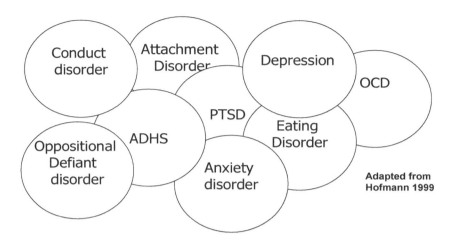

Figure 3.2: The Diagnostic Puzzle

3.2.1. *Susan – Different diagnoses at different developmental stages*

Susan first presented aged 8 years with ADHD which was then managed with medication. Aged 11 years she had developed an eating disorder which took a year to stabilise. She was having recurrent nightmares of monsters and dying and believed it was bad to eat; it made her sick. She was subsequently referred for EMDR therapy for her recurrent nightmares. The recurrent nightmare of the monsters was targeted and during the process the dissociative barriers dissolved and Susan recalled that she had been abused by a friend's father who had given her chocolate to eat and then made her perform oral sex when she was 5 years old.

3.3.   Treatment opportunity window

One of the things that therapists may not explicitly think about when they start conceptualising assessment and treatment is whether the child and family are in the appropriate treatment opportunity window for psychotherapeutic interventions. We have become more aware of this as our EMDR skills have grown.

Curiously, for some children and their families, the EMDR therapy has seemed less effective than for others. Our experiences have shown that for some children (recently arrived refugees from war zones, others recently moved from neglect and abusive families to foster homes, survivors of very recent earthquakes or manmade disasters) the basic needs for the survival of the physiological self and its safety and security is paramount (Maslow, 1943). Using the Treatment Opportunity Window model below it can be seen that different psychotherapeutic opportunities are possible at different periods as the treatment opportunity widens.

For example, a young child recently arrived from a war zone with some family member may need at first to learn to survive in the new country by learning the language, how to cope at school, about the new culture and how to integrate themselves and their families into this. In addition they may carry the responsibility of translation for their parents and have to take on parental roles in order to help get the family's needs met.

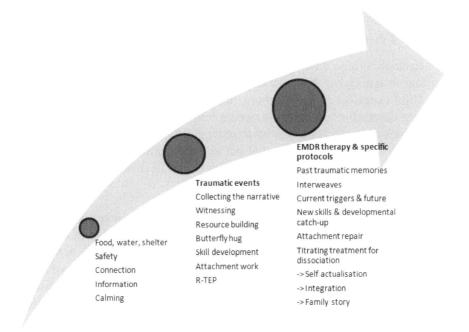

Figure 3.3: Treatment opportunity window

Also consideration needs to be given to what daily life stressors may also be affecting the treatment opportunity window. For example, if in the process of settling into a new culture the child refugee becomes the object of bullying at school, the window will likely close and an end to the bullying and safety re-established is needed before it can open again.

The therapist also needs to ask themselves what kind of therapy work they are expecting the child to do: are they thinking of working on core beliefs when the most pressing need for the child may be to be able to sleep at night when the nightmares of the war images are preventing it. Following the treatment opportunity window helps to guide this process. In the case above, the work firstly should be towards normalising the child's life experience by connecting, giving information and working on establishing a healthy sleep pattern. This could be achieved by working on the most intrusive traumatic nightmare or image using the R-TEP protocol (Shapiro, 2001) adapted of course to the developmental level of the child. Further therapeutic opportunities open up as the child becomes more stabilised and contained and is capable of achieving greater tolerance and resilience.

3.4. Trauma vulnerability and treatment duration

When thinking about what may constitute a trauma in childhood, it is important to remember that a trauma may be caused by any life event that the child experiences as disturbing and can include the embarrassment of wetting themselves at school, or being bullied. Similarly, cultural beliefs and rituals may affect how traumatised a child may become by any given event. However it is also true that not all those children who are exposed to disturbing life or traumatic events develop PTSD or chronic traumatisation.

Figure 3.4 indicates trauma vulnerability and likely trauma treatment duration using EMDR. What makes some children more at risk of developing traumatisation than others is an ongoing debate and subject of research. The research into trauma in childhood indicates that the younger the child is at the age of traumatisation, the more severe the impact is likely to be on their developmental trajectory and on their developing brain if it is not treated.

Research also indicates that the more personal the trauma may be in impacting on primary attachments, the more devastating its traumatic consequences will be for the child, thus a father killing mother would have a greater impact than a minor road traffic accident that did not seriously disrupt attachments.

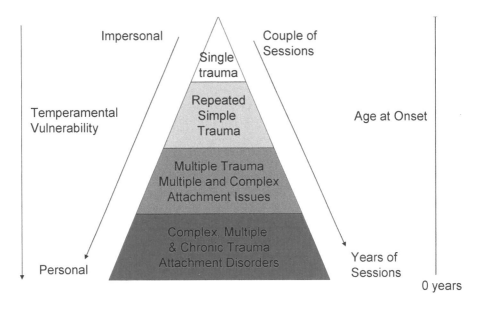

Figure 3.4: Trauma vulnerability and duration

Having said this, we have noticed that even healthy attachments can be numbed by trauma but as soon as the trauma is treated they regain their equilibrium. Disruptions in attachment and attachment disorders create greater vulnerability for children as they are not safe in the world with their caretakers. Further, the greater the number of traumatic experiences and their chronicity, the more likely they will increase the fragility and sensitivity of the child if they are not treated.

How the child perceives the trauma has also been found to affect their vulnerability to traumatisation. Temperamental vulnerability from genetic factors, social and familial contexts will also affect how the child reacts to traumatic situations. What may not affect one child may have quite a devastating impact on another, like being made to stand up and read out aloud in class and feeling humiliated by this.

More recently it has also been suggested that pre-traumatic risk factors may be predictive of the vulnerability to develop post-traumatic stress and that parental PTSD may be associated with biological changes that render offspring more vulnerable to the effects of trauma exposure (Yehuda and Bierer, 2008).

3.5. Applying the treatment triangle to clinical work

In our clinical experience it becomes clear that the earlier we can intervene in reducing the traumatic consequences of a traumatic event for a child, the better the outcome may be. It seems that no matter how severe the event may be (traumatic bereavement, domestic violence) the earlier we can reduce the child's suffering the more we prevent the installation of specific traumatic filters or dysfunctional neuronal pathways from developing from states to traits. Unaddressed these would then become the ways through which the child would come to view the world and respond maladaptively, being organized inappropriately by the past traumatisation. Early intervention prevents the development of inappropriate rigid coping strategies which can characterize the behaviours of untreated older children and adults traumatised in early life.

We have found that the longer the period of time between the traumatic incident and the start of the EMDR therapy is, the longer and more complex the therapy will have to be in order to modify the more pervasive distortions in the adaptive capacity and behaviour of the individual. We have found that early intervention with young children exposed to extreme traumas has helped to prevent the development of later complex traumatisation as they have progressed through childhood and adolescence even though they have had to cope with significant family changes. Complex trauma can be treated simply if treated early if not it will become complicated by its own complexity, similarly to the treatment of pain, when it can be stopped early.

3.6. Summary

In this chapter we have discussed the diagnostic tree as a way of conceptualizing how to apply EMDR to many different disorders where trauma or significantly disturbing events are the root causes of their disorder. We have discussed how different diagnoses may be applied with different presentations of the child at different stages of their development and how EMDR therapy may used. The treatment window helps the therapist to plan the timing of therapeutic interventions according to the child's or adolescent's needs and the treatment duration triangle helps to guide how long this therapy may take and what factors will affect this.

Chapter 4

Getting Started: Integration of Child and Family Contexts

4.1. Child and family history

Fundamental to successful EMDR therapy is a detailed and clear history of the child, its family and its parents and their cultural beliefs and values. This provides the platform on which good treatment planning can be built, enabling effective focusing of the targets and leading to successful treatment outcomes.

4.1.1. *Jill and Simon – Which child to treat*

A 6 year old girl, Jill, was referred for a medico-legal assessment following a road traffic accident in which both, she and her younger brother, Simon, aged 2 years, had been sent flying across the back seat of the car. She had sustained a mild head wound which had healed well. She was not showing any signs of post-traumatic stress in her play or her daily behaviour. In the course of the assessment, her mother commented that her son had lost interest in playing with his cars following the accident. He was also described as hyperactive with a poor concentration span and temper tantrums. It transpired that his temper tantrums were specific to the evenings and when mother went out.

In play, Simon then demonstrated his guilt for the accident's occurrence and his fear for his mother's safety. She had told the children frequently in the course of daily travels to sit still and not argue or they would make her have an accident. He had been arguing with his sister at the time of the accident. It was also he who had flown across the seat and bumped into his sister whilst she bumped into the door. The family had not thought to consider the traumatic effects on him, he had been uninjured and they had been concerned in case there had been serious brain injury to their daughter. Simon had not been referred for medico legal assessment.

4.2. Where to begin and with whom

One of the most difficult things for clinicians starting to use EMDR therapy with children is to answer these two points. How do they choose what is relevant, what is irrelevant and what is safe for them to start working with, in order not to re-traumatize, destabilize, or overwhelm the child. We aim to give some guidelines about this below, but would also emphasise the importance of regular supervision for the therapist in order to learn and become more comfortable with the information selection process.

It is good practice at the outset to get informed consent from the parents and consent or assent from the children as far as this is possible. There may be legal factors which may contaminate the work. In cases where there are custody battles going on, child care proceedings, or litigation, therapists need to ensure that they are aware of the legal responsibilities that they have with respect to the above in their own countries.

4.3. The child's history

During the first phase of history taking, the therapist needs to pay attention to the developmental history of the child including his pre-natal history and birth, physical health, what has characterised his development and how he has integrated different stages like walking, talking and socialisation at school.

It is also important to get a clear understanding of his sleep patterns as childhood psychiatric conditions can lead to or exacerbate sleep problems, similarly insufficient or disturbed sleep can interfere with the child's ability to regulate emotion and behaviour leading to mental health problems and these alternately cycling can persist for extended periods of time impairing the child's functioning across many areas and may affect their availability to process during EMDR therapy and with memory processing. Sleep problems are generally under reported.

There is a strong link between sleep alterations and psychosis and between suicidality and insomnia (Bruni et al., 2011). It is also important to note that sleepiness in young children can take the form of increased activity with irritability, aggression and symptoms of ADHD or social withdrawal (Zarowski et al., 2011). Sleep deprivation, erratic sleep-wake schedules or delayed sleep phases are also common in adolescence especially in today's world of Facebook, the internet, twitter, computer games and mobile phones and poor sleep hygiene, (Raffray et al., 2011).

4.4.   The family history

The family history is also essential as it contains information about the context, which events have impacted on the family life, the life cycle of the family (Carter and McGoldrick, 1980) and traumatic events outside of the family. The concept of a combined developmental and traumatic timeline, including the events impacting on the family, allows us to understand in a dynamic process the evolution of the family and its individual members and in which context these events occurred.

4.5.   The trauma and developmental timeline

In our work with families, the trauma and developmental timeline allows us to highlight and delineate a detailed history of traumatic incidents and in particular pre-verbal and inter-generational events. This enables the therapist to be aware of these and how they are linked to different stages of the child's development and where it may have been disrupted.

From these markers of the incidents over time, the therapist, family and child can make the skeleton of a narrative of the child's early life history and development. The narrative will help the child in the complex process of integrating fragmented sensations, experiences, emotions and images. With the bones of the narrative it then becomes possible, when the child is sufficiently stabilised enough, to use this narrative in EMDR therapy. Subsequently, in further EMDR therapy sessions, each marker may become a target in its own right for EMDR therapy processing.

4.5.1.   *David – The trauma and developmental time line*

David aged 3 years 8 months old, was referred because he was displaying behavioural problems in his foster home. He had been in foster care on two previous occasions before at the age of 2 years 11 months being placed in a long-term foster care placement. By this stage it was realised that he would not be able to return home and it was hoped that an adoptive placement would be found for him. The construction of the trauma and developmental time line highlights the incidents that he went through in his early development and allows the therapist to be aware of his family's dysfunctional dynamics and potential attachment difficulties as well as his potentially compromised developmental opportunities.

Table 4.1: Trauma and developmental timeline

Age in months	Child	Mother	Father
– 9	Conception – unplanned pregnancy	Domestic Violence (DV) victim drug & alcohol abuse	DV perpetrator drug & alcohol abuse
Birth	Complex birth drug withdrawal symptoms	DV victim	
0 – 13	Poor weight gain & feeding problems & eczema	Post Natal Depression DV victim	DV perpetrator
9	Learns to sit alone		Left the family
13	Witnessed severe DV & injured	Mother DV - injured – Refuge	DV perpetrator – charged
14	Walking & severe Temper tantrums	Financial problems	Father in custody
16	Physical injury to face (?abuse/? accidental)	Mother denies injury	Released on bail
17	Found in street (neglect)	DV victim - Mother drunk	DV perpetrator
17 – 22	1st Foster care placement – speech developing eating problems & behaviour problems	Mother has new partner	
20	Remains in foster care		Overdose ?suicide
22	Returned to mother – eczema recurring	Temporary housing	
30	Delayed language poor weight gain	Mother new partner + DV	
35	In house fire – child playing with matches	Mother drunk & burned	
35 – 37	2nd Foster care placement – new carers & behaviour problems	Mother has baby	
37	Return to mother & new baby	Post natal depression	
38	Reported raiding dustbins - not substantiated		
39	Witnessed mother's attempted suicide	Attempted suicide	
39 – 44	3rd new foster carer – separated from sibling. Behavioural problems. (sexual abuse?)	Mother in hospital then in mental health hospital	

The information above was organised with the help of the social worker, the foster parents and access to the Court Report of the Expert Witness. By drawing on all these sources of information the therapist is able to build a complex picture of events that the child himself may have found particularly disturbing.

From this knowledge base, the therapist is able at her discretion, to help his current foster parents, social worker understand and develop insight into some of his behaviours relating to his early experiences. In this way, they are helping them to gain a narrative of the child's life experiences and the child's development. By providing this context, the foster parents develop a greater insight and ability to cope with and manage the child in his daily life. The narrative helps the foster parents to make sense of the emotional, regressive and acting out behaviours that the child may have.

4.6. The therapeutic contextual narrative

The commonly held knowledge creates a therapeutic contextual narrative in which the main adult caretaking network share the same knowledge. They are then able to work together from the common script, instead of knowing, or owning, a fraction or small part of the child's history and context. This creates an environment that is containing for the child and helps in his affect regulation and attachment potential. This forms another layer to the integrative process as the child is held in the real world in daily life in a context he may never have experienced before.

With the therapeutic contextual narrative, it is possible to provide the child with links to his past and present, and enables the child to connect former fragmentary senses of self with his current self and come to understand himself in a more holistic and global way. This is very long term work and requires considerable energy from the therapist to organise such a containing world. We will return to a discussion of this complex work later in the book.

4.7. History of family dynamics

In the history taking we need to consider the factors that may have placed the child and family at risk in the past. How safe have this child and family been? Sadly we have found that the issue of family or domestic violence is unfortunately bypassed all too often in the history taking phase. As we mentioned earlier, EMDR therapy is effective as a treatment for past traumatic events and is not a therapy to help the child cope in a situation of ongoing stress including domestic violence. Therefore in this situation it will be essential to address the violence and work towards stopping its occurrence before being able to start the EMDR therapy with the child. We will discuss in Chapter 9 some of the ideas we have on domestic violence. We have to constantly keep in mind that the child is dependent on the family context and is organised and shaped by the relationships between the child and the family members.

When assessing children, we find that the family dynamics and the quality of the attachment patterns between the members, as well as the child's functioning, are of importance. Is the family functioning healthy and are the attachment patterns more or less secure and organised, or disorganised? We need to be able to see the child as part of the larger system and to zoom back and forth, from the narrow focus of the child to the larger one of the family, when considering the treatment plan. This is illustrated in the following diagram of family layers shown in Figure 4.2.

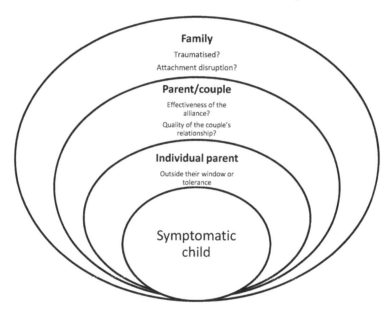

Figure 4.2: The family layers

4.8. Integration and symptom definition

The process of integration facilitates the dynamic conceptualization between the individual and the family. It challenges us to widen our thinking and therefore the definition of the presenting symptoms in terms of intra-psychic, or interactional, or both. Figure 4.3 illustrates the idea of the integration between the intra-psychic and interactional thinking. This also requires an integration of the past events that illustrate the changes over time (the diachronic dimension) with the present interactions (the synchronic dimension).

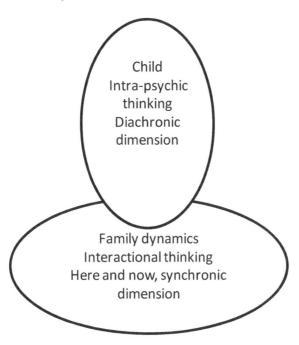

Figure 4.3: Integrating the diachronic and the synchronic dimensions

4.8.1. *James – The family dynamics*

Returning to James, who we discussed earlier and who was in a ferry disaster. He received further therapy sessions around the traumatic memories during which other traumatic elements of associated information arose, were processed and linked together. In a later therapy session it also became apparent that he was angry with the whole family and felt alienated from them. He told the therapist that this was because they all had known what had happened in the ferry disaster and he did not. He felt that this had been deliberately kept as a secret from him. The trauma had disturbed the family functioning and dynamics. The trauma damaged his pattern of attachment to the family as he did not feel he belonged and he had become the scapegoat. The trauma was still alive and was still being transmitted; it was not yet a story that the family could talk about (Delage, 2008).

4.9. Symptom definition

From a contextual point of view, the child's presenting symptom could be a problem that is a characteristic of the child's, or it may also be a symptom that is characteristic of the family's dysfunction and related to a complex family situation. The family also might be going through a difficult phase in its life cycle and the expression of this family difficulty can be expressed by the development of a child's symptom (Carter and McGoldrick, 1980). Further, a symptom may be characteristic of a simple trauma, but may also be a characteristic of complex and multiple traumas.

Clarifying the symptom definition will help us to define the treatment planning and the following steps of whom to invite to the subsequent sessions: the child alone, the child with mother, the parents or the child and the whole family. How this is conceptualised by the therapist depends on their own clinical training, orientation and world view. It is pertinent to comment here that fathers often seem to be left out of the therapy. Should the therapist be as insistent that the father be present at the first session with the child in the same way that they insist on the mother being there, or for example, does the therapist accept the mother's definition that father's work prevents him from coming to participate in his child's treatment? This issue is larger than this book, but is a question that we feel all therapists should ask themselves when working with children and adolescents.

4.9.1. Anna – Symptom definition

A young mother phoned about her 3 year old daughter, Anna, who was refusing to go to nursery school. She would scream and cry in the morning before going to school and mother felt very bad having to carry her there and leave her. Anna had also become afraid to stay in her bedroom alone, although she had had no problem previously. Her 5 year old brother was not a concern. Asked about the children's father and if he was living at home, the mother said "*yes*". She was invited to ask him to come with them for the first appointment. Her answer to this question was typical "*he works a lot and I am not sure he could not make it*". It was emphasised that it was important for him to come to share his ideas and his views of the situation too.

When the family was seen it was observed that Anna was clingy and stayed close to her mother, whilst her brother went to play. Father appeared more distant and isolated and mother did most of the talking. Gradually during the interview, the different life stressors they were go-

44

ing through became clear. Father had started his own business and was working long hours. Mother was working 4 days a week and doing most of household chores. Anna's brother had just started primary school. At this point it was unclear what sort of therapy might be needed.

When father was asked if he could be more involved in the daily routine, he suddenly started to cry and expressed how he was losing his temper and shouting a lot. The children became very quiet, watching father cry and mother's reaction. The question of safety arose immediately. What did father mean when he said he was losing his temper?

The parents were seen together for the next session. Mother seemed very uneasy with father's reaction and large differences in their parenting styles emerged. Mother voiced being very tired with the way things were going. Father talked more about being overworked, having a *"short fuse"* and feeling really uneasy with his behaviour. As often with a family going through this life cycle phase of young children, two careers and some financial strains, their marital relationship was suffering and they were drifting apart.

Father was asked if he would be willing to come for a few sessions of EMDR therapy to help him with his anger management and he agreed. Following treatment the marital and parental relationships became safer and the children felt more contained. It was then possible to address Anna's fears of attending nursery using EMDR therapy. This broader perspective early in the treatment allowed the therapist to plan treatment for the most appropriate point of entry within the family.

Figure 4.4 can help us understand the dimensions of a presenting problem and illustrates the symptom's definition.

In the first quadrant the child presents with a minor transitory problem of normal development and apart from some reassurance and psycho-education to the parents and child no further intervention is necessary.

In the second quadrant the symptoms can be defined as relating to the child only and the family functioning is healthy. Thus the therapy lens is narrow and will focus on treating the child only. In this condition the parents may, or may not, become co-therapists in the treatment of their child and it is the clinician's clinical judgment that will determine whether this is appropriate or not. On the whole where the family functioning is healthy enough we would like to have a parent(s) silently observing during the EMDR therapy sessions with the child, provided the child wants this. When we do this we recommend positioning the parent behind the child, but from where we can observe their non-verbal communication and also elements of their attachment and attunement behaviours. We ask the parents to remain quiet and non-interventional during the processing unless asked to participate in some way, for example giving the child a comforting cuddle during the re-experiencing that they were not available to do, for whatever reason, when the event originally occurred.

• Minor symptom of normal development • Safe family functioning • Psycho-education *1. Brief intervention*	• Linear thinking • Healthy family functioning • Symptom belongs to the child *2. Child therapy*
• Circular thinking • Presenting symptom indicates and underlines family dysfunctional dynamics *3. Family therapy*	• Linear and circular thinking • Symptom belongs to the child and serves a function in a dysfunctional family *4. Child and family therapy*

Figure 4.4: Child/family symptom definition

In this way the parent can become a co-therapist in the child's treatment and the child heals more fully.

4.9.2. *Henry – Identifying when the symptoms belong to the child*

Henry aged 6 years, who came from a healthy family, developed severe recurrent nightmares of monsters chasing people and ripping them apart and showed symptoms of sudden personality change and disturbance, for which his parents could not identify any cause and were extremely worried. He was treated with EMDR therapy. During this therapy the target was the picture he had drawn of the nightmare. Through the processing it became evident that he had watched an adult-horror film on television late one evening after his parents had gone to bed. The therapy was able to allay his disturbance and the insight that his parents gained from this information enabled them to understand what had happened to him, to modify their parenting skills and help the child feel safe to carry on with his daily life. They also put a parental control on the television and un-plugged the set at night when they went to bed.

The third quadrant highlights how the child's presenting symptom is a manifestation of the underlying dysfunctional family patterns. The child's problem is a clue to some family suffering and the clinical focus is going to be on family therapy. In this case working with the child alone would not resolve the dysfunctional family dynamics. Here we have to widen the therapeutic lens to accommodate the broader family context. Further discussion of this is outside of this book and we would refer the reader to the literature on family therapy.

The fourth quadrant illustrates the complexity of both child and family suffering. In this situation, the symptom belongs to the child and also serves a function within a dysfunctional family. We observe this in com-plex traumatic situations where both child and family are hurt. In these cases we need to knit the therapeutic work with the child together with the family therapy in a process of integration.

4.9.3. *Louis – Identifying when the symptoms belong to both child and family*

Louis aged 12 years, came to the consultation with his two parents. His mother had referred him because she was worried about his school and home behaviour. She had emphasised that he had been adopted at age 2 1/2 years in Russia. As usual the whole family was invited to the first appointment to be able to get as much information as possible to develop a treatment plan. Louis was a very bright young boy who liked to play sports and was very good at making and fixing things. He said he was a little bored in school and had a hard time doing his homework. His adop-tion from Russia was discussed. The parents didn't have much informa-tion about what happened before the adoption and why he was put up for adoption. The only thing they knew was that his biological mother was very young.

During the discussion, it was observed that the parents put a lot of em-phasis on the adoption (diachronic dimension) and less on what was actu-ally going on at home (synchronic dimension). As is often the case, the child was put in the centre of the discussion, *"we are here because of him"*. When they were asked questions about the family life, a lot of traumatic issues emerged. Mother had a severe alcoholic-dependency problem following a major car accident. She was recovering, but in the process of her recovery had made a suicide attempt. Father seemed very controlling and strict with Louis. Asked about violent behaviour, father acknowledged that sometimes in the past he has slapped and shouted to discipline Louis. There was quite a bit of tension and difference between the parents about what to do with Louis and how to raise him. Mother seemed closer to him and in some ways was protecting him from father whom she found too strict. During the discussion, Louis was very quiet and tried to stay neutral in his answers when asked questions.

The clinical question was what to do next? Should the work be on some potential traumatic pre-adoption memories, or on the current family functioning? The answer seemed clear, in order for Louis to feel safe enough to work on the past he needed to be safe in the present. It was decided to see the family for another session before thinking of working with Louis. The difficulty was how to convince the parents to come back for another family session, knowing that they thought that the problem was with their son. It's always a very delicate task to create a link between the child's symptom and the family functioning, when contextualising it.

After a few family sessions, through the family narrative, Louis and his parents were able to talk about mother's suffering, difficulties with alcohol, tension between the couple, and father's intention at one point to leave the family. Subsequently, Louis's behaviour greatly improved. It was now possible to see him alone for a few sessions and explore with him any specific painful memories around his life in the family and his adoption. These then became targets for the EMDR therapy and were successfully resolved.

4.10. Child and family preparation

4.10.1. Physical and medical conditions

When preparing the treatment plan it is essential to find out about the child's physical health and whether they may have a condition that may compromise their safety during the EMDR processing. There may be medical conditions, which could affect the decision to use EMDR therapy or not and also the mode of bilateral stimulation offered. Those that come to mind include, asthma, eye conditions, epilepsy and heart conditions, although this is not an exclusive list. Whilst these may not completely exclude the use of EMDR therapy, appropriate advice from the child's medical doctor would need to be sought as to whether this sort of work would be possible and which ABLS mode would be advisable. We need to plan with the parents in advance what they might want to bring with them to the session to enable it to proceed safely. For example, for a child with asthma, the parent might want to bring the child's nebulizer just in case an asthmatic attack could be triggered.

We have found over the years of clinical work using EMDR that it can be an effective therapy for numerous conditions embedded in more overall complex, multi-modal eclectic treatment programs, including: psychological aspects of coping with chronic disease, pain (including migraines); medical conditions (including diabetes); syndromes and developmental disorders (including Autistic Spectrum Disorders); and other disorders including eating disorders, dissociative disorders and reactive attachment disorders.

The elements used to calculate the treatment duration using EMDR (Chapter 3) are just as relevant for treatment planning of the EMDR therapy component of these overall complex treatment programs. Integrating the EMDR therapy into the overall treatment program requires multidisciplinary planning and monitoring. Its execution may also be dependent upon other aspects of the condition, for example if a child has traumatic memories underlying their anorexia, it may not be possible to start work on these memories until their weight has stabilized at a healthy level (minimum Body Mass Index for example of "BMI" 17). Then EMDR therapy may be applied, but the contract needs to include that it will only be continued provided that the BMI remains healthy.

4.10.2. Parent's availability to participate in treatment

Are the parent(s) able to commit to attending with the child regularly for as long as the therapy continues? Are there secondary gains that might undermine in the effectiveness of the treatment planned? For example, whether there is any litigation underway; or what role does the symptomatic child play in the family and does their sleep disturbance and continuing nightmares act as effective means of reducing parental arguments in the evenings as they have to attend to the distressed child.

Further, are the parent(s) planning to come to therapy sessions to help their child, or could they use the therapy as a battle ground? A systemic analysis of the family functioning is pertinent to evaluate if the child is stuck in an interactional coalition process between its parents. A coalition is defined as an alliance between a child and a parent against the other parent. It is often the sign of a dysfunctional family hierarchy (Minuchin, 1974) where the child is being involved in a conflict between the parents. For example, a mother through an alliance with a child may use him to fight with the child's father, or the father with his alliance with the child may set up the child as a way of getting even with her. The therapist needs to ascertain whether the parents have given the child implicit permission to participate in the therapy without fear of splitting loyalties or retaliation and this needs to be made explicit in the family. Before any therapy can be undertaken, it is important for the therapist to establish, as with all cases that the safety of the child is paramount.

4.10.3. *Paul and Lisa – Safety first*

Paul aged 10 years and Lisa 7 years old were brought to consultation by their mother because of Paul's behaviour. He was being physically violent towards his sister and verbally abusive towards his mother. Their parents were going through an acrimonious divorce following domestic violence. Paul had also experienced physical violence from his father. The parents had joint custody and the children spent every alternate week living with their father. The therapist needed to know that Paul was safe with his father.

The therapist also needed to establish whether the father was in agreement with this therapy as otherwise the children would have been placed in an intolerable conflict of loyalty between their two parents. Here one has to be aware of the legal requirements relating to therapeutic interventions with a child in their Country. Is it necessary to have the agreement of both parents if they are separated, divorced and share joint custody of the child?

As stated previously we choose to see the whole family at first to try to understand the family dynamics, the nature of the presenting trauma, its impact on individual members and family functioning. However, in the above case it was mother and the two children who finally attended therapy after Paul's safety had been established. The children's father was aware of the therapy, but decided not to participate.

4.11. Affiliation

We need to work with the widest window of therapeutic intervention that we can achieve in order to plan for successful treatment. As with any therapeutic treatment, when using EMDR therapy, it is necessary to create a therapeutic alliance with the parents and the children. The ability to move therapeutically from top-to-bottom and bottom-to-top of the family hierarchy will depend on the position the therapist occupies within this family system. When all the family members are seen together first, the therapist has a greater degree of freedom of movement to work later on with any of the family sub-systems: the couple, the children, or an individual family member.

There is a logical coherence in this therapeutic approach of successive encounters, if the therapeutic level of affiliation moves from the highest level possible, the group, to the individual. But there is a risk of logical incoherence when the therapist, after initially affiliating at the individual level, wants to move to the other levels of the family system later on and organises therapeutic encounters with the parents, or the family as a whole. His individual affiliation level invalidates him from affiliating at the group level. The therapist is the child's therapist and only the child's therapist. This change of level puts the therapist at risk of facing an uncomfortable situation characterised by feelings of uneasiness, conflicted loyalty and betrayal of the child (Silvestre, 2010). Meshing together the contextual, the relationship and the individual levels, acts as a guide for the therapist in treatment planning.

4.12. Preparing the parents and affiliation

One of the key ingredients to achieving successful therapy with the child is successful affiliation with the parents or caretakers. Just to remind ourselves, affiliation is an interactive process which enables the creation of a therapeutic relationship with the patient being either: a person, or a group. This ongoing dynamic process, which is more a therapeutic skill than a technique, provides the umbrella under which all the therapeutic transactions occur (Minuchin, 1974).

In this process the therapist joins the parents in a positive framework by entering and listening to their world views and associating with their world map, with the objective of finding and enhancing positive resources and support for the child throughout their therapy. This process is empowering and where possible the goal of child and adolescent EMDR therapy is to incorporate and empower the parents in the process of healing their children.

Having parents present and available to interact, when appropriate during the sessions, enables the parents to also develop a more comprehensive and shared narrative of the experiences that their child has undergone and gives the parent insight into the working of EMDR therapy and their child's thinking processes.

Parents need information about trauma and its effects on the child's behaviour. They also need to know how EMDR will work for their child and the potential problems arising. They need to monitor and keep a diary of changes in their children's behaviour during and after sessions including: changes in eating patterns, sleeping habits, feelings of being tired and the rare possibility that their child might experience an abreaction. We explain that ABLS may be given in several different modes, eye movements, tapping and sounds. We also explain that EMDR therapy is different from hypnosis as it is an integrative process, not a dissociative process.

We also need to explain that the child may experience high levels of arousal during the therapy, that this is the remembering, reconnecting and integrating process and that the child during this time is safe in the therapy room with them, rather than being alone in the experience as they were when it first happened. In this way the parent is then able to understand that the soothing and calming presence they offer is helping to heal their child in a naturalistic way.

The inclusion of the parents in the sessions of treatment with the child depends on the child's age, the nature of their problem, the quality of the attachment, the child's wish to have the parent there or otherwise and the emotional availability of the parent to cope with the child's distress. Preparation of the parent may also include the development of a narrative story for a young child's traumatic experiences. Discussion of the development and use of the narrative can be found later in Chapter 6.

4.13. Parent(s) level of traumatisation

We need to evaluate and address the level of each of the parent's own traumatisation prior to the treatment of the children. Doing this will strengthen the parent's affect regulation and ability to safely contain their children's affect dysregulation during EMDR therapy. Persisting traumatisation in the parents maybe a risk factor for PTSD in children and children's symptoms may be related to the presence of symptoms in their parents (Yehuda et al., 1998).

The parents or caretakers need to be able to believe, respect and validate the child's emotional experience. They need to be able to tolerate the child's affect and at the same time manage their own emotional response so that it does not override or divert from the needs of the child. If they are able to do this, then they may become co-therapists in the EMDR therapy, acting for the child, particularly the very young one, as their "*safe person*". When the child is no longer in the care of a parent, then similarly, affiliation with the main caretakers of the child is equally fundamental, though this must also be interwoven with their affiliation with the wider social network involved in the care of the child.

The regulation of the child's affect is fundamentally linked to the quality of the attachment between the parent and the child and the quality of the parents' relationship; these influence their fundamental sense of security. Clinical practice has taught us that the child's affect regulation depends greatly on the parent(s)' ability to regulate their own emotions and the type of attachment the parent(s) have developed with the child (Main, 1993; Delage, 2008).

4.14. Preparation for the child

During the preparation phase the child's current developmental level needs to be assessed by observing the child's behaviour, speech, language comprehension, capacity for imaginative play and temperamental qualities through talking with them, drawing and play. The child needs to know that the therapist is someone who helps children when bad, sad and scary things have happened to them. It is often useful to cite a few examples including what has been known to have happened to the child in the middle of these in a neutrally-toned way (Harris-Hendricks et al., 1993; Pynoos and Eth, 1986). This then enables the child to feel able to talk, draw or play about the things that have happened to them.

With younger children, the use of play materials can be helpful and these can include toys such as an ambulance, police car, play people, dolls, doll's house furniture, telephones and many other items that may be relevant to what the child has experienced. It is interesting to note that traumatised children tend to ignore the soft comforting toys like teddy bears and that their play is often restrictive, mechanistic, repetitive and joyless and does not have the free-flowing range and spontaneity that is characteristic of healthy childhood. In their initial behaviours in their first sessions, the children will demonstrate traumatic referents (Terr, 1988 & 1991). The reader will recall that James who was a victim of the ferry disaster constantly, joylessly and repetitively played with the water during the initial session until he was stopped.

4.14.1. *Jenny – Traumatic referents in pictures*

Similarly in her initial session, Jenny who was 6 years old and had witnessed her father kill her mother, drew a picture of a bleak beach with a big sun and a palm tree and spent a lot of time detailing the cicatrising of the bark on the palm tree. This cicatrising of the bark was the traumatic referent to what the child had seen: her mother slashed with a sword over and over again. The bleak beach was symptomatic of her dissociation from the traumatic event.

The therapist needs to understand the child and their perspective of what the problem is, as this may be very different to the adult's perception of the trauma. Alan who was just toddler when his mother was murdered by his father, presented in his first session as mute and withdrawn. He showed little interest in the array of toys and chose an ambulance and some small play people and played repetitively with these. He kept putting play people in and out of the ambulance and driving it up and down, but always left one behind. For the child, it was not the murder itself, but the abandonment by the mother which occurred when the ambulance drove her away, leaving him behind, that was the most significant traumatic event.

The therapist needs to be aware that the child may in fact have co-morbid symptomatology. For example, clinical depression and PTSD are often under-diagnosed in children and adolescents and may indeed be co-morbid. Symptoms of these are also often missed by parents and teachers, and this is particularly so the younger the child is. Sometimes this occurs because the child becomes more withdrawn; and sometimes it can occur because the adults themselves cannot bear to think of what the child might have experienced. Returning to the case of Alan, who witnessed the traumatic death of his mother, it was not until he was 7 years old that he was referred by his general practitioner for problems with his behaviour and social relationships. It was during the assessment that the connection was made between his behaviour and social relationships and his traumatic bereavement.

4.15. PTSD symptoms in young children

Further symptoms of PTSD in young children are often under-diagnosed because of the inadequacy of the DSM-IV and ICD 10 criteria to cover this age group. The symptoms include recurrent nightmares, sleep problems, repetitive compulsive joyless play, regression, hyper-arousal or numbing of affect, new separation anxiety and clinginess, and new fears (Scheeringa et al., 1995). As previously mentioned the PTSD Semi-Structured Interview and Observational Record for Infants and Young Children (0 – 48 months) is a very useful tool in assessing the above (Scheeringa et al., 2003). In practical terms, clinically, we have found these alternative criteria have been useful in diagnosing PTSD in children up to the age of 7 years.

The Children's Revised Impact of Events Scale (CRIES) can be very helpful as a means of screening for PTSD in school aged children. The Children's version of the Post-Traumatic Cognitions Inventory; and the Depression self-rating scale for children are helpful screening tools and are translated into many languages. These measures have been developed by the Children and War Foundation and can be found on their website (see Annex).

4.16. Screening for dissociative tendencies

Of particular interest is the concept of dissociation derived from the world of adult mental health. We propose for children and adolescents to define dissociation developmentally as a lack of connectivity, coherence and integration; a failure in the child's ability to integrate, assimilate or associate information and experience to develop an integrated coherent sense of emergent self. These responses, which develop from multiple causes including: a defence for a traumatic experience, a flooding of emotion and information and breaches or ruptures of attachment and they disrupt processing in EMDR therapy.

Thus screening for dissociative children is strongly recommended, as this group requires much more careful treatment planning, longer periods of stabilisation and therapy, itself, needs to be titrated very carefully. The Child Dissociative Checklist and the Adolescent Dissociative Events Scale (Putnam, 1997) are useful ways of screening for this.

Markers that may help to alert us to the dissociative child may include the following symptoms: the child going into day-dreams, trance-like states, appearing spaced out, regressing rapidly and unexpectedly, denial of known painful and traumatic experiences, and the child hearing voices and the presence of imaginary friends. This is not an exhaustive list and the reader is referred to the Guidelines for the Evaluation of Dissociative Symptoms in Children and Adolescents published on the web by the International Society for the Study of Dissociation (see Annex). How to manage dissociative behaviour if it occurs during a therapy session is discussed later in Chapter 10.

4.17. Summary

In this chapter we have looked at how to integrate the child and family contexts. This integration is being achieved through the history taking, the trauma and developmental time line, the therapeutic contextual narrative and symptom definition. The process of integration will guide the therapist in his work with the child and her family and provide him with a platform on which good treatment planning can be built and effective targets identified and focused on.

Chapter 5

Preparing for Safe Processing

5.1. Resource activation

The resources of the child and its family need to be explored by the therapist. Different questions can help our thinking: what have they been able to mobilise to cope through difficult traumatic times? Who has been able to help them, what has been helpful, what has been least helpful and what do they need for the future?

In this stage the therapist needs to develop positive resources that may help the child during treatment by enabling a positive body state and feeling to be achieved. These are then used to help to moderate the child's affect if they become too dysregulated during the EMDR processing. *"The core of a resource is a positive body state"* (Hofmann, 2002). These positive resources could incorporate many different things including a safe place, a time when something special happened, a moment of achievement, the use of a superhero or a hug from their parent. A useful resource is that developed by Wizanksy (2006) which offers a play-based route entitled *"Footsteps through the Maze"*.

We also test out the value of the parent's physical contact or 'cuddles' for helping the child feel better whilst in the preparation phase. This is usually a source of some amusement and delight. Further, it may be that the parent will be needed as a safe person for the child. For younger children modelling the ABLS with the parent helps them to feel able to play too. Sometimes transitional objects and other toys can be used to help the child feel secure. Safe places for children in contrast to most adults are often places when there is great activity rather than a general sense of calm and peace, for example riding a skate board, or playing a sport. Such activities may be particularly pertinent to those who are perpetually hyper-aroused and for whom sitting still may in fact induce flashbacks and unpleasant memories of past traumatisation. Making children active in the process may help them to feel more contained.

5.2.   Parental participation

The parent's participation in the treatment process is important particularly with young children and becomes less so as they move into adolescence. However, we want to emphasise that the decision of whether or not to keep the parents in the room does not rest with the child, as the therapist needs to make a clinical decision about whether it is appropriate for the parents to be there at all.

In cases where the presence of the parent is contra-indicated, the child should not be offered the choice. Where the situation is unclear, a clinical judgement needs to be made about the situation, as some children may not be able to say what they really feel when the relationship with the parent may be too enmeshed or they may not want to disappoint or upset them.

5.3.   Children's safe place

For very young children, safe place is often seated on their parent's lap when the attachment is healthy. Safe place is a resource for the child that they can use during the processing when emotions become too distressing, to end incomplete sessions and at home and in other contexts when they feel distressed. The safe place (or positive resource) enables the child to escape from the pressure of the EMDR processing by a form of controlled dissociation. Children need to feel safe in the real world before EMDR therapy is started. Safe place will not soothe a child who is re-exposed to trauma in his everyday life.

The child needs to find a safe place or a positive resource. In order to help them they will be asked to think of one, describe what it looks like, what that makes them feel like when they think about it and where do they feel it in their body. This may be done through a variety of different ways, talking and imagining, drawing or creating it in other ways with toys and materials. This is then installed with its positive body sensations by a brief set of ABLS. There is no scale to evaluate safe place and no need to do this.

In installing safe place for children, as a rule of thumb, we have to keep in mind the developmental level of the child and the generic safe place protocol may be reduced to simply installing the safe place with its positive body sensation with just a very few, slowly delivered, ABLS. At the end of this very brief intervention the child usually reports feeling happy or happier. Installation as above may then be done again to increase this until the child reaches a point where it does not change any further.

Below is an example of a safe place drawn by an autistic boy who was 12 years old. The two images were drawn spontaneously by him to show that he was actually playing a game on his "Game boy".

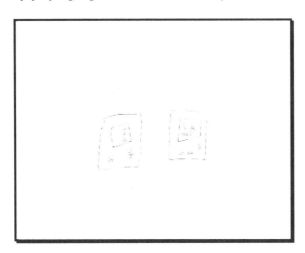

Figure 5.1: Example of a safe place drawing

The use of safe place is often a good indicator of a child's readiness to begin the EMDR work. Sometimes, if a safe place can be very hard to find this is an indicator that the child needs further stabilisation before desensitisation is undertaken. If we find that even with a small amount of ABLS that a child's safe place, or other resource gets disrupted and breaks through to negative material, or becomes neutral, or numbed, or the child reports feeling less happy, then the child is not yet ready to begin the work of desensitisation and further stabilisation is required.

5.4. The child's pace

The golden rule for working with children and adolescents is to work at the pace of the child, being mindful of the safety factors and being willing to interweave other activities into the sessions. Sometimes specific resources may be required to deal with specific issues. For example, the installation of Super Mario and his powers helped a 9 year old boy, who was severely physically disabled, to get the strength in EMDR therapy to look at the traumatic memories of numerous painful surgical interventions and psychological scars over the past eight years.

5.5.   Metaphor

We find it helpful when explaining EMDR to children to use a metaphor of a splinter of wood getting into their finger. This enables the child to realize that although something bad has happened and it hurts that it can heal, though initially it might be painful when the process of removing the bad thing is started and that it will then ease, feel better and once re-moved will heal naturally.

5.6.   Breathing

We teach the children how to do abdominal breathing, breathing in push-ing their abdominal muscles out at the same time so the breath goes deep into the lungs whilst counting to 5 or more, then holding this breath counting to 5 or more and then breathing out slowly whilst relaxing their abdominal muscles counting to 5 or more. We practise this with them. After they have learned the principles of this, the therapist will remind them to do this at the end of each set and will also do it with them during the processing in the desensitisation and installation phases. Any others in the room at the time will also be asked to do the same in synchronicity with the child.

5.7.   Stop signal

In this preparation phase, the child is taught a "Stop" signal and this is practiced so the child can become aware that in the therapeutic setting, "Stop", actually means that a grown-up will stop when they tell them to do so. This may need to be demonstrated, as many times children ask adults to stop doing things they do not want for example, combing their hair or using a licked handkerchief to take a grubby mark of their face and they do really need to understand we do mean we will stop.

5.7.1.   Andrew – The importance of the stop signal

The importance of the stop signal is illustrated in the case of Andrew aged 7 years 6 months who suffers from haemophilia. No one else in the immediate family had this condition and he felt 'different' because of it. He had also been through a very traumatic experience as a result of a cir-cumcision operation 8 months before being referred. During the recovery period the bandage was kept on too long and it required a very painful and unpleasant removal, during which he was held down by his parents, doctors and nursing staff.

His referrer commented that he was constantly unhappy, very emotional, cried easily at small incidents and was often angry but unable to say why. He also cried in his sleep and had developed sleep walking and a negative attitude towards his parents and siblings. His concentration had deteriorated and he was easily distracted. His personality change from being a formerly happy, though quiet child, dated from the time of the surgery.

Andrew had lots of bad dreams and described one recurrent one where he went to cuddle his father and he turned into a monster. Despite this bad dream he felt safe when cuddled up with his parents playing a game. He also had flashbacks of being in the bath whilst the bandage was being removed. He did not like this and this picture came often in the playground, in class, at home and at night. He wanted this picture to go.

The EMDR procedure was described and the importance of Andrew being in control of the process was emphasised. He was taught the stop signal and to visualise a television in his head that he controlled with the remote. Asked to bring up the horrible picture on his television, Andrew said he had it. He did not want to say any more about what it was like or how bad it was. When asked how he was feeling, he said "*It feels scary and sore.*"

After 2 sets of ABLS his body became quite rigid and his face strained and pale and he said "STOP" with his teeth tightly clenched. He was reminded that he was safe in the therapy room with his mother and that nothing bad was going to happen there. He was just remembering something that was bad and that it had happened a long time ago when he was only 6 years old. After a short while he was ready to go again. After a further 2 sets of ABLS, he said "STOP". Andrew was clearly reexperiencing the pain of the procedure and his face was contorted.

At this point some therapists can be tempted to stop the procedure altogether as it appears to be evoking so much pain for the child and they may not realise that this is the remembered pain of the past that the child still carries and not something they have created in the child. The protocol teaches that to stop altogether at this point would leave the child in the middle of the traumatic processing. Whilst Andrew needed to touch base with his safe place, he needed to have the stop signal to make the processing tolerable for him and to help him control the pacing of it. He also needed to be helped gently to continue the process through to the end. Andrew was asked if he was willing to continue and said he was.

Two further sets of ABLS were done before Andrew again used the stop signal. Andrew illustrates how a child can regulate the pace of the desensitisation process in order to stay within his window of tolerance. Subsequently, Andrew was able to tolerate 3 more sets of ABLS before requesting a stop and then a further 11 sets of ABLS. By this point he had processed the painful traumatic memory and he became more talkative and gave more of a spontaneous commentary. We often find that children tend to give more commentary as they process through the trauma as language becomes linked to the sensory-motor traumatic memory networks. Andrew ended his processing by smiling and saying, "*I have put in a nice picture of me playing in the bath with all my toys*". He then wanted to draw on the board and his bravery and mastery was played out in various ways. After this session, his nightmares vanished and his sleep walking stopped. He was no longer plagued by flashbacks and he regained his former momentum and happier self.

5.8. Therapist's comments

The therapist in this case found the processing was stretching her own capacity to tolerate the child's pain and did not really believe that the processing was completed so rapidly and thus continued to review his progress over the next 2 years during which he remained symptom-free. It taught the therapist to trust the process and always go at the child's pace. The sorts of changes we see in Andrew happened very quickly indeed, they were very intense, but the channels were short and he passed through them very quickly.

In retrospect and with more experience, perhaps more could have been done for Andrew at the start to reduce the painfulness of his experience if the therapist had had a greater knowledge at the time that pain itself might come up during the processing by developing a pain control positive resource. The resource developed, the television, did not seem to have the appropriate qualities as it was empowering visual and auditory channel control and not the sensory pain channel. Further the resource was one suggested by the therapist rather than one that the child had developed for himself at the therapist's suggestion. This example highlights the need of regular supervision when working with traumatised children as the therapist is regularly stretched when confronted with a child's pain and suffering.

5.9.   EMDR with the child's parents

On occasions the therapist may be able to offer EMDR therapy to either or both parents individually as required. Whether this is going to be feasible will depend on many factors including both practical considerations and on their degree of traumatisation. For example, the therapist may decide to do a few EMDR therapy sessions with the parents as a way to stabilise them before working with the child.

The questions the therapist faces here are twofold, how many sessions with the parents and how to conduct the work with the parents and the child?

This is a matter of clinical judgment for the therapist; do they feel able to offer this or do they need to refer to an adult practitioner. In very complex cases, where mental health issues are present a referral to adult services may be necessary. It's a delicate balance between risking loosing treatment coherence for greater resources; and retaining the larger vision in order to understand the family and the child perspectives at the risk of lacking the resources needed.

As we have often found in clinical work, the parents will not necessarily follow through the recommendation to seek outside and complementary help. Sometimes when they do try to do this their problems are seen as too trivial to merit adult mental health services.

Sometimes the therapeutic alliance with the parents has been built upon the trust the parents place in the child therapist because they can also identify with what the child therapist is saying to their children. It can resonate with their own early childhood traumatisation and it is their inner young child that responds to the child therapist's containment. These cases can be very difficult to move on to adult therapists. One of the key indicators is the coherence of the parents' own narratives of their past life and life events and the degree and severity of disturbance they may be experiencing (Main, 1993).

Qualitative markers in their narratives during the family interviews can help us to assess this. We look at their communication skills, their emotional flexibility, their extent of emotional expressiveness, their coping skills and their abilities to establish appropriate boundaries and a healthy functional family hierarchy. We feel it is worthwhile if the therapists can help the child and parent(s) similarly, as a way to maintain strong treatment cohesiveness provided they have the skills and training to do this.

But in very complex cases, or when mental health issues are present, it may be necessary to refer on to specialist adult therapy services.

5.9.1. *Timmy – Preparing the parent*

Timmy aged 4 years, was referred for EMDR therapy following a time in hospital when he had been critically ill with a twisted intestine that became infected. Surgery was required and other medical procedures had had to be undertaken, which left him very traumatised and unable to cope with any further medical examination. In the history of what happened, his mother and father described how difficult the time had been for them waiting for Timmy's condition to be stabilised sufficiently to be able to undertake the essential surgery. When Timmy had finally been taken into surgery, mother had dozed off in his room on ward. Mother awoke to find that Timmy's bed had been completely stripped and thought in consequence that her son had died and no one had told her. She experienced a period of frozen horror. When father returned she discovered that her son had not died and that he was still in surgery.

Thus when considering where to start with therapy, it was clear that before being able to work with Timmy's traumatisation, it was important to help mother with her own traumatic memories of what she had thought happened. This then freed her to be able to offer Timmy the safe emotional containment that he needed during therapy and to tolerate his very painful and terrible memories. She was given 4 sessions of EMDR therapy.

This case contrasts with the earlier case of Michael whom we discussed in Chapter 1 in which his mother required 2 years of therapy for her own chronic early childhood traumatisation.

5.10. Summary

In this chapter we have discussed different elements which are necessary for safe processing of traumatic material. We have talked about resource activation and parental participation as resources through their ability to build coherent narratives and be the safe person for the child we have also raised the importance of breathing, the use of the stop signal and the safe place for the child. Considering these and also working at the child's pace are the key ingredients for the therapeutic journey.

Chapter 6

Working with the Child

6.1. Assessment of the EMDR target

Assessment of the child forms the third phase of the EMDR protocol. This phase consists of a detailed assessment of targeted memory, which in children is affected by their developmental and cognitive levels. As we all know in adults it consists of image, negative cognition, positive cognition, VOC, emotion, SUDS and physical sensation. As we have already discussed in Chapter 2, the developmental model of EMDR consists of the adaptation of protocol according to different developmental levels.

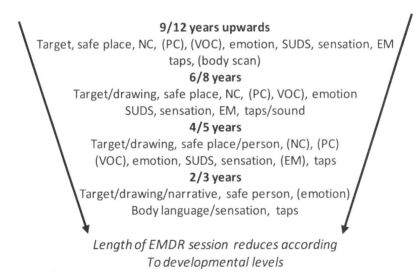

9/12 years upwards
Target, safe place, NC, (PC), (VOC), emotion, SUDS, sensation, EM taps, (body scan)
6/8 years
Target/drawing, safe place, NC, (PC), VOC), emotion
SUDS, sensation, EM, taps/sound
4/5 years
Target/drawing, safe place/person, (NC), (PC)
(VOC), emotion, SUDS, sensation, (EM), taps
2/3 years
Target/drawing/narrative, safe person, (emotion)
Body language/sensation, taps

*Length of EMDR session reduces according
To developmental levels*

Figure 6.1: The developmental protocol

The items in brackets represent the elements of the standard protocol that the child may not being able to come up with and indicates that the intervention will have to be adapted for the developmental level.

EMDR Therapy needs to be carefully timed to each individual's needs in overall treatment plan of the family. It needs to be carefully titrated so as not to overwhelm fragile small windows of tolerance. The window of tolerance is discussed in greater detail in Chapter 7. We have noticed clinically that traumatic memories are stored at the developmental age and stage the child was at, when they first experienced them. Different versions of the child protocol need to be used to target memories stored at different age levels as we saw with James in Chapter 2. However, it must also be said that once the memories start to process, the child becomes more able to access the material and the developmental protocol can thus be expanded exponentially until they reach their current developmental level.

6.2.   Target identification

The focussing of the target for EMDR treatment requires a great deal of care. EMDR therapy may be likened to a laser surgery and the more focussed the target is, the more effective the treatment will be. The target may consist of multiple fragmentary traumatic perceptions including, visual, auditory, olfactory, tastes and sensations. As a therapist we may need to be proactive in helping the child identify these perceptions, and may need to give the child educative guidance on the differences between feelings and thoughts and help them by offering selections. Sometimes with younger children, of necessity, parents select the child's targets.

Targets can include nightmares, traumatic events, stomach aches, headaches and other symptoms; or something that makes them sad, angry, scares them; or something that made the child feel worthless, guilty and bad; or the worst thing that ever happened to them as well as other things that the child wants to work on. When treating traumatic bereavement the normal grieving process requires the recall of the loved one in many different contexts. With traumatic bereavement, every time the loved one is recalled, the traumatic images arise first and interfere with, or prevent the recall of happier memories. We need to treat the intrusive traumatic images first.

In supervision we often meet EMDR therapists who are struggling to identify what they should be targeting in the therapy. This is one of the most difficult clinical decisions to make, though in time with practise it becomes far easier. A common problem is that the therapist may assume that because something bad has happened in the child's world that the child may still be distressed about it, but in fact many children spontaneously heal from such effects and the key to this is establishing how the child feels about it now.

The target needs to be a problem that has a significant negative emotional valence and something that has sufficiently disturbed or traumatised the child and is affecting the child's world, daily life and behaviours. If the negative emotional valence is too low the EMDR therapy is unlikely to produce change as the memory may not really be distressing.

Often children themselves do not understand what has caused their problems, but they do know what is upsetting for example, nightmares, and these become their targets. They may become distressed by the sounds of screeching brakes or ambulances, the smell of smoke or burning rubber, the feel of puckered, scarred skin, and many other things.

6.2.1. *Jim – Targeting a nightmare*

Jim aged 4 years, was referred because his sleep had become very disturbed with nightmares, in the day he was very anxious, withdrawn and clingy with his mother and had lost his adventurous personality. The family were very concerned because he had seemed to literally just change overnight. His nightmares of monsters were used as the target. They always came in the dark in his dreams. As he processed these he commented that Captain Hook was going to get him in the car. When his mother was later discussing this, she worked out that around the time of his change of personality one of the other children had become very ill; she had had to collect medication that night and had to take all the children with her. She had parked right outside the chemist and dashed in to get it. The children had seen a video of Peter Pan that day as a treat. Around the same time the family had been experiencing a number of worries and stresses related to the health of relatives and finances. Jim successfully processed the nightmare and thus his fears. The parents gained insight into how these had arisen.

6.3. Examples of targets drawn by children

In Figure 6.1, the child witnessed the aftermath of a house fire in which 6 people perished. Four of those were children. The bodies were taken out in body bags and this is what she might have witnessed as she lived next door.

When thinking of adolescents we have noted, although we can use the generic protocol with most of them, that they still use it in a different way to adults because neurologically they are still developing. They can often over or underestimate their feelings and have still to develop a realistic perception of the future.

Figure 6.1: The aftermath of a fire

They also find it difficult to put feelings into words and often respond with repetitive words for example, *"the same"*, *"the same"* after each set, but on further questioning we find that in fact the images, feelings or sensations may well have changed. At this point we advise the therapist to be mindful of the adolescent's body language and other non-verbal cues as these may well reflect the changes that they are not describing and they may also need to be proactive in helping the adolescent identify changes.

6.4. Desensitisation

The developmental protocol adheres as closely as possible to the standard generic protocol only differing when developmental levels prevent the child being able to follow the latter. Integration of the developmental perspective does not mean model drift. This developmental protocol can often be mistaken as a licence to do something different.

When working with children, the common mistake is often to assume too greater degree of flexibility and thus abandoning the theoretical rigour that underpins the therapy. For example, not returning to target and obtaining SUDS when the child says that he is now experiencing something more positive and the therapist making the assumption that the child is now in the installation phase. In this case, it may mean that the child is experiencing some relief, but the target may not be fully desensitised. True to the model one must go back and check. We also know that by going back to the initial target, we may discover that a new associational chain may be opening up. Thus all the ingredients that go into making the therapy need to be retained.

6.5. Common problems encountered in supervision

We often find that the therapist does not respect the need for minimal intervention and often talks too much to the child during the sets of eye movements or taps. Sometimes the therapist makes assumptions that prevent him from following the child's own idiosyncratic thinking and may ask leading questions, which can lead the child's thinking in certain directions in attempts to please the therapist. This takes the child off the task and interferes with their own processing. This can also happen with non-verbal cueing such as the therapist inadvertently touching his own head whilst asking the child where in the child's body he may be feeling something. As we know, children are more suggestible and more likely to want to please the adult and follow their directions. Children are more sensitised because of their neuro-development than adults to the non-verbal body language of adults around them. They are therefore more likely than an adult to follow the therapist's non-verbal expressions and body language.

6.6. Promoting attunement

A further common problem is that the therapist struggles to find the child's own level and pace and takes them too fast, or too slow and for too long, or not long enough, through each set. Learning to regulate the sets to each individual's pace is easier to achieve when one remembers that this is a process of attunement to each child. The speed of bilateral stimulation is geared to the fastest pace that the child can tolerate. ABLS can be eye movements, tapping or sound. Mechanical devices can also be used, but we are not advocates of these because we find that the degree of attunement between the child and the therapist is poorer and less containing. Sometimes they may be used, but it is important that the therapist maintains the control of the regulation of the sets and maintains good visual contact with the child and attuned to their non-verbal cues. In this way the therapist can maintain the affect regulation and containment for the child. We also add a note of caution, just because a machine has the capacity for auditory, visual and tactile stimulation does not mean that these should be employed simultaneously. To do this risks hyper-stimulating the child and putting him outside of his window of tolerance.

The standard generic protocol uses visual, tactile or auditory stimulation and the developmental protocol adheres as far as possible to this with the minimum of changes necessary. Some clinicians and children find it difficult to cope when the clinician taps directly on the child's hands or knees and so they use pens or wands instead. We feel that this can interfere with the attunement at times. We suggest that the use of a large cushion and the tapping of the child's hands on the cushion may be a way round this. Alternatively, the therapist taps at one end of the cushion and the child at the other with the therapist modelling and controlling the sets for the child. This latter method is a good way of promoting attunement and helping a restless or hyperactive child become actively engaged in the process.

Further problems are encountered when the therapist is not careful enough in the setting up of their therapeutic and physical environment to enable them to engage in a therapeutically containing way with the child. For example, the wrong positioning of the chairs, their size and heights which could prevent the child from being able to place their feet on the ground, which diminishes their sense of balance and stability. Further, the positioning of the chairs may lead to problems such as the therapist's face being in the child's line of vision during the eye movements. The therapist often forgets that the chairs need to be placed close enough together, but in the "*crossing of ships in the night position.*" One of the possible solutions we have found when working with a child who finds proximity and sitting still difficult is perhaps to utilise an office chair on wheels. This enables the child to move around freely between the sets and be gently brought back into positioning for the next set of ABLS. Ideally, the children need to be at the same eye level as the therapist and the degree of physical proximity between the therapist and child needs to be carefully thought through. This is because the relationship, particularly through the attunement that the therapist establishes with the child, will facilitate the child's affect regulation.

The breathing at the end of each set, depending on the age of child can be made into a game. The therapist and child do it together and when the parent is in the room they should be advised to do the breathing as well. This helps to regulate the affect not only of the child but also the therapist and the parent (observers should also be advised to do this.) Doing this we have discovered that it is an on-going protective factor for all in the room.

Another common problem in the desensitisation phase, when starting out as an EMDR therapist, is the tendency to try to regulate the ABLS by concentrating on counting them and thus not paying sufficient attention to the child's body language and its non-verbal cues. Pacing the ABLS should be done by watching for these non-verbal cues and using these as a guide that change may be occurring and stopping the set shortly after seeing a non-verbally-cued change. Whilst note-taking between sets is possible, we find that we must be mindful of maintaining the attunement with the child and be careful not to take too long in case it breaches this, however the pause created by note taking can also take a positive consolidating role.

Similarly, the therapist must guard against inadvertent extraneous interruptions, for example, they must never answer a ringing phone or distract in any way as this will disrupt the joint attunement and focus. However having said this, it is surprising how focussed children are during the processing and how little their concentration is disrupted by outside noises and phones ringing in the background.

6.7. Parents presence in desensitisation sessions

Having done preparation work with the parents in advance we often ask the child at the beginning of the desensitisation phase whether their parent(s) will know how to behave properly, to sit quietly and not interrupt, talk for the child, or laugh at what they say. In this way the child gets an understanding that the therapy is for them and their parents can be present but not very active in the session.

The child is offered the alternative of allowing their parent to go for a nice cup of coffee in the waiting room. We do not recommend that the parents or carers leave the waiting room during the session, as there may come a point at which they may be needed and thus they have to remain available. Again we would emphasise that the decision of whether or not to keep the parents in the therapy room does not rest with the child but with the therapist.

With very young children we have also found that sometimes it is less invasive to the child if one of the parents, guided by the therapist actually does the tapping of the child themselves. They are naturally attuned to their children and they intuitively know the pace. In this way we are utilising the naturalistic healing that a parent provides in a semi-structured way. We have noticed this form of intervention is also healing to the parents who become empowered in their capacity to help their child and stop feeling guilty and helpless in the face of their child's distress.

Guidance must of course be given about not using this outside of the therapy room. The therapist needs to be the guider of the processing by monitoring the child's body language, as many of the changes coming are most apparent in the child's body posture, muscle tension and flexibility and in their facial expressions and other physical gestures, rather than in their language. In our experience the processing seems to bring changes firstly in the physical sensations, then the emotions and finally in the cognitions. Interestingly parents watching their children during the desensitisation process pick up on the changes in the body language of their children and we can see them visibly relax as the child starts to do so and sometimes, even seconds before we can see the child does so.

As we briefly mentioned previously, when the parent is present during EMDR therapy with the child, we recommend that they are seated behind the child in such a way that the child will be least able to see them and pick up non-verbal cues on the parent's face during the treatment process, but also where the therapist can see the parent's non-verbal signals. The parents will need prior preparation so that they understand what is going to happen and why they sit this way and why they need to remain passive until cued to participate by the therapist. In addition the parents do need to be reminded not to follow the fingers of the therapist during the sets, or they too might become triggered and start processing their own material. (This advice should also be given to observers who may be in the room or watching through a one-way screen or watching videos of the processing.)

6.8. Teenagers and parents

We have been surprised at how many teenagers have actually wanted their parent in the room with them. In particular of note when given the choice, contrary to what many might expect, are the numbers of teenage girls who want their mothers with them whilst working on their traumatic experiences of rape. As stated previously, it is important to work with the mother first to ensure that they are able to be appropriately emotionally available to the girls during this processing.

We have found that when processing rape, the girls particularly respond to the security of mother's hug at times as a form of physical positive resource during the processing of the most frightening aspects of the event. Boys, when also so victimised benefit from the presence of their fathers in the sessions. The parent is in this way able to provide the comfort, support and love that they had not been able to do at the time it happened. It must be remembered here that neither the therapist nor the parent need to know the details of what happened in order to help the child process their difficult material. It is enough to know that things are changing between sets and to be able to offer empathy and attunement. The only time we may have to ask more is when the processing gets blocked in order to offer a supportive interweave.

It is helpful to give an educational interweave that lets the child know that they are not alone in their experiences and many others have suffered the same or similar. Likewise, it can be beneficial to offer educational information that their experiences are like those of other victims of an assault, it is an assault, albeit with a different weapon, but nonetheless an assault. Similarly the child needs to know that when the time is right and she finds the right partner, the experiences of love, giving and sharing will be different. Further for younger children, additional therapy may be needed when they are older and revisit their past experiences in the light of their developing cognitions, emotional and moral development.

Having parents in the room during desensitisation can at times become problematic and affect the processing as some children do try to protect their parents from the events which they have found distressing. This also needs to be considered as far as possible, though often the therapist may have no inkling at all of what might be in any particular child's inner world, or what may be dissociated there and which may be uncovered by the EMDR processing in the desensitisation phase.

6.8.1. *Jane – When a parent's presence can inhibit processing*

Jane aged 15 years who had mild learning difficulties, insisted she wanted her mother in all her sessions. Her mother had been very appropriately supportive of her and there was a healthy positive attachment between them. She was working on the traumatic break-up of her relationship with her boyfriend, which had precipitated self-harming behaviour. However, her behaviour had not undergone much change over 3 sessions despite her seemingly positive processing within each session.

It was decided that Jane should be seen alone for the next session and she agreed to this. It was within this session that she went on to disclose chronic sexual abuse by her step-father that had started when she was 9 years old. She had not wanted her mother to know of it as it would upset her.

Thus the therapist must always be mindful of what else could be interfering with the processing and make opportunities to explore these. In this particular case, Jane had been prior to the therapy, totally unable to tell anyone about what was happening and it seemed that it was the EMDR therapy and the therapist's attunement which gave her the trust to finally put into words what had happened and was still happening to her.

A common error made by those starting out with EMDR therapy with children is the debriefing of the parents within the child's sessions. Whilst some discussion about the child's work, progress or difficulties can of course be helpful in the session's closure (not during the desensitisation or installation phases), most of this should be done in a separate session afterwards with the parents alone.

Children live in the present and as they progress into adolescence they may want to engage in more discussion about the sessions. This is reflective of their developing tendency and capacity to review and revise their autobiographical narratives. Again clinical judgement needs to be employed to ascertain how much discussion needs to be done and with whom. Thus, sometimes it may be helpful to discuss with the parent and child to help the construction a more adaptive narrative.

Our recommendation is to follow the child's or adolescent's lead in this respect, being mindful again of the principle that the therapist should stay out of the way of the processing not only during, but after it. Every child has their own idiosyncratic way of processing material and therapists cannot pre-judge how something is going to progress as the child will in the therapy find its own unique resolutions that no therapist could have imagined. Children are empowered by the therapeutic process and lead in the work that they need to achieve and they can display amazing courage.

There can be a tendency when starting out as an EMDR therapist to become awed and excited about the revelations that come up in the processing and with this a strong desire to share these with the child and parent at the end of the session. Again, a brief comment may be helpful but it must be remembered that the child has completed this process for themselves during the therapy and thus does not need any lengthy explanation about the process itself. It could even be re-traumatising rather than helpful, as one child commented at the end of his EMDR therapy: "*It's ancient history; it's yesterday's newspaper!*"

6.9. Channels of information

In children these channels of information are short and have fewer associational chains. As the children become younger it is important for the therapist to remember this and to be proactive in helping the child make associational links by asking them if they have experienced another time when they thought that, or felt that, or had the same sensation. We have found that older children, too, when considering earlier memories, need the same sort of prompts to access these, simply asking them to "*float back*" to the first time they could remember similar thoughts or feelings may be too abstract for them to access.

6.9.1. *Mary – Processing using float back*

Mary was 15 years old when she was referred for school refusal. She had suffered severe bullying at school and had become a recluse rarely venturing from the family home at all. When asked to "*float back*" to the first time she could remember having felt abandoned and in danger, she recalled incidents from when she was in primary school and fell out with her friends and was socially isolated. However, when this was desensitised and she was asked if there was any other time she had felt abandoned and in danger, she then went on to recall being 3 years old and breaking her leg whilst in the care of a relative and having to go to hospital without her mother. Much of her clinginess to her mother vanished after she processed that earlier event and realised that she was now 15 years old and did not need her mother to look after her as she could look after herself now.

6.10. Use of the child's drawings

Another consideration in supervision relates to the use of children's drawings and what to do with them, particularly when the child draws the most disturbing image as the target to be processed. We need then to remember as therapists not to show the original drawn target during the desensitisation and installation process as this may be re-traumatising to the child as their image of it will have been subtly altered by the processing. We advise that it is better to just ask them to remember the first picture they drew. This is in keeping with the standard protocol when we ask the client to go back to target we do not then describe this to them in any detail at all, but allow their memories of it, changed as they may be because of the processing, to be the guide. During the processing the target image is fading and altering in subtle ways and even when the adult returns to target the image that they are actually imagining could have changed. Along these lines the drawn target once the processing has started must not remain in the child's vision. Similarly, if a child is drawing what comes up between each set, again these drawings must be turned over or removed once the next set of eye movements or taps has begun.

Should the therapist keep the drawings made during the processing or should the child be allowed to take them home? In our opinion the child should not be given the drawings made during the target selection and processing to take home. What happens in the therapeutic context needs to be held within the therapeutic context, whether it is drawings, videos, recordings or other such material. The drawings are a part of the child's therapeutic process and do not belong to the child or the family. The therapist may share at their clinical discretion the general focus of the session but needs to be mindful not to respond to specific questions from parents who may want to analyse them and advise them that this is the child's own idiosyncratic processing material,

The parents should be advised that any discussion about the child's drawings or processing is not to be carried out later at home with the child as it is a matter of respecting the child's therapeutic space, unless the child spontaneously brings it up. The only exception to this is the drawing of the safe place or other positive resource that the child may want to take home as it has become very important for them. Again the parents need to respect and accept what the child wants to say about the picture or processing without questioning it any further. We do not ask that the child bring it back but give the child the chance to draw it again if they want to, but we often find they want to draw new ones. EMDR therapy, like any other therapy, requires that the therapist sets appropriate boundaries and rules.

6.11. Developmental interweaves

Having said all the above, it is of course important for the therapist to intervene when for example, the processing is stuck or looping by either the introduction of an interweave (cognitive, emotional, sensory or educational); or if the child is beginning to dissociate.

After each set, the child is asked with the minimum of suggestion about *"what is coming up"*, or *"what are you noticing"*, or *"what is happening"*, or *"what are you feeling"*. We often find that after starting the process the child will spontaneously tell us with the minimum prompt of *"umm..."*

what is coming up for them after each set. Sometimes children are unable to respond to a specific question like *"what are you noticing"* and then we may ask *"what are you feeling"*. However, often the set may have stopped at a point of transition in the child's processing between one thought/memories/feelings/sensation and another; and at this point it is advisable just to say *"OK"* and do another set. The questions for the therapist to ask themself during this processing are the following; is the child at a point of transition and is continuing to process; or is the child really stuck; or does the child have the developmental capacity and knowledge to be able to continue to process?

6.11.1. *Johnny – A need for a developmental interweave*

Johnny took his tricycle into the garden and found an enticing puddle; he rode through it with glee splashing up the mud and water. When he got home he was in trouble because his clothes were covered in mud. The next day he took his tricycle to the puddle again but mindful that he had to keep his clothes clean he took them off and put them in the basket, then he rode through the puddle. He was perplexed on his return to the home to find he was in trouble again. What had he done wrong this time?

In the above example it is clear that he needs to have some form of educational information to help him understand that the context is broader and link this to his existing knowledge.

6.12. Examples of interweaves that have been used

One child processing the murder of her mother started to loop around "I am scared that he is going to come back and get me too". The interweave proposed by the therapist was "I don't understand because you tell me he is in prison for the next 15 years. How old will you be then and will you still look the same and how will he find you when you have already moved twice?" A short set of ABLS was administered after which the processing started to move again with the child realising that "he won't know where to find me, I will be 23 years old and I won't look the same."

Another child whilst processing the death of his father got stuck on "I did not know he was going to die, I could have stopped it if I knew." The interweave offered was "I don't understand, you were only 5 years old. How could you have known and how could you have stopped a disease that even the doctors, who are all grown-ups, could not stop." After a short set of ABLS the child was able to say: "It would have been better if he had told us. He didn't because he wanted us to be happy" and again this was enough to get the processing moving again.

In a third case a young girl was processing the death of her mother and became stuck around "Mummy used to drink lots. I wanted to stop her but I couldn't." The interweave offered was "Children can't stop grown-ups doing things. Even other grown-ups can't always stop them doing things. Who else tried to stop mummy drinking?" Her response after a short set of ABLS was Granny and Daddy tried to stop her. Daddy had fights with her and Granny tried to hide the bottles but they could not stop her. And again the processing was able to continue.

Sometimes when processing gets stuck it is helpful to ask *"what would help?"* followed by a short set of ABLS. This often enables a resource to be created by the child in the moment that fits exactly to the child's need. They will have their own unique resolutions, which they will achieve using their own creativity. Allowing them to draw this and then installing it with another short set of ABLS often unblocks processing.

6.12.1. *Rodney – Spontaneous resource development drawing*

In Figure 6.2 example, Rodney aged 8 years old who was abused by a paedophile drew the picture in response to the question of what would help. The picture is in two parts the first being on the left hand side.

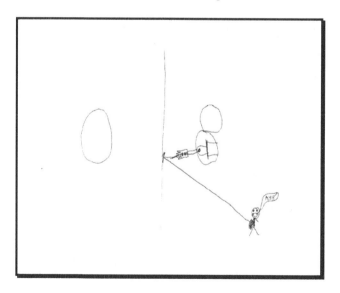

Figure 6.2: Resource development – 01

This depicts a camouflaged laser gun cover built into the wall. The second half of the picture shows how it is used when unsuspecting vampires arrive. The laser is fired from behind the vampire onto a mirror on an adjacent wall and hits the vampire in the back, whereby he dies, "*Arr*".

6.12.2. *Dan – Spontaneous resource development*

The picture in Figure 6.3 was drawn by Dan aged 7 years who had been in a road traffic accident. He was experiencing flashbacks of the incident and could not get these out of his head and was looping. He drew a flashback helmet to deal with his problem. It is worn with a chin strap on which there are control buttons. It collects the flashbacks that are circulating round and round and pulls them up like a stream of photograph film and then the laser zaps each one in turn until they are all removed.

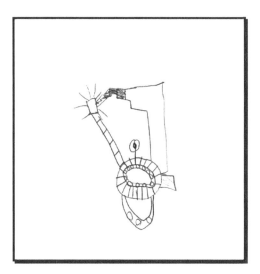

Figure 6.3: Resource development – 02

Thus, working with children does not mean losing track of the EMDR methodology and thinking process, but also using developmentally appropriate mediums. Below are two techniques for adapting the protocol developmentally for pre-verbal traumatic memories and group interventions.

6.13. The narrative technique

This technique developed by Joan Lovett (1999) can be very helpful for the work with young children those whose difficulties are based in their very early childhood and also for children with learning difficulties. The narrative is a language scaffold to a disturbing event developed using an age-appropriate vocabulary and creates links between the cognitive, emotional and sensory information. It can be given in the first person or the third person or using an animal or similar, depending on the parents' and clinician's evaluation of the child and which would be best for them.

Governing this clinical decision are the following: the child's age and developmental level; their need to go through it as a *"once upon a time story..."* or as a *"question and answer"* style dialogue between the parent and therapist, or between the parent and the child; and the child's ability to take an emotional distance from the traumatic situation. This includes things that would be familiar to the child's daily world so that they can identify with it including transition objects and other comforters. It has three parts: a beginning, middle and an ending. Whilst the narrative contains the bones of the facts, these have to be presented in a child-sensitive way.

The beginning introduces the family and familiar contexts that relate to the child's world and home situation including transitional objects. Attachment cues can also be put in here to add to the child's sense of security, for example, her mother singing her a certain favourite song (Bar-Sade, 2008). This represents the installation of safe place of the generic protocol.

A middle in which the traumatic incident is described with the sensory-motor information (target) and what the child may have thought about herself (negative cognition may include it's my fault or I am bad/naughty) in the situation and with additional information to help the child integrate it into a more realistic understanding.

An ending in which an appropriate, constructive resolution is given, which allows for the development of closure and this may include educational interweaves and installation of positive cognitions.

6.13.1. *Phillip – Narrative of road traffic accident*

Phillip was 2 ½ years old when he was referred. He had been in two road traffic accidents. In the first one, he had escaped from the house and had run into the road where he had been hit by a passing motorist and was thrown some meters into the ditch on the far side. He was 16 months old at the time. He suffered only soft tissue injuries and was said to have made a full recovery.

He had subsequently been involved in another road traffic accident when he was 26 months old in which the family car containing himself and his parents was hit from behind. He was referred for therapy following this second accident. He had become obsessed with cars, very attention-seeking, extremely clingy and also developed severe night terrors. His parents described how his personality had changed from an active curious child to this very clingy one.

The decision to work on the second accident first was taken because this was the one that had triggered his behaviours and distress and was thought to be the worst for him. The narrative built by the parents and the therapist started by describing a little about his toys and home. It then went on to describe how he and his parents *were travelling in the car when they had to stop to let an ambulance go by. The driver behind them had not been so careful. He bumped them. It had given everyone a fright and made a big noise. He had cried but nobody was badly hurt, though his mother had to have a check-up but she was fine. After this they all went home and Daddy's car was fixed, then they bought a new one."*

Phillip was seated between his parents on a sofa with cuddled up to his mother with her arm around him. Whilst his mother was telling him the story his father was tapping him continuously on the knees. The therapist guided the pace of the story telling by signalling to the mother to pause between sentences and watching to ensure that the child remained within his window of tolerance during this process. The narrative was given in one session and the decision taken to tap throughout as this would help this very young child maintain the continuity of the story.

Phillip chose to spend the final quarter of the session playing with the cars in a more constructive non-repetitive and reparative way and also chose to finish doing this quite rapidly in order to draw on the whiteboard in spontaneous and happy scribbles. His parents were asked whilst Phillip was playing how they felt the session had gone for Phillip and what they noticed. They both reported changes in his body posture and demeanour and that he seemed more relaxed, they too reported feeling better seeing the changes in him. His parents were advised to keep a diary of his behaviours in between the sessions.

At the start of the second session his parents reported changes had occurred. Phillip was not so obsessed by cars any longer, he was playing with a greater variety of his toys and he was sleeping better although he still had some night terrors. He had also begun to talk about what had happened about this road traffic accident and they were able to answer his questions and offer him reassurance appropriately. Curiously he had also begun to talk about a red car and a lady in a handkerchief. This really surprised his parents at first and then they realised that Phillip was referring to the first road traffic accident. In the first accident he had been hit by a red car driven by a lady who was wearing a traditional Muslim headscarf.

A narrative of what happened to him in the first accident was then developed for the third session. Again Phillip chose to sit between his parents and cuddled into his mother who had her arm around him whilst she told him the narrative. Father again tapped. Phillip added just few words of his own and mentioned a helicopter. This again surprised his parents because although the air ambulance service had arrived at the time of the accident, Phillip had not in fact been taken in it, but had been driven to the local hospital in an ambulance with his parents. They affirmed that the helicopter had landed in the field next door and it had made a loud noise, it had come to help him but he did not need it and it had gone away again. Thus they were able to incorporate his information into the narrative.

In the fourth session his parents reported that Phillip's sleeping had settled and he had became his previous cheerful and curious self. He was now talking to them about both accidents and asking questions. By the fifth session Phillip had settled down, was no longer asking questions and had moved on in terms of his development.

We have noted that during the processing of very early non-verbal memory as the narrative progresses, the language can help the child link his sensory-motor experiences to language and then he becomes able to contribute verbally to what it is that he wanted relief from, or even take ownership of the processing himself. In Phillip's case he was able to contribute to the narrative by remembering the helicopter. If he had been able to take ownership of the narrative by contributing more, it would not have been necessary to continue with narrative, but to allow him to process independently using the next phase up of the developmental protocol.

With an older child, using the narrative might involve giving just a small portion of it at a time and then pausing to take a breath and asking the child what has come up for them; giving pauses in between the sets may enable the child to become more participant in the procedure. If the child then starts to provide their own material, as previously said, the narrative form itself may no longer be required, as the child then accesses for themselves their own memories and associations that need to be processed, rather than the narrative material, which is just a guideline and not a substitute for their own individual thinking.

This type of narrative helps empower the parents to be proactive in healing and resolving the child's trauma and thus developing their own resiliency. It also helps the clinician's focus and understanding of the family's cultural belief system of the traumatic incident.

6.14. The four field technique

This technique was developed by Jarero et al., (2006). It was designed to be used in group settings: classrooms and sibling groups. It had initially four stages. In the first stage the children are asked to draw a safe place and identify where in their bodies they feel this positive sensation and write it down if they want to. They are then asked to install this safe place using the "*butterfly hug*". This is a means of tapping whereby the children cross their arms and tap their hands on the opposite upper arm. In the second stage the children are asked to draw the image of the worst moment of the traumatic incident. They can write what the negative thoughts or words they had about themselves when looking at this. They are also asked to evaluate the SUDS level they experience when looking at the drawing and thinking about their negative thoughts and write it down. They are asked to notice any body sensation and to start tapping until a new picture comes up for them.

Stage three is the next drawing of the new picture and they are asked to look at that and doing the tapping again until another picture comes up. Stage four is the next drawing that comes up for them. They are asked to evaluate the SUDS level and then are instructed to go back to their safe place drawing and do butterfly hugs again. This is known as the four-field technique because of the four drawings; however the clinician can expand this by asking the children to do more drawings according to their clinical judgement and the time available.

The original four-field technique was invented as a rapid intervention for a disaster zone affecting a large number of children. In our clinical experience we have found this technique valuable in working with sibling groups who have experienced the same traumatic event. For example a 5 year old and her 9 year old brother were both able to jointly process the illness and death of their mother from cancer simultaneously using this protocol though their thoughts and images were uniquely their own. The sharing of this experience helped the children reconnect in their re-attachment to each other.

This is a useful first therapeutic approach, but some children may need more individual work on specific issues following this treatment. It can work as a screening tool in helping to identify those who need more help (Korkmazlar-Oral and Pamuk, 2002). However, it must be remembered that children may need to revisit their traumatic experiences in the light of their developing cognitions, emotional and social maturation as they progress throughout childhood and particularly if they are re-triggered by subsequent life events.

6.15. Installation phase

Questions encountered in supervision include the following: What is the speed of the bilateral stimulation during this phase of installation? The speed of the bilateral stimulation is just as fast as for the desensitization phase and in both instances as fast as the child can tolerate. Another question is what do you install if you do not have a positive cognition? The therapist could install the positive emotion that the child experiences and ask them also what this makes them think or offers a positive cognition at the end of the strengthening of this "*so you feel ... so this means...*" Or, with a very young child the therapist could ask the parents for a positive cognition and install what the parents are saying is good about the child-like "*You are great, you are doing well, we are proud of you...*"

A good rule of thumb is to install whatever comes up that is positive for the child and continue until it cannot get any better. That is to say we are installing something that was not necessarily being defined as a positive cognition during the evaluation phase.

6.15.1. VOC evaluation

We are often asked how, following the developmental protocol, can the VOC evaluation be in tune with the child's developmental level. We all know from the standard generic protocol that the VOC is about thinking of the initial target together with the positive cognition and asking "*how true do the words... feel to you now on the scale from 1–7?*" The VOC requires the ability to meta-communicate by describing and linking two levels simultaneously: the connection between the target and positive cognition on one level and "*how true it feels today in the present*" on another level. The VOC, therefore, requires a more abstract broader perspective in connection with the target, an exercise we have found difficult if not impossible sometimes with adults. Children live in the present and do not think much to the future and even in adolescence this concept of the future may not be yet fully formed.

For example, for one child the negative cognition was "*I am going to die*", the positive cognition was that "*There will be a trampoline*", so when the ghost in his nightmare throws him out the window he will bounce! The therapist helped to reframe that by asking "*does that mean that you will be safe*" and he said "*yes*". The therapist is in this instance, helping the child connect by providing the higher order concept of safety that the trampoline represents in his concrete thinking.

Sometimes the therapist may be able to see a physical precursor of change from negative to positive when the child flushes up the neck, displays an upturning of the lips and gives a little murmur. These physiological signs are linked to heart rate coherence and precede the child's recognition of positive feelings.

6.15.2. Yawning

We have also noticed that children, when material has started to shift from negative to positive content will start to yawn. Yawning may be a process of resetting homeostasis or equilibrium, after a change has occurred in the body state; it provides more oxygen to the brain and increases relaxation. Thus this can be a physical indicator of change occurring. However, sometimes this yawning accompanied by a sense of fatigue may actually be a part of the processing itself. Children often report fatigue after completing or towards the end of desensitization. If this occurs the therapist should ask them to notice that and tell her when something changes and the ABLS should be continued. This in itself may be enough to shift this fatigue to a more general state of alertness after a couple of sets. When the child indicates a change has occurred, the ABLS is stopped and the child instructed to take a deep breath and then say what has changed. After which installation continues as usual until it is completed. Sometimes children will not tell the therapist a change has occurred but the therapist can detect this from watching the body language of the child and should stop ABLS shortly after seeing this and then follow as above until installation is complete.

Having said this, there are two other different manifestations of yawning some may come from genuine fatigue from a long day at school or from having stayed up to late the night before. This yawning is often accompanied by a rubbing of the eyes and drooping eyelids but they remain grounded in the present.

The other manifestation of yawning and fatigue may be heavier and accompanied by a general state of drowsiness and distance. In contrast to the yawning previously described this occurs during the desensitisation phase and when it is clear that the processing is not yet completed. This is an indicator that dissociative behaviour is occurring and in this instance the therapist needs to be proactive in encouraging the child back into the "*here and now*" and grounding them in the present. Further discussion of this can be found in Chapter 10.

6.16. Body scan

This phase can be confusing for children depending on their age because they have to hold image, positive cognition and scan for tension in the body. When they can't do that, what could the therapist do and what is important to keep? "*How does your body feel now...*" is a question that respects the child's level of development. If there is no tension the nice sensation can be installed. The younger child will often know how their body feels now, but we often only get a confused response because the processing has already finished and the child is wanting to move on to other activities. If this is the case, move on with them. If the child does talk about some tension the therapist does what he has learnt to do in the standard protocol.

Many children and adolescents in our clinical experience process the body sensations and tensions during the desensitisation and installation phases, they are not so discretely differentiated as in adults and we may not have to do a special process to get there. Children's feelings and sensations are much more closely linked to their body and there is less of a distinction between them. The younger the child is the less differentiated the feelings and sensations are, for example, they report things like anger in their fists and feet in contrast to adults who would tend to report a tightness in the throat and chest. When the emotions subside for children frequently the sensations spontaneously do too.

As we have often discussed in this book, at the end of the session it can be helpful to engage the parent's support of the child's positive body state by giving him a hug or a cuddle. This aids not only the positive reinforcement of the body sensations but also is re-nurturing the quality of attachment between the parents and the child.

6.17. Closure

Wherever the child gets to in their processing within each session, the therapist needs to leave enough time to close down the material for the child in a safe, containing way. Closing the session safely by spending time in play, relaxation or containment exercises and other activities is very important in EMDR therapy given the intensity of the work and the levels of arousal that the child may have reached during the session.

Parents, too, need to be alerted to what may come up after the session and the changes they may see in the child. They need to keep a diary of this as children are unlikely to be able to monitor these for themselves. Asking the parents to do this keeps them involved in the treatment and therefore allows them to work with the therapist and not against him. The parents' participation is always a crucial part of working with children and it is a therapist's responsibility to pay attention to this.

How do we know when a session is incomplete with a child?

As we have discussed, children and adolescents only partially adhere to the adult scales and their measures are often wildly inaccurate using the adult criteria. We may assume that if a child can tell us that his SUDS are not down to zero that this will be an incomplete session. If a child tells us that his SUDS are zero, this may not be a reliable indicator that he has finished desensitizing and this will need to be re-evaluated in the next session.

The therapist also needs to use their clinical judgement to assess just how uncomfortable a child's body language is and how it may still be being triggered to gauge how far the processing may have gone. The therapist may get an inner feeling of incongruence when listening and watching the child's behaviour. This incongruence is a perception that something is incomplete; something is lacking fluidity, is not coherent and remains unresolved; despite the child expressing something positive this is not being reflected by his body language. The therapist needs to trust their own feelings as a marker of this incongruence.

Some children may report positive changes have occurred, but again the therapist must use their own clinical judgement to ascertain whether this means they have actually entered the installation phase, or are just experiencing some relief from processing the distress. In either case, the processing is not complete and incomplete session procedures still need to be followed.

The therapist can then ask the child to leave the difficult material in some contained way in the therapy room for example, in a strong box, a filing cabinet or cupboard. The child can also draw, or write, or in some other way indicate what is still bothering them and put it inside. Again we emphasise that children do not go home with any of the process drawings other than the safe place or a specific resource. Towards the end of the session it is helpful to bring the child's focus back into the present everyday life by talking about, or playing with things and asking about what they are going to be doing after the session ends.

6.18. Re-evaluation

When children return for the next session it is interesting to see what has changed and what has not and it must be remembered that the metabolising of material may have continued to occur after the session ended and the child might be in a different place to the one they were in when they left the session. This is where the feedback from the parents and carers is essential, because children live so much in the present they do not realise things have changed. It is normal now, so the terrible problems of the previous session may not even be remembered, or may be referred to as something that happened a long time ago, or is "*rubbed out*" or "*gone*".

With older children we ask them to go back to the target and think about how much it bothers them now and ask them to rate the SUDS. If there is still a degree of disturbance or something else disturbing has come up, then this will need to be processed. In clinical practise we have found that those children who get positive gains from a session of EMDR will come back to the next session with their own agendas of what they want to work on next. We have noticed that the positive experience of EMDR therapy is empowering the children and adolescents who then want to take ownership of their own therapy with the therapist guiding them.

6.18.1. Helen – Asking for further therapy

Helen was 3 years old when the therapist worked on recurrent nightmares with her using EMDR therapy. A year later she told her mother she needed to see the lady who did the clapping game with her again. This was after her nightmares had been re-evoked following her father's request for access.

The therapist needs to be aware of how the parents and the family are reacting to the child's change. As we previously mentioned, the child's behaviour needs to be understood through the lens of the family dynamics. If the child is at peace now, what other difficulties or problems could arise? We have seen many times that the child's difficulty can act as a distracter from the parents' or couple's tension. The therapist in their treatment plan will need to address such issues to prevent some potential relapse with the child's behaviour. They will need to see either the whole family or the parents, or refer them to another practitioner if they do not have the appropriate training for this.

6.18.2. *Matthew – Treated and seeking help for his family*

Matthew aged 8 years, came to therapy because he was having some behavioural difficulties in school with the other children and was struggling to learn. When seen with his parents, the focus was mainly on his behaviour. It was decided to see him alone and Matthew chose what he called his "*soft poo-poo*" as his target. When work with him was completed he told the therapist it was time now to help his mother and father because they scream a lot.

In the re-evaluation phase the therapist also needs to be mindful of the three prongs to the protocol. Once the past traumas have been resolved there may still be work to be done on current triggers and building a future template.

We have noticed that when children are diminished in their emotional, cognitive and social growth due to trauma, they may have a lot of developmental catch-up to accomplish after recovering from their symptoms. Some of this, particularly with young children, may occur in a process of accelerated physical development. However, there may also be more work needed with their parents or school to help them with their post-traumatic growth and developmental catch-up.

When the children are reviewed sometime after therapy is completed, we notice that they eat well, thrive and grow healthily and that they become more spontaneous, happier and at peace. Parents make comments like their children are blossoming or blooming and even that they think their learning has come on in leaps and bounds.

6.19. Summary

In this chapter we have described working with the children through phases four to eight, from desensitisation to the re-evaluation phase of the EMDR protocol and how this adapted to meet developmental needs. We started with the assessment of the target and how this might be achieved. We have talked about the importance of attunement in the sessions and how this may be achieved working at the pace of the child, together with how to utilise spontaneous resources during the desensitisation. We have also discussed having parents in the sessions and when this is helpful and when it may not be.

Chapter 7

Resilience and the Window of Tolerance

7.1. Resilience

Resilience is a much debated topic and there are many factors which help children to develop coping mechanisms and good resiliency (Cyrulnik, 2002). Resilience can be defined as a bio-psycho-social and cultural process that allows for new post-traumatic growth and that organises itself inter-subjectively in relationship with another (Cyrulnik and Jorland, 2012). Resilience needs to be seen as a dynamic, evolving, adaptive process and not as a static and immutable characteristic (Delage, 2008).

Resilience can be considered as the capacity of one person to successfully be able to live and to develop themselves in a positive and socially acceptable way, in the face of stressors or elements that could have created a negative outcome. Resilience is a multi-faceted process that interweaves individual characteristics (cognitive, behavioural and intrapsychic) with the family's psychological competencies to express and regulate affect (Anaut, 2012).

Good attachment with competent, caring and protective adults will help the child to internalise good affect regulation and boundaries. Familial support and parental emotional functioning are strong protective factors that reduce the impact of trauma, as well as enhance the child's ability to cope (Cohen et al., 2000). The family's resilience capacity enables it to help manage the child's suffering in a positive, empathic and supportive way in the face of adversity. When the parents are able to do this, they increase the child's affective adaptability and the quality of their attachment to each other, which in turn further increases the stability of the family's foundations.

A positive worldview in which the children take appropriate responsibility will enable them to develop a degree of mastery and success in their daily life. It may aid the development of a more positive sense of self and contribute to a feeling of being able to cope. Having adaptable and easy going personalities promotes positive social interactions and helps them live positively in a socially acceptable and adaptive manner. Thus despite exposure to distressing incidents, which contain high risks of negative outcomes, many children healthily attached and resilient do not in fact suffer from traumatisation as a result of their adverse life experiences.

On the other hand, clinically, we have noted that even in healthy families, trauma can disrupt healthy attachments. Emotional availability between the parent and the child may become mistimed or delayed and thus not as soothing as it would naturally be. This resolves after therapy is completed. In addition, in our clinical experience we have noted that the internalisation of resilience is a developmental task of adolescence. Whilst it is possible to help younger children heal from their traumatic experience using EMDR therapy, it is our experience that re-exposure to further traumatic events may well be re-traumatising for some of them despite good resources and support of the family. Whilst again this can be treated, they seem to remain vulnerable to further traumatisation until they are able to become introspective and reflective in their thinking (when they develop meta-cognitive capacity), which capacity develops in adolescence and enables the development of self-reflective capacities and self-regulation.

It is important to note here that older children and adolescents with complex post-traumatic stress disorders have difficulties in regulating their emotions, self-soothing, tolerating strong emotions and labelling emotions. They also have poor impulse control and are often self-destructive or take dangerous risks.

When working with children and their families it is important to evaluate how well they are coping in their daily life, what has been most helpful for them, what has been least helpful and what they think might help them in the future. Looking at their family strengths allows us to think about their level of resilience, both as individual family members and as a family system as a whole. How does the family characteristically cope with problems in their daily life and what is their ability to jointly handle problems and solve conflicts on an individual level and as a family group? Further, how does the family protect the children, educate them socially and how do the members communicate and express their feelings?

Studying the family's narrative can give useful information on the type of narrative that they are transmitting to the future generations. As previously stated, one needs to consider whether they are narrating a story of the past adversity or whether they are still frozen by their traumatisation and unable to work to a positive resolution of the past traumatic event, in which case they may be transmitting the trauma and not the story.

7.1.1. <u>Wendy –Impact of past unresolved trauma in family on therapy</u>

Wendy aged 14 years old, was referred because of her severe OCD, her school refusal and her selective mutism. She appeared frozen in her demeanour, could not give eye contact and only uttered a few words in a low whisper. Because Wendy was so overwhelmed, cut off and remote the therapist decided to see her mother on her own in the next session. Her mother explained that Wendy, when 12 years old, had been exposed to some sexual exploration by a neighbour's 13 year old son.

Mother said that she could really identify with Wendy because of her own experiences of being sexually abused also aged 12 years and she has shared this with her to support her. Mother explained that she had been subjected to this by a paedophile aged 43 years who had groomed and abused her over a period of 18 months. It had ended when she had finally told her own mother what was happening. Mother agreed that she still felt very traumatised by her past despite having had CBT treatment and having taken the perpetrator to Court when she was a young adult. The therapist then proposed that she might benefit from some EMDR therapy for herself to help her contain and provide healthy support to her daughter and not be reactivated by her daughter's actual trauma. Below is a summary of mother's processing in the two sessions of EMDR therapy around these issues.

In her first session, mother reported that she was 'gutted' that it had happened to her own daughter too, why had it happened again? She felt like a bad parent because of it. She felt very let down and cannot trust people. She saw what happened to her daughter as being the same as what happened to her as they were both kids. In the subsequent set she wondered whether perhaps this had transferred to Wendy's experience. In the next set she realised this made them both see the experiences as the same when they were not. As the processing carried on she began to realise they were not the same thing. Her daughter's experience was a one-time childhood fumbling and experimentation, whereas her abuse lasted a long time. She felt she hasn't helped her daughter and doesn't want her to feel the same way she feels, in terms of low self-worth.

Mother went on to process she felt damaged and unconfident. In terms of what happened to her daughter, she feels that her daughter is not worthless, but *"lovely and brave"* and *"not damaged goods"*. She hated that what happened to her is affecting how she sees what happened to her daughter, as it is very different. She describes her own experience as *"far more sinister and a lot longer"*.

Mother felt that she had a longer sentence than her abuser had had and did not want to carry it anymore, *"it's his burden"*. She never really realised the impact it would have, as she buried it when she was growing up. When mother had told her own mother, she responded that no one would ever love her and she was a dirty little girl. Her mother eventually apologised to her when she was an adult, for being unkind, but she had been mentally ill herself.

She felt she needed to tell her daughter that the two experiences were completely different; her daughter's experience hit her own trauma and affected how she comforted Wendy. Towards the end of the EMDR session, she expressed how it's much harder to remove emotions and experiences in the heart that it is in the head. She had let it control her as that is all she knew. She said she needed to tell her 12 year old self what she would tell Wendy and wanted to believe it. She knew all this in her head, but found it much harder in her heart.

In the second EMDR session, mother had a sense of sadness and real frustration that her head did not marry up with her heart. She wished she did not believe what her parents had said, criticising her all the time. She felt a bit silly she could not pull herself together and when asked by the therapist what is stopping this, she explained she had internalised their voices. She did not want to get hurt anymore, wanted to put a wall up and not let anyone in other than her children and husband. She really wanted to break free. There was an emptiness in her heart, even though she has a great family and kids, she still did not feel happy and then felt guilty, it is like walking under a shadow. She said *"I've always responded in the same way, it's my fault, it's about me. Have I just been responding as a little girl for all these years and that's how I've been dealing with stuff, but why have I been doing that, why am I still thinking like a little girl? If I was an adult I wouldn't blame myself for everything. I'm thinking like a 12 year old"*.

She would like to run away and put the inadequacy in a box and bury it but running away was not an option. Mother questioned if Wendy is running away too and following her pattern. She's always dealt with things this way, as that's *"how I did it when I was 12"*. She realised that it was a decision she could make. Everyone has their own issues, men and women, just because they don't talk about it doesn't mean they aren't there. Mother recognised she did have a choice and could decide how to respond. It was the trauma she went through that took away the ability to make choices. She no longer had to respond as a 12 year old.

The above example illustrates the complexity of the impact of the past unresolved traumatic events on the current disturbance in the child and family. Of course in such a complex case the overall treatment programme included not only EMDR therapy for the mother, but also EMDR and CBT therapy for the daughter and family therapy. Of significant note were changes in the behaviour of the child as the mother processed her own traumatisation. As mother found her voice so too did Wendy.

7.2.   Window of tolerance

In a state of homeostasis the autonomic nervous system oscillates between states arousal and de-arousal, swinging between sympathetic arousal and parasympathetic de-arousal. When trauma is experienced by the individual this homeostasis is disrupted and the loss of balance of this process creates greater swings in the levels of oscillation between arousal and de-arousal (Bradley, 2000).

These swings can take the individual outside of their comfort zone, in other words outside of their optimal level of arousal and de-arousal and can result in either hyper-arousal (adrenergic), a state in which the child is hyper-vigilant, distractible, unable to concentrate and experiences symptoms of intrusion, or hypo-arousal (serotonergic) a state in which the child experiences symptoms of avoidance, denial, surrender, numbness, freezing and ultimately submission. As previously mentioned Perry et al., (1995) have defined two continuums of behavioural adaptation in coping with trauma that they hypothesized as states becoming traits in younger children exposed to repeated traumatisation over time.

The concept of the "window of tolerance" (Ogden and Minton, 2006) illustrates the optimal response capacity of a person in the face of a traumatic event. The perceived information from the external and internal context is integrated and response that is most pertinent for that event will depend upon the capacity of the window of tolerance of that individual. The comfort or treatment zone corresponds to the optimal space for therapeutic work within which the individual can cope with the experiencing of difficult emotions, sensations and cognitions without the feeling of losing control. Above or below this window, the individual is entering a zone of hyper/hypo excitation where the person is flooded and numbed by the emotions which are taking over.

When the window of tolerance is small the capacity of the individual to respond within their comfort zone may be easily overwhelmed or exceeded. The individual will then respond with either hyper-arousal or hypo-arousal. In these states the individual's integrative cognitive capacity is replaced by reflex responses (Siegel, 1999). Thus the larger the window of tolerance is, the more the individual will be able to express a flexible response to stressful elements with a lesser emotional susceptibility.

As clinicians, in treatment planning, we need to evaluate the window of tolerance that the child may have. Affecting the child's capacity to participate in the therapy will be: the chronicity of the traumatisation, their temperamental disposition, the quality of the family attachments, the degree of personalization of the trauma, the age of the child at the onset of the traumatisation and their intellectual capacity and resilience factors including the resilience of the family and its attachments. The Treatment Duration Triangle described in Chapter 3 illustrates this. This information is obtained through the history taking and also by the essential clinical evaluation of the child himself. We have noticed that the clinician may miss that the child's window of tolerance is being exceeded in some way and may mistake this for non-compliance.

One of the rules of thumb for working with children using EMDR is how easily the safe place or similar resource can be installed. When the safe place is hard to find or breaks through quickly to negative material this is a clear indicator that the whole therapeutic process needs to be slowed down as this indicates that the child has a very narrow window of tolerance. This is done by more stabilization, pacing sessions more gently, breaking into smaller units the traumatic material to be processed, or working with the least disturbing first and also building more resources to help them cope before undertaking the desensitization process.

7.3. The constant installation of present orientation and safety

The Constant Installation of Present Orientation and Safety (CIPOS) technique (Knipe, 2008) has been adapted for children (Eckers, 2009) and can be another way of gently beginning the process. This technique is helpful for those children for whom the fear of the fear of the trauma itself is too frightening to begin to work on the trauma. The focus is to help the child to begin to confront the thought of the trauma in a way that does not overwhelm them and helps to stabilise them in the present time so that they may become desensitized enough to be able to work through the trauma itself at a later point. The child is held safely in the present with the therapist doing playful things and is very gradually exposed to the memory of the traumatic situation in a carefully titrated way.

The child is asked to draw a picture of the traumatic situation. The drawing is then turned face down. The child is engaged in a positive activity such as catching a ball. The good feeling the child experiences in their body whilst doing this is then installed with brief ABLS. The child is then asked to look at the drawing for three seconds and the drawing is then turned face downwards again. The child is praised for their courage and then the positive activity is repeated and the good feelings installed again. This is continued by repeating the sequence several times. The child might then be invited to look at their picture of safe place instead of doing a positive activity. The traumatic picture is then confronted increasing the time of exposure from 3 to 4 and then to 5 and more seconds. In the next session the sequence is repeated again. If such a direct approach is still too overwhelming, it is suggested that a soft toy or similar attachment object of the child's be used to look at the pictures instead and then asked what the toy's feelings are. The above continues until the child is able to tolerate looking at the picture.

When working with very vulnerable children, as with adults, the golden rule is that working slower than faster achieves better results in the long run. We know that the size of the window of tolerance is directly linked to the quality of the child's attachment experiences. The poorer the quality of attachment, the smaller the window of tolerance is likely to be and the more the therapist will have to work at establishing this in the therapeutic alliance and within the family.

The aim in therapy is to gradually and delicately stretch the window of tolerance over time to cope with greater degrees of distress. This is achieved through a combination of using the attunement with the child, resource building and in desensitising the whole process to an appropriate pace for the child to develop greater resilience, resolution of the traumatisation and integration.

As can be seen in Figure 7.1, the window of tolerance is first evaluated in the assessment phase. Over time and with therapy, this window is gradually enlarged by the processing of past dysfunctional memories as demonstrated from the interval between "therapy time 1" to "therapy time 2". This process may take anything from several sessions to several months to achieve. The goal of the therapy is to develop a level of tolerance that enables the child to cope with most adverse experiences and stressors in everyday life in a more flexible and adaptive way.

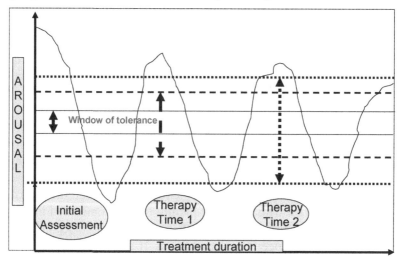

Figure 7.1: Stretching the widow of tolerance over time

But we want to emphasise that the stretching of the window of tolerance needs to be put into a contextual frame in which the therapist's own window of tolerance may be looked at as the scaffolding framework within which the parent's and child's windows of tolerance can be enlarged in therapy. These are intertwined.

EMDR therapy is very powerful and in our experience, the therapist needs to learn to expand his own window of tolerance in supervision as a part of the process of acquiring competence in the therapy. It can at times, as already mentioned, feel quite challenging for the therapist as strong emotions can be engendered and feeling comfortable containing these can be difficult, until the therapist is familiar enough with the process and learns to trust it and has developed the skills to manage this. As the therapist becomes more familiar with and comfortable with the EMDR processing, they learn to attune to each individual child more finely and thus develop greater synchrony with them. Attunement may be defined as the capacity of the therapist to accommodate, harmonize and synchronize their behaviours, demeanour and pace to the individual child.

EMDR therapy, by its methodology, also helps to regulate emotional arousal by shaping this during the processing. At the start of each set the traumatic material is aroused engaging the sympathetic nervous system and at the end of each set the taking of a deep breath re-engages the para-sympathetic nervous system. We always teach the therapists to take the deep breaths with the child to promote the attunement between them and also to re-regulate the child and also the therapist after difficult material the child may be bringing up. It is a joint process of engagement. As we have said previously the therapist's capacity to tolerate and hold the child's affect during processing is quintessential.

This process of attunement helps to keep the child within their own window of tolerance and to cope better with the gradual stretching of it and reduces both abreactions and dissociation. This is why high quality supervision as the therapist is developing is crucial and needs to be maintained after they have become competent as all cases are unique. Further, we would refer the therapist to their own professional body and to the National and European EMDR Associations Codes of Ethics and Practice as guiding structures.

We may liken the windows of tolerance of the therapist, parent and child to Russian dolls with the therapist containing both parent and child, the parent contained by therapist containing the child and the child safe to grow. The therapist enables the parent to learn to tolerate the child's distress and helps with the child's growing in capacity to a healthy level of tolerance for their age and stage of development. The aim in therapy is to help the parent and child grow to places where the therapeutic scaffolding is no longer necessary. At this point the therapist needs to recognise that ecological changes for the family and child have been achieved and learn to let go so that the family can resume its own dynamic developmental trajectory without him. Our clinical experience has taught us not to expect the expected; and the way in which each family and child will reach resolutions will be unique and individual to them.

Focusing again on the window of tolerance, both hyper and hypo arousal responses are often seen in working with children when they are moving out of their window of tolerance. The child may show their uneasiness to the therapist by avoiding behaviours, for example, by asking to play, changing the subject, asking to go to the toilet, or simply blanking off with a loss of affect and a glazed stare into the middle distance. Or they may do this by exhibiting hyper-excitability with the child becoming very agitated, moving around constantly and unable to stay focused.

The work consists of the therapist developing a therapeutic attunement and alliance with the child by first respecting the limits of his window of tolerance. The process of attunement between therapist and child is essential and helps to regulate the non-verbal affect, to hold and contain it. This process is similar to that of a parent regulating and soothing a young infant. We consider this attunement between therapist and child a key element of the work because of the social dynamics involved in this process of mirroring, imitation, contingency and synchronicity.

We have found that one of the most difficult things to teach in supervision is how to develop this attunement. Some therapists seem naturally able to use this, whilst others struggle to read the children and their signals and adjust their behaviours accordingly. The key to attuning to the child is identifying, reading and responding to the whole body language not just their facial expressions and expressed words.

Children are less able to explain complex feelings and have fewer facial expressions due to their developmental levels. This attunement between therapist and child cannot be replaced or mimicked by only a machine bleeping or flashing lights. Affect regulation of the child depends greatly on the quality of the relationship with the therapist as an external regulator. As we mentioned before in contrast to children, adults do not depend as much on the quality of the relationship to regulate their affect, they have internalised to a greater extent their own mechanisms for doing this. In this way children differ developmentally from adults.

7.4.   Mechanical ABLS and attunement

We are concerned that multiple mechanical stimulation (for example, lights, vibrators and headphones simultaneously) are commonly being presented as a way of working therapeutically using EMDR with children who are thought to be motivated by these 'high tech' interests. We are worried that this may be being used without adequate thought to what this simultaneous mechanical stimulation may be doing to a child. Without the protective factor of being emotionally contained in a therapeutic attunement, the treatment is missing the essential social communicative scaffolding and linkage and thus may be reducing the level of the child's security.

It is important to realise that the therapist is part of the therapy not just a vehicle through which robotic actions are performed. EMDR therapy is not just a mechanistic process but is more global and is being regulated by the emotional attunement of the therapist helping the child maintain one foot in the present and one foot in the past. It is thus a form of congruent communication with the therapist regulating this process within each set.

Siegel (1999) suggests that at moments of mis-attunement when incongruence and incoherence occur there is a feeling of disconnection. In EMDR, the interactive therapist can address immediately the disconnection and interweave this back into a congruent continuity. This cannot be repaired within the sets using mechanical stimulation, which lacks the flexibility and the possibility to finely retune and reintegrate the process. Repairing attunement is interactive and when the disconnection is acknowledged the process can move on to reconnect. Understanding this is important as these markers of disconnection can help the therapist recognise dissociative tendencies in older children and adolescents as well as in adulthood.

The mechanistic process using machinery creates predictable repeated patterns without variation, except when adjusted for between sets and not within sets and we hypothesise it is creating a lack of flexibility and spontaneity in responsiveness, which is quintessential to human self–regulation and fluid adaptive capacity. As Siegel (1999) has stated, in trauma, rigidities to the flow of energy can lead to difficulties in adaptation as the mind flows to the extremes of order (rigidity) or chaos, with the oscillation flipping between these poles preventing the individual from achieving the highly complex, internal or interpersonal states that can be seen as the essence of mental health.

Further, we are also concerned about how over-stimulating such a barrage of multiple alternating bilateral stimulations may actually be to the child's emotional capacity to cope with traumatic material. When using the standard protocol, one mode of alternating bilateral stimulation is normally employed, whether it be hand taps or eye movements or auditory. In advanced workshops, one has sometimes seen the trainers using more than one modality to help to stimulate processing of material when needed.

With children the use of more than one modality of stimulation may overwhelm their window of tolerance. Safety first is the main consideration and only stimulating them enough to do the processing is required. EMDR desensitisation may be likened to a gas cooker flame, which once it is ignited should be burning at a steady speed without reducing the gas so low that it goes out, or increasing it so high that it becomes a conflagration. To date, to the best of our knowledge there do not appear to be any studies that compare the use of a single mode or multiple modes of mechanical stimulation with the therapist administrating the ABLS in the child and adolescent population.

7.5. Summary

In this chapter we have described how the window of tolerance is a key conceptual element in EMDR therapy with children. We discuss how the therapist's own window of tolerance functions as the scaffolding framework within which both the parent and child's own windows of tolerance can be enlarged in the therapeutic process. We also discuss attunement and express reservations of the use of mechanical ABLS devices which could inhibit attunement and overwhelm the child's window of tolerance.

Chapter 8

Attachment and Family Dynamics

In the previous chapter we discussed the notion of attunement and its importance in the EMDR process. In this chapter we plan to explore attachment and family dynamics in some greater detail and their relationship to EMDR therapy. As we all know, a child does not exist alone, but within a family context; and family dynamics and attachments are fluid and change over time with changing circumstances and life events.

Beginning at the beginning, the infant exists and its needs are defined initially by crying, hunger, sleeping and a set of primitive reflexes. These signals are shaped by the carer who intuitively learns to differentiate a hunger cry from an anger cry from a tired cry from a pain cry and to attune and respond to these intuitively in different ways, some of which is biologically determined by oxytocin levels and some of which is socially determined by the parent's own life experiences. Thus the infant learns to understand itself in a more sophisticated state-based and relationship-dependant way and a process of internalisation of these affect regulation blueprints begins and in this lie the origins of attachment blueprints.

The continuity of the movement between these states is mediated and given coherence by the carer who sets harmonious boundaries, rhythmic patterned routines, constancy and predictability in their responsiveness. As the blueprints are internalising they start to become operational and emotional expressions of the child's emerging sense of self start to develop. Interruptions, incongruences, inconsistencies and disharmonious ruptures affect the quality of this evolving sense of self from predictable states. Thus disruptions in attachment may be seen as the primary traumas, they jeopardise the very integrity of the infant and without the continuing care of the parent or carer the infant maybe endangered and could even die.

In this book we have also emphasised the neuro-developmental nature of childhood and adolescence with processes becoming more complex and sophisticated as the child matures physiologically and neurological and in the light of their growing experiences of the world both interpersonal and environmental. Through these and their internal sensory motor responses the child evolves.

8.1. Attachment

Attachment is the fundamental element that characterizes the nature of the relationship between the child and its family. Attachment theory was first conceptualized by Bowlby (1969). Attachment consists of a combination of ways in which the child and parent are mindful of each other, communicate and relate, through attunement, contingent communication, reflective dialogue, repair, emotional communication and coherent narratives. Secure attachment enables the child to explore the world from a stable base and take risks. To develop a secure attachment the parent's response needs to be quick, warm, coherent, predictable and validating. Insecure attachment occurs when the parent's response to the child doesn't meet these criteria.

Patterns of attachment were described by Ainsworth et al., (1978). In a secure attachment through contingent communication the parent perceives the child's signals, makes sense of them and gives a response that is appropriately timed. The child reciprocates and an interactive communication is established. The signals include eye contact, facial expressions, voice tones, bodily gestures, posture and the timing of these.

At times contingency does not occur and then there is a rupturing in the attunement and a need to repair this. Rupturing can occur because the parent or child is tired, distracted or preoccupied. It can also occur when a child's behaviour needs to be contained by limit setting and also because of guilt, anger, depression or other emotional distress. Repairing attunement is an interactive task, firstly acknowledging the disconnection and then reconnecting. Through the sharing and joint reflection of positive and negative emotions, the child learns to differentiate feelings and to make them tolerable internally. This leads in time to the development of empathy and compassion.

Developing coherent co-narratives and storytelling are important in the development of interpersonal communication, in making sense of other people and the social world. The parents' ability to understand themselves and their worlds enables the child in joint communication to facilitate the development of secure attachment. Main (1993) identifies that the most robust predictor of a child's attachment to a parent is the coherence of the parent's autobiographical narrative. The question is not whether the parent was traumatised but whether their mind is still in a state of lack of resolution or whether they have made sense of their life.

Disorganised or disoriented attachment develops when the parent's behaviours with the child is characterised by frightening or frightened behaviours. These behaviours can create paradoxical and problematic situations for the child which they cannot resolve. The parents are thus unable to soothe or emotionally regulate the child appropriately given their behaviours and the child may be prone to developing dissociative symptoms as a result (Liotti, 1999 and 2009). This is because the child is pulled in contrary directions; it approaches for comfort and nurturance but then finds the proximity dangerous and needs to withdraw in a classic double-bind situation. This well-studied and described clinical situation of double-bind can be seen as an example of disorganized attachment and its consequences on the child's psychological functioning. The child is unable to find the appropriate response that is satisfying to the parents.

For example, domestic violence between the parents can often be the source of an insecure or disorganized attachment in the child. When the attachment is unstable the child is not held safely emotionally, is not soothed and thus does not develop their inner ability to contain their emotion. The parents are unable to set the model of emotional regulation that the child needs. The parental relationship does not play its containing role of helping the child to maintain his level of emotion within his window of tolerance or by helping him to come back into his window of tolerance through secure and predictable soothing behaviour.

8.2. Family dynamics

When there is a traumatic event it is likely to impact not only on the child but also on other individuals in the family. The attachments in the family can become dysregulated and disrupted, even in healthy families with good secure attachments. Thus it is important always to consider the impact not only on the individual but also the family as previously mentioned in Chapter 4. Often parents may be suffering from significant traumatisation themselves and unless the trauma is treated in the adult, the child may not be able to achieve a full recovery. Whilst many parents may have some significant traumatisation themselves, this is often insufficient a disturbance to trigger adult mental health services to intervene in their treatment. The discovery of underlying traumatisation in the adults may often only be made in the context of the family assessment and treatment opportunities may also be limited to this arena. It is a matter of clinical judgement as to what point traumatisation is sufficiently interfering with the adult's normal life and mental health to warrant a referral to an adult mental health service.

Similar criteria to that outlined in Treatment Duration Triangle (Chapter 3) may be used to guide this assessment together with an assessment of the parent's narrative. Thus the more complex, multiple and personal the traumas are in the parent and the earlier their origins are, the more likely they are going to need to be referred on for treatment in their own right. With less complex traumas in relatively intact parents, who would not be deemed sufficiently serious for an adult service, the clinician may wish to offer focussed short-term treatment before treating their children. As previously mentioned, parents can often be co-therapists in the treatment of their children and helping them to attain the best emotional space to be available to support their children is important in treatment.

When trauma impacts a family it can cause loss or injury to the family bonds. For example 70% of couples who have lost a child will divorce in less than 18 months after the child's death (Cyrulnik, 2006). Trauma also creates a loss of communication between family members, unpredictable expressions of emotion and feelings of isolation, and there can be a loss of emotional and sexual intimacy within the couple's relationship.

We therefore need to work with the whole family to reduce traumatic consequences for the children and to create a context of safety. This work enables the therapist to help the parents regain their attachment competency and thus improve affect control in the whole family and help prevent family relationship breakdown (Delage, 2008). Family dynamics can help the child to contain her emotion when her cortex cannot do this by itself. It is important to work with the family to stop the transmission of trauma to the next generation and to do this by transforming painful traumatic events into a narrative through which things can be said with a distance as a story, as mentioned previously.

Working with the family becomes more difficult when the parental roles are unsafe, when there is continuing domestic violence and continuing risk to the children. The children are not safe and they may be being continually re-traumatised. The priority is to stop violent behaviours and to ensure the safety of the children. It also can be problematic to work within the family context when the children's care is being shared by parents who are acrimoniously separated or divorced and thus the children's loyalties may be divided. In this latter case the therapist needs to be mindful of engaging all the family members possible and to be careful not to put the child in a conflictive situation. The therapist needs to be aware of child protection issues and their Country's legal regulations with respect to working with a child when the parent is separated and who has parental responsibility.

Attachment, when it becomes traumatic creates problems for the child as the family boundaries are unclear, unspecific and chaotic (Erdman and Caffery, 2003). Marvin (2003) has observed a link between the four primary attachment patterns (Ainsworth and Bell, 1970) and the four patterns of family structure (Minuchin, 1974). He associates the secure-child and autonomous-parent healthy attachment style (secure) with the adaptive family structure. He associates the anxious-avoidant child and dismissing-parent attachment style (avoidant) with the disengaged family structure. He associates the anxious-ambivalent child and preoccupied-parent attachment style (ambivalent) with the enmeshed family structure. Finally Marvin associates the disordered, role-reversed child and abdicating parent style (disorganised) with the incongruent family hierarchy structure. We have found this linkage between the individual and family perspective particularly helpful in conceptualizing and integrating our EMDR work with children and their families.

EMDR therapy thus has to be embedded in a variety of other therapeutic approaches to meet the needs in complex families where problems exist within individuals and within the family dynamics. The role of the therapist is to develop a global vision of the above and create integration using multiple interventions. In particular the therapist needs to pay attention to ruptures in family relationships and individuals within the family becoming isolated, for example, fathers can too often be forgotten because they do not want to/or are unable to come. The therapist must not forget to invite them.

Figure 8.1 helps to conceptualise the complexity of the interaction between the individual characteristics, the attachment patterns and family dynamics that are needed to build this complex vision.

Of course it must be remembered that trauma can have consequences not only at a child level or at the family level, but may also reverberate in the wider social systems surrounding the child, in particular their schooling and other professionals involved in the child's life. The therapist needs to be aware of these potential different levels and consider engaging these social elements in the course of the therapy as appropriate. Complex trauma requires the interweaving of needs at an individual, family and social level.

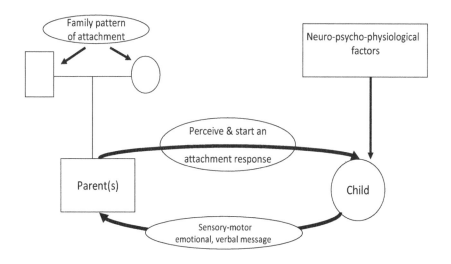

Figure 8.1: The complex vision: Intra-psychic and interactive

8.3. Fostering and adoption

Unfortunately in today's world not all children can be left in the care of their natural parents as they may have been exposed to neglect, abuse, and other traumatic events whilst in the care of their parents and may have suffered significant harm either physically, psychologically or both as a result. Others may have arrived in care because of the death of their parent.

The task of parenting a child who is a stranger to the new family is a great one. Firstly, the parent has to learn and understand the child's temperament, fears and previous life experiences that the child has had and integrate them into their family life. They have to learn to map onto and attune to the child and its needs, its rejection of them and its fear of them. In turn the child has to absorb a whole new life, many things may be unfamiliar and strange and the way their new adults manage and treat them may be very different to their previous ones.

They may find it hard to link their past sense of self with their current situation. They also will at some levels be grieving for the loss of their past worlds and they may also be suffering a sense of abandonment and be conflicted by issues of loyalty. Can they be loved by the new parents, can they accept the love of the new parents, what does the love of the new parents mean and does loving the new parents mean they have to reject their previous family? They may also fear that their new adults are just as unpredictable and potentially dangerous to them as their old ones were and whether it could ever be safe to attach to them at all because of a lack of internal safety and a fear of being rejected again. The child may feel a need to test out the safety level of the new family.

Before a child can attach to a new family they need to grieve their losses and detach from their past relationships. Most children entering the care system will have suffered significant disruptions to their attachments and multiple complex traumatisation. Simply loving these children and providing a stable home and consistent parenting is not likely to be enough to address their needs. For the new adoptive parents there may be very high expectations of their own performance as parents and of how they may be able to transform the child's life and world. There are also likely to be pressures on them from their understanding of the system's expectations of them as good, competent parents rather than 'good enough' parents.

Whilst initially, the placement may receive professional support as time goes by, the parents often feel isolated, a deep sense of their own failure as parents and a fear of asking for help because this may threaten or jeopardise the child's placement with them; or if they are foster parents, their credibility and licensing as a foster family.

One of the first tasks for the therapist is to engage not only the new parents, but also the care system around the child to ensure that there is adequate communication and transmission of information; and to develop the trust and safety in the social system surrounding the child including the school and the family. Networking between the agencies and the new family is important in developing this.

The family needs help to develop confidence in the system to support them during the difficult times without feeling criticised. They also need to feel supported in their parenting by the therapist in helping them to develop their insight and expand their own windows of tolerance to be able to parent the child. The therapist needs to develop a platform on which they and the parents co-operate into developing a co-therapeutic role in working with the child, whilst at the same time creating an affiliation with the child and maintaining an openness that enables the parents to be able to express their frustrations, worries, strengths and weaknesses thus expanding their resiliency. This will involve a lot of psycho-education about, not only the dynamics of adoption, but the symptoms and behaviours associated with complex traumatisation.

The therapist should help the parent map onto the child and its idiosyncrasies and to attune and build a synchronous communication between them and child. The parents need to understand that aspects of the child's behaviour reflect the developmental level at which the traumatisation occurred and that the child might present as much younger than their years in some respects, particularly in relation to emotional, social and moral development. The therapist should help the new parents identify, recognise and manage their own grief at what the child has experienced before coming to them. Working with them through EMDR can strengthen their emotional availability to the child in the child's subsequent EMDR sessions and their resiliency in coping with the child's processing of painful memories.

Whilst the child processes such painful memories the adoptive parents can become an active positive resource, by the development of a brief, claiming narrative and perhaps also hugging them or other appropriate physical nurturing contact. For example, the following well known to attachment therapists may be given together with the ABLS: *"Mummy and Daddy are very sad and sorry that this happened to you and if they had known you then and been there they would never have allowed this to have happened to you and they are going to look after you now right up until you are a grown-up yourself and even after that."*

This work strengthens the bonding and attachment between them. Adoptive parents need to understand the fragility and vulnerability of the child's internal sense of safety. They need to be aware in their words and actions not to threaten or jeopardise this, but rather to nurture and heal. Thus, bearing in mind the notion of the Russian dolls previously discussed, the therapist is helping the parents to help the child.

In our experience with adoptive families, the same role names are used for the parents as were used for the biological parents, namely for example, "mummy and daddy". Whilst, more recently there has been some social attempt to vary this, it is still confusing to a developing child when the differences are not kept alive. In our experience of working with adoptive children, whilst in early and middle childhood the children's behaviours are manageable but difficult for their adoptive parents, in adolescence they can tend to explode. This is because in this phase of development the adolescent is renegotiating their attachment relationship and the boundaries.

What has become evident particularly since we have used EMDR therapy with this group is that many of the children have 'fused' the two or more mummies, or daddies in the past with their current ones. In this way they have come to ascribe all their early negative experiences to the hands of their current caretakers.

Their past is still alive; the children are viewing their adoptive parents through the dysfunctional filters acquired from their biological family experiences. It is thus very important in our opinion to be clear helping them in the differentiation of these two. Ideally this should be done at the start with the naming role being differentiated. However, it seems that this is a hard task for the adoptive parents to understand so early on as new parents, as their primary wish is to become the child's mummy and daddy. One of the ways of doing this is to help the child understand that they have both biological parents and 'grow-you-up-parents'; the ones that made them and the ones that they are going to grow up with and live with.

8.3.1. *Peter – Separating past from present*

Peter aged 14 years was referred for his opposition defiance both at home and at school. His adoptive parents who had raised him since he was 3 years old were at the end of their tethers. In the EMDR processing of his anger at his mother and father Peter revealed past hurts and neglect. When these were discussed with his parents, it became clear that these incidents related to his life with his biological parents. In the therapy a cognitive interweave was used with Peter asking him how old he was when it happened. He was able to say it was when he was very little and lived in the brown house. His adoptive parents had never lived in a brown house, but his adoptive mother recalled that in the life story book (that Peter had and which he had not looked at for many years) there was a photograph of his biological parents standing in front of a house painted brown.

In Peter's next session the photograph was shown to him and he exclaimed in some surprise that he had two mothers and it was not his current mother who had done that but his birth mother. His behaviour changed considerably after that and he was able to process his anger at what had happened to him in the past, with his adoptive mother supporting him in this.

As can be seen above, the therapy can help the child and parents connect in terms of the child's past and present experiences and develop a dynamic co-narrative that they can all share in the present and build upon in the future.

8.3.2. *Katie – Separating birth mother from adoptive mother*

Katie aged 6½ years old was brought to the therapist by her adoptive parents. She had been adopted aged 2½ years in Haiti and brought back to Europe. Her biological mother had died when she was just 2 months old. She was reared by her father until she was 19 months old when she was placed in an orphanage as he was no longer able to care for her. However he has kept in contact with her and Katie sees him regularly on visits back to Haiti. Her adoptive parents said that Katie had seen many different therapists but her problems persisted. She remained very difficult to cuddle and avoided physical contact; she had a lot of fears, nightmares and problems concentrating at school.

The therapist met with the parents, Katie and her younger, adopted, non-biological sister aged 3 years, who also came from Haiti. Her parents were seen to be safe, containing secure, accepting, empathic, resourceful and loving and were trying to do their best. Targets were identified together with the parents whilst the children played.

In the subsequent session a photo of the biological mother was used as the first target. Katie with her adoptive mother processed sadness of her loss. In the subsequent session the target was a video of the adoption taken by the adoptive parents in Haiti, it showed her, them and her biological father and family. It also showed their return to Europe. A narrative form of EMDR was used with this video, titrating the content and sets to Katie's pace.

The parents were seen to engage them in the therapeutic process by sharing information about the adoption process and the consequences on child development. They were seen in between Katie's sessions and sometimes at the beginning of her sessions. Initially, a parent or parents were in the sessions with Katie, but as the work progressed this varied and Katie was seen alone. In later sessions more current targets about her daily life were worked on including school difficulties and issues of racism there, current fears and bed wetting. A variety of modes of ABLS were used: tapping on her feet initially with the early memories; and later butterfly hugs with her drawings; and then eye movements with the current fears and bed wetting. The modes of ABLS followed the developmental targets in keeping with the developmental protocol.

As can be seen the therapist was interweaving family and individual sessions to meet the complex needs of the situation. This helped Katie and her family to integrate her past life with her current life and her position within the family. After completing the work with Katie, the therapist received a Christmas card which can be seen in Figure 8.2 on which she drew both her adoptive and her biological mothers. This illustrated to them that she had integrated her past with her present.

Figure 8.2: Integrating past with present

8.4.   Summary

This chapter emphasises how a child does not exist alone but within a family context. Family dynamics and attachments are the main characteristics, changing over time with changing circumstances and life events. EMDR therapy therefore has to be embedded in a variety of other therapeutic approaches to meet the needs of complex families where problems exist within individuals and within family dynamics including reconstructed families.

Chapter 9

Domestic Violence

9.1. The complexity of domestic violence

Domestic violence is the most prevalent crime today affecting children within the family although the prevalence is largely under-reported with estimates up to one in four to five families being affected in some countries. Often the perpetrators are not prosecuted, though the prevalence of prosecution varies from country to country and in the United States from state to state.

It is frequently underestimated in the population and we have found that therapists neglect to ask about its occurrence in the family. The therapist may have difficulty in understanding and being comfortable with the idea that working with domestic violence requires a conceptual shift from private-confidential psychotherapy to public psychotherapy with respect to the country's legal and social requirements, where the safety and protection of the children are paramount. Domestic violence is firstly a crime; and secondly a personal/relationship problem.

When considering working with domestic violence the therapist must always ask themself the following questions: is the family safe in reality in the present; what will need to be in place before the therapy can begin; who is going to need therapy, who can we treat and in what order should they be treated; and what are we going to treat? Working with domestic violence is a complex treatment.

Domestic violence is often inter-generational, being transmitted from one generation to the next by observation of it in the family context. The violence that is witnessed and experienced in childhood increases the risk of the child developing violent behaviours as adults in their couple relationships, either as perpetrators or as victims (Carlson and Dalenberg, 2000). However of course, not all children will repeat the cycle of violence because of their own resilience, life experiences and other positive supportive attachments.

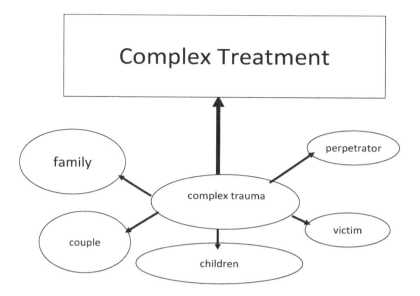

Figure 9.1: Complex treatment for domestic violence

In 2004, a European survey, found that worldwide, male domestic violence was causing more deaths and handicaps to women aged 15 – 44 years old than were caused by cancer, malaria, road accidents and war combined. Research undertaken by the National Child Trauma Stress Network (2003) found that children exposed to domestic violence were 15 times more likely to be abused than others. There was a 30 – 70% overlap between child abuse and a serious risk of sexual abuse. Further, battered women were twice more likely to abuse their children than others. Children exposed to domestic violence had double the rate of psychiatric problems than others; and abused, neglected children exposed to domestic violence were three times more likely to drop out of the education system.

Christen et al., (2004) define domestic violence as the behaviour of a man or a woman that is characterized by their willingness to destroy their partner, or whatever belongs to them and to scare them. The perpetrators use power and control without respect for the other person's integrity and uniqueness and tend to view the other as less human than themselves. The perpetrator's behaviour is a dysfunctional expression of aggressiveness that is often learned through family and social patterns and it is a form of communication that blocks verbal dialogue and transforms the victim from a person to an object.

The perpetrator's attachment tends to be hyper-anxious and disorganized with greater allegiance to the family of origin (more of a son and less of a husband) and with a very low capacity for differentiation which causes a high level of emotional dysregulation. They have a small window of tolerance, which under stress causes a flooding over the cognitive processing during which their capacity to reason and talk is diminished. They are therefore limited in their response repertoire and a frequent cognition when using EMDR with this type of perpetrator is "*I have no choice...I am lost... I am powerless...*" The emotional flooding itself re-traumatizes the perpetrator and their response is either violent or dissociative. It re-traumatizes because it reactivates past traumatic material. This is cyclical, the more violent he becomes the more re-traumatised he becomes and as this escalates, the only way out becomes more violence.

Domestic violence is rarely a single incident, but is more a characteristic repetitive way of functioning. Finney (2003) in her summary of key findings on alcohol and sexual violence cites several studies below that indicate that alcohol, which is often cited as the root cause of domestic violence, may not be so. Mirrlees-Black found that only 32% of domestic violence acts were committed when the perpetrator was under the influence of alcohol. McCord described alcohol as a contributory factor to violence rather than the cause of violence. McGregor described alcohol abuse as not the cause of violence, but as an excuse after violence.

9.2. The cycle of violence

The cycle of violence first described by Walker (1979) illustrates the interaction characteristic between the perpetrator and the victim. The relationship begins with a honeymoon phase during which the perpetrator is courting the victim and feeling secure because of the proximity with the partner. The daily stressors gradually create a distance and undermine the perpetrator's sense of security in the relationship, and heighten his fear of abandonment. This reactivates his underlying insecure, disorganized attachment and at this point the perpetrator is flooded and unable to talk about what he feels and violence ensues. After this, the perpetrator feels remorseful because he realises he is destroying the object of his love and makes reparation. The victim interprets this as insightful understanding of what the perpetrator has done and as proof of change and responds to his need for proximity. At this point, if a couple presents for therapy there is no window open for change and therapy is not an option. The cycle repeats, but little by little the victim starts to distance themselves, their self-esteem and self-worth diminishes and they become more helpless and powerless.

The opening for change will only come when the level of violence has been such that is has required the proactive intervention of external agencies: for example the police, child protection services and medical services. Opportunities for intervention diminish as the control over the victim increases through the perpetrator's verbal, physical and sexual violence and isolates them and erodes their external social resources. Within this closed interactional system, the dynamic is further fuelled by the control issue in an explicit way for the perpetrator, who feels he is being controlled by the victim, almost as though he has given her the remote control over his emotions; and in an implicit way for the victim who keeps trying to understand him, help him, make him change and save the relationship, regardless of the price and to the detriment of her own protection and self-worth.

We need here to differentiate between domestic violence and couples who use violent transactions as a way of regulating their relationship. In the latter case, even though it is not a case of one partner controlling the other, the actual level of symmetrical violence may be very high and will be equally damaging for children in the family. In this case, the therapist has to prioritize child protection needs over any consideration of the privacy and confidentiality of the couple's relationship.

Figure 9.2: Cycle of violence

Over time the intervals between the honeymoon phase and the acts of violence become closer and closer and this cycle spirals to a point where violence becomes almost a daily routine.

9.3. Prevalence of domestic violence

Domestic violence is more likely to be perpetrated by men than women. Fusco and Fantuzzo, (2009) estimated that 73% of men were perpetrators, 13% were women and 14% were joint perpetrators. 67% of victims and perpetrators were married or living together at the time of violence and 43% had children at the home at the time of violence. There is a tendency to minimize or underestimate children's exposure to domestic violence in the family. A common statement is that the children were in bed asleep and did not witness the violence. However, Fusco and Fantuzzo found that 95% of the children experienced sensory exposure to the domestic violence, 4% only saw it and only 1% of the children did not witness the domestic violence in any way. They found that when the perpetrator and victim were both the parents, the child was more than 3 times likely to be directly exposed to domestic violence events.

The significance of emotional abuse, the witnessing of domestic violence and verbal abuse, on the development of children is illustrated in some findings from a study by Teicher et al., (2006) on childhood maltreatment. As a part of this study, symptoms and exposure ratings on the Dissociative Experience Scale Score were collected from 554 subjects aged between18 – 22 years of which 68% were female. These were compared with 250 controls that had no history of exposure to abuse or other forms of early adversity. The subjects were categorised into three groups of maltreatment: emotional, physical and sexual abuse. Within the emotional abuse group were three sub-groups: domestic violence, verbal abuse and both. This emotional abuse was found to have a much more significant effect size on self-reported dissociation than either the physical abuse or the sexual abuse groups.

9.4. Family role disruption

Domestic violence disrupts the family roles and in particular it seems the father's role. Cummings et al., (2004) found that the quality of fathering was negatively correlated with marital conflict. When marital conflict was present this quality was more likely to be compromised than the mothering. Fathers also displayed less engagement with and higher negativity to children when marital conflict was present.

Battered women's lives are often enmeshed with their abusive partners through their children. They display ambivalent attachment to their abusive partner and are at risk of re-victimisation by subsequent partners and by the wider social system. They suffer from feelings of abandonment, isolation and learned helplessness. They are characteristically vulnerable, with weak self-esteem and poor assertiveness. In EMDR therapy with these survivors of domestic abuse one of the most frequent cognitions is *"I am a failure...I am worthless..., I am a bad mother..."*

The quality of the parent-child attachment is damaged by domestic violence. There is an impaired affect regulation between the parent and child and a numbing of the attunement between them. Some of the minimisation that mothers do of their children's exposure may be related to the above. The victim and the children may become traumatic reminders for each other, particularly if the child identifies with the perpetrator role and physically resembles the perpetrator. There may also be some role reversal with the child in some ways becoming the parent of the parent.

Domestic violence in early childhood shatters the developmental expectation of protection from the attachment figure. The parent by their violent behaviour becomes a source of danger rather than of protection. The child has nowhere to turn for protection and support and this creates irresolvable fear and a double-bind relationship for the child.

9.5. Treatment issues

Working with families with domestic violence is complex, particularly when both parents are perpetrators, as the child is more likely to be exposed to witnessing it and is at greater risk of physical harm. Without intervention the situation is likely to continue to recur.

In cases where there has been domestic violence it is essential for the therapist to firstly establish whether the violence is continuing or not; and whether the family and children are actually physically safe. As we have said previously, the therapist cannot be a bystander to domestic violence but needs to intervene to protect the children according to the laws of their country. One should remember that EMDR and other therapies are only effective when the traumatisation is finished and the family is safe and their basic needs for food, shelter and safety are met. EMDR therapy cannot be effective in the face of ongoing trauma, or when basic survival needs have not been met.

Figure 9.2 is a picture drawn by a 7 year old girl of her target memory of the domestic abuse perpetrated by her father and which left her mother, baby brother and herself homeless. In this family, the domestic abuse was chronic. In therapy the child expressed that the worst part was being thrown out of the house with nowhere to go. The chronic domestic violence was part of her everyday life experience.

Figure 9.2: Target memory - 01

Figure 9.3 is a picture drawn by a 6 ½ year old boy of an attack made on him and his mother by his father whilst they were asleep in his mother's bed. In this incident his father hit him with the boy's toy train.

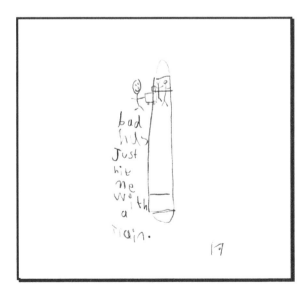

Figure 9.3: Target memory – 02

EMDR therapy needs to be integrated and intertwined into a comprehensive treatment plan for the family and individuals within it. It needs to be carefully timed to each individual's needs in the overall treatment plan of the family. Again we recommend that the therapist consider treatment for the parents prior to treatment for the children.

9.6.   Perpetrators

Ideally, the perpetrator needs treatment though this may not be possible in many cases with the perpetrator who may no longer be allowed to see the family and may indeed be incarcerated. The treatment for the perpetrator is often ordered by the Court and may consist of individual therapy and/or group therapy programmes into which EMDR therapy can be incorporated (Shapiro, 2012).

9.6.1.   *Andre – Treating the perpetrator*

Andre (aged 45) came to treatment with his wife Isabelle (aged 42). She had previously filed a complaint with the police department for his violent behaviour. They were still living together and had two teenagers a boy aged 17 and a girl aged 14 years. During the first session the couple's dynamics and the history of his violent behaviours were explored. She didn't want to end the relationship, but she was very tired by the repetition of the violent behaviours that had been going on for the past 20 years and had reach her limits.

As often observed in this situation, he felt that he was violent because of her and what she was doing. Smith and Silvestre (2011) describe how it is essential to work with the perpetrator on his understanding of his violent behaviour and his acceptance of his own responsibility for this before starting any couple counselling. The therapist therefore decided to refer him to a group counselling for perpetrators and meanwhile described to both of them the treatment process. Firstly, he needed some individual sessions and in parallel she needed some individual sessions to evaluate what kind of help she needed for herself (e.g. to be referred to a woman's group or individual psychotherapy).

The couple sessions were put on hold until the level of security between them was sufficiently developed to prevent them from the danger of relapsing into violent behaviours.

André agreed to go to the men's group and to see the therapist alone. EMDR therapy was used to target old memories of being inadequate and not loveable. André's mother had died when he was 8 years old and he often referred to his wife as a surrogate mother. His father remarried when he was 12 and he had a difficult time with his stepmother. He had felt abandoned regularly by his father when he realised that he was always taking his new wife's side. The negative cognition "*I am lost*" served as the central organizing point. His anxious attachment was very insecure and as often observed, he secured himself by controlling his wife Isabelle.

Any movement of autonomy she took was understood by him as another abandonment, she became his thing, he needed to always know where she was, what she was doing and with whom. Gradually the therapy moved on to more recent targets of his violent behaviours when he had felt threatened by her functioning. Her shift work with its irregular hours was a continuous stressor.

We have observed in our practice with perpetrators that one of the strong arguments in favour of EMDR therapy is the fact that they don't have to talk a lot about what happened and to be challenged again by their difficulty in expressing themselves. Instead of that they feel more able to focus on an old or recent memory and through the standard EMDR protocol to connect it with ideas, emotion and body sensation. Their memory of images are always very powerful and they regularly express some surprise when they see how they are still reacting to them with so much intensity. EMDR therapy bypasses the difficulties in verbal expression that are so characteristically pre-eminent within the perpetrator population.

André was amazed by all the connections he made during his EMDR sessions especially when he realized that he was not being asked to talk. He had previously tried to undertake a "talking therapy" but had stopped very rapidly, not seeing the purpose of talking and unable to explain his behaviours. It is our experience that EMDR therapy seems to boost the recognition of the perpetrator's own responsibility for his violent behaviour and furthermore enhance the quality of the couple's work later.

André was able to understand his wife's position differently by the time the couple's therapy started. He kept acknowledging during their therapy that he had changed the filters through which he was looking at his wife's behaviours. He was reacting less to her, being less vulnerable and feeling more in control.

In our clinical observation, the therapist has to act as a central organizing point during the EMDR individual work, the couple's work and later the family work. By doing so he reinforces the level of attachment and of security. It is the enactment by the therapist of the process of handling a multi-level intervention therapeutic approach and an example of EMDR therapy in context.

For example, a group was run by one of the authors of this book for 6 incarcerated adult male domestic violence offenders. They ranged in age from 21 years to 65 years old, were volunteers and were incarcerated from 2 years to 15 years and two had murdered their wives. EMDR therapy was part of a broader therapeutic programme. The use of the Butterfly Hug and the drawing technique was chosen as it was particularly well adapted when working with a group of inmates because they didn't have to talk to each other about what they had done to their partner; confidentiality and safety in prison are important issues not to be overlooked.

9.6.2. Group Therapy for perpetrators

The group first looked at psycho-education issues including gender role, control issues and child education. During the second stage, the group was given some theoretical information on the brain functioning, in particular the relation between the reptilian, emotional and cortical brain, the window of tolerance and emotional flooding. They were also given information on inter-generational transmission of violent behaviour and its effects.

In the third stage, they were taught breathing techniques for relaxation and the use of the safe place was developed. Then in the fourth session, the group was instructed to think about the worst picture that they had in their mind when thinking about their violent behaviour. Although the work was done by drawing, some still made comments as they processed. These included *"I gave her everything..."*, *"She was my mirror..."*, *"She was a thing for me..."*, *"If you leave me I will kill you and then I kill myself..."*, *"I thought she was my mother..."*, *"I don't know what happened to me..."*, and *"I became crazy ...the light went out..."*.

In certain circumstances, after violence has stopped and the perpetrator's therapy has been completed successfully, with the perpetrator having been able to demonstrate that he has taken responsibility for his action, is genuinely remorseful and demonstrate significant change in his behaviours, couple therapy may be undertaken. More research needs to be carried out in this field and it is an area where integration of a couple's relational dynamics and individual EMDR perspective is needed. To describe further the treatment with couples is outside the scope of this book though there are adult therapists who specialize in this work integrating EMDR.

9.7.   The partners as victims

Therapy for victims includes building resources and desensitizing their past traumatisation with EMDR therapy and additional group therapy for survivors of domestic violence. Often mothers present with children whose behaviour has become attention seeking, clingy, demanding and aggressive following the breakup of the violent relationship. They may often been in temporary housing or a woman's refuge and finances may be very strained and they may have fled with nothing more than just the clothes they were wearing at the time. Although she is seeking help for the child, her own numbness and traumatisation needs to be addressed, so that she can be appropriately soothing and containing of the child's disturbance. These are often people whose own morale is so low that they are incapable of seeking treatment in their own right, but in the context of their child's needs are more amenable to help for themselves to help their child.

Battered women's lives are often enmeshed with their abusive partners through their children and they are often unable to put the relationship behind them because of their children's needs. They may also present with ambivalent attachment to their abusive partner and this is one of the reasons they find it so hard to leave their unhappy situations. EMDR therapy may work on specific incidents of violence, but also on poor self-esteem, poor assertiveness, vulnerability and dependency learnt from their past family and relationship experiences. Targets may also include guilt towards their children for failing to protect them, the stressor of the traumatic reminders of the perpetrator that the children may evoke in a variety of ways, including their physical resemblance and mannerisms.

9.7.1.   *Owen – His mother's perspective*

One mother who was subjected to 15 years of domestic violence from her ex-husband reported the following about their son, Owen, then aged 14 years old: *"I feel like I haven't bonded with him and I thought it was because of his autism but I don't think it is because – as he's grown it is like he has turned into his dad. So I can't bear him touching me it makes me repulsed when he tries to cuddle me - I don't like it ... It feels I am being abused by Owen now because of the things that he says. I don't know how much he understands because of his autism - well I don't think he does –*

125

he doesn't understand what he is saying - but he's having such an effect..."

At the end of her first session of EMDR therapy she said she was feeling really positive and that she wanted to give Owen a cuddle and kiss him goodnight that night and feel comfortable doing it. She subsequently reported feeling considerably happier at her next session; she was relaxed about cuddling him and talking to him. She felt a weight had been lifted off her shoulders and felt that they had become a lot closer.

9.8. The children witnessing domestic violence

As we have already, mentioned most children living in homes where domestic violence has occurred are likely to have witnessed this in one form or another. For many of the children domestic violence is a way of living. One child in therapy who was witness to domestic violence and also physically abused by his father in front of his mother said *"I always thought it was normal."*

There are many consequences for these children, a loss of safety and protection. In many cases the protector becomes either a source of danger or is reduced to the likeness of another helpless child. This can create irresolvable fear and nowhere for the child to turn and may cause disorganized attachments and in the longer term, maladaptive dissociative coping styles and lack of an adequate flexible defensive response repertoires. The child may internalise unsafe internal models of the world and a sense of distrust, suspicion characterized by problems with boundaries, relationships with others and a loss of empathy. Problems can also arise for the children when they become identified with either the perpetrator or victim.

9.8.1. <u>Bonnie – Witness to domestic violence</u>

Bonnie aged 9 years, was referred for anxiety problems after experiencing a variety of traumatic events. She lived with her older brother and mother. Her father had left the family when she was very young after a violent attack on her mother. The traumatic memory of this event was still affecting her and was used as the target for one of her sessions.

Bonnie described how she was in her bedroom and she heard the door being broken down. She ran to her brother's room and he hid her under the covers. Outside the room her mother started screaming as her father hit her. He knocked her to the floor and she could hear her mother crying

126

and her father swearing before he left. Her mother was near the sofa and she and her brother got some toys and a blanket for their mother. They put the blanket over their mother and got some pillows to make her comfortable because she felt sad and because Bonnie knew mother was not very happy. Bonnie and her brother stayed with her mother and Bonnie added she hated her father.

Asked what the worst bit, Bonnie said it was the breaking down of the door. Her negative cognition was "*I am helpless*" and her positive cognition "*It's over.*" Her VOC was 2 and the emotion was feeling "*really upset*" with her SUDS at 10 and her sensation was "*In my heart because it just feels like it has been ripped apart.*"

What follows is the verbatim description of the EMDR session where the ">>" indicate a set of ABLS.

>>   *Just hard to explain*

>>   *Feel a bit happier because it is all over*

>>   *if it happened again I would know what to do, try to stop it*

>>   *feel angry, really angry with dad, can't forgive him, why didn't he talk to her rather than do that*

>>   *if I had been bigger at the time I would have stopped him*

>>   *I feel confused about why did he have to do that when he knew that me and Tom would get really upset, confused, why did he do it in the first place*

>>   *I just feel lonely, no one loves me only Tom and mum*

>>   *feel really anxious and scared because I don't know what is going to happen next*

>>   *think it is just going to happen again and get worse*

>>   *it feels like the world is closing in on me and a black hole has swallowed me up because of dad everything has gone black*

>>   *one of my family has left me and I just have mum and Tom*

>>   *just trapped because of my dad in the house. I wanted to get some help but feel really guilty; not helping makes me really guilty and anxious*

>> *I feel like a little bit excited not scared and anxious. When I grow up I can stand up to him and not feel scared and show him what he has done*

>> *when I grow up I will give him a taste of his own medicine, tell him what he has done and then I will feel happy because he will know mine and mum's pain and what we have been through*

>> *my brother is really nice, always been there for me that's why I say he is my hero*

>> *I didn't know what was going to happen next >*

>> *I felt really guilty and thought it was my fault being really naughty and getting him angry and that's why*

>> *I just thought I did something really bad without really noticing it and got my dad really angry*

>> *come to think of it I don't think it's my fault, dad is selfish and only cares about what he wants to do*

>> *if I had done anything wrong he would come to hit me and not mum*

>> *don't think mum did anything wrong, think dad might just have been drinking*

>> *maybe it was not my fault or mum's or Tom's*

>> *I feel he is not sorry*

>> *I still feel confused and still don't understand why he got so upset*

>> *feel if I still lived with him I wouldn't know what he was really like and he could have hurt us*

>> *I don't forgive him because he should have known we were here, he is just really selfish and thinks of himself*

>> *when he comes now he brings presents and treats me like a baby, I don't like it. It is not what I want. I want to be a family again but I know that can't happen*

>> *feel a 100% relieved, it's all over because I can just forget about it now and live my life without that thing bottled up in my head.*

At this point the therapist guided Bonnie back to the target and she reported her SUDS were 0. A further set of ABLS was given and then Bonnie reported that her VOC was 7 after another set of ABLS she reported her VOC was 100 and her session was then closed. In subsequent sessions Bonnie went on to work on other aspects of her worries not related to the domestic violence.

The above example illustrates just how alive the traumatic memory is in the present. The incident that Bonnie related happened 6 ½ years previously. As the session progresses we can see all the different channels that her thoughts and feelings progress through including anger, confusion, worthlessness, fear, identification with the perpetrator and guilt. She finally comes to a resolution that is over and she can live her own life. She is not organized by the past anymore; its maladaptive cognitions, emotions and behaviours.

9.9. Implications for therapists

Returning again to our analogy of the Russian dolls where the therapist contains the child, domestic violence can create very powerful counter transference and the therapist needs to consider how they are feeling and containing their emotions and taking care of themselves, to avoid developing secondary traumatisation. This is particularly pertinent when considering EMDR therapy which requires intensive attunement and affect regulation on the part of the therapist; and where emotions can run very high and abreactions can occur. Secondary traumatisation will undermine the therapist's ability to regulate the child.

9.10. Summary

In this chapter on domestic violence there are a number of questions that the therapist always needs to keep in mind. They are: is the family safe in reality in the present; what will need to be in place before therapy can begin; who is going to need therapy; who can we treat and in what order should they be treated; and what are we going to treat? Working with domestic violence is very complex but EMDR therapy can help to bring positive changes to battered lives and transform inter-generational trajectories by helping families to pass on a story not a trauma.

Chapter 10

Developmental Perspective of Dissociative Tendencies

10.1. Theories of dissociation

The concept of dissociation developed in the world of adult psychotherapy. Historically, Janet's (1889 &1907) clinical research was the first to describe and recognise the critical link between trauma and pathological dissociation. He considered pathological dissociation to be phobias of memories to thoughts or memories of old traumas that were expressed as excessive or inappropriate physical responses. He also observed that it was as if the patients had lost their capacity to assimilate new experiences and as if their personality development had stopped at a certain point.

Modern theories of dissociation are largely built upon the early work of Janet. Dissociation has been defined in numerous different ways from many different professional and theoretical perspectives and a variety of models developed. However, there does seem to be an overall, general consensus that some dissociative behaviour is normal; and that there is a distinction between normal dissociative behaviours and dysfunctional or pathological dissociation.

As previously stated dissociation is a concept derived mainly from the world of adult psychopathology and the phenomena described differ in many respects from what may be seen in childhood and adolescents. A recent model of dissociation in adulthood is that of Structural Dissociation developed by van der Hart et al., (2006). There is a vast body of literature about models of dissociation in the adult population that is outside the scope of this book to address; for a review of this see Dell and O'Neil (2009).

10.2. A developmental perspective

As our experience of using EMDR as clinicians has become more sophisticated, it has enabled us to see things in children that we had not realised before. We learn to see how EMDR therapy enables thoughts, emotions and sensations that were previously not connected, for whatever reason, to begin to flow together in a process of connectivity, differentiation and coherent integration at their own developmental level. This leads to an achievement for the child of new connectivity, which enables resolutions to be unique and adapted to the individual child and is neuro-developmentally mediated. The therapist becomes the conduit of this process helping to initiate and guide it, but hopefully not interfering with its natural flow.

Siegel (1999) proposes that living organisms have a natural tendency towards integration. Integration refers to the collaborative linking functions that coordinate various levels of processes, within the mind and between people. Integration is also how the mind creates a coherent self-assembly of information and energy flow across time and context. Thus integration creates the subjective experience of self, establishing a congruity and unity of the mind as it emerges within the flexible patterns in the flow of information and energy processes of the brain. These processes are both within the brain itself and in its interaction with others. Siegel states that neural integration is fundamental to self-organization and to the capacity of the brain to create a sense of self. Dissociation may be conceptualised as a disruption in integration of various processes, including memory, identity, perception and consciousness.

In our clinical practise using EMDR therapy we have become more aware of the dissociative behaviour through observation of the phenomena of: distancing and spacing out; glazing over; sudden loss of all affect; extreme symptoms of fatigue and lassitude; sudden regression in voice tones and language and body language. These dissociative tendencies tend to be more frequently observable in our more vulnerable children and adolescents suffering from complex multiple traumatisation and attachment disorders. Twenty years ago we doubt whether either author would have been able to identify more than a handful of children and adolescents with dissociative tendencies, as we did not have the framework to do this, nor did our professional training include this.

EMDR therapy has opened up for us a new lens on the nature of integration and dissociation, as these can be observed in the clinical setting with children and adolescents during EMDR therapy and can influence the duration, the effectiveness and course of therapy. Without adequate screening, preparation and stabilisation of our more vulnerable children with dissociative traits, they may actually be wounded by the EMDR as it may knock down protective dissociative barriers which in children who are insufficiently protected and have limited defence mechanisms are very thin and permeable. It has thus become very important to try to understand this dynamic more clearly and how to manage it. It seems from our clinical observation that integration and dissociation are at opposite ends of a spectrum in processing. Clinically, the task has become how to understand this dissociative behaviour and manage to protect and hold our children and adolescents safely in the therapeutic process, whilst at the same help them to heal.

We, in trying to understand dissociation, have felt a need to orientate to a neuro-developmental and evolutionary perspective. Infants and children are beginning the process of developing senses of self and personality structures and these are fluid, dynamic and not yet stable. The brain organs that serve the higher-order integrative functions in adulthood, the prefrontal cortex and hippocampus, have yet to mature and will only do so in late adolescent and early adulthood (Perry, 2008).

Further, the various action systems function relatively independently from one another in early childhood. Our world is populated by children defined by their neuro-developmental immaturities and their fluid neuroplasticity. Thus we find the use of terminology extrapolated from adult psychopathology, in particular the use of diagnostic labels of infantile dissociative disorders, to be unhelpful and stigmatizing of a child's future potential personality development and life opportunities.

Because of the dynamic developmental process in childhood and adolescence we propose from the clinical perspective that incoherence, underconnectivity and lack of integration may be better described as dissociative tendencies which may take the form of states in younger children and dissociative states/traits in older children and adolescents. These can take different forms and affect the developing child and their sense of self in different ways at different stages of development.

Throughout this book we have repeatedly emphasised that no child exists alone, but exists with a context of the family and its attachment patterns, as well as the wider social context. Siegel (1999) is helpful here in our thinking, as he integrates attachment research with the neuro-developmental research and suggests that the developmental roots of dissociation lie in the dynamics of interpersonal relationships. Much of a child's development occurs through interpersonal interaction, which is why attachment plays such a fundamental role. Interpersonal disconnection has a profound inhibiting effect on developmental progress.

From our perspective, a natural part of early childhood development is a world that is populated with make believe and fantasy play; fairies and mythical creatures, which can be as real as diggers and dinosaurs and within which imaginary friends including "*Binky bonker*" and "*Fee-Fam-Foom*" thrive. Similarly, flowers can be as big as houses and the process of integrating factual information about the real world and the differences between reality and fantasy is a developmental task.

Early childhood particularly is filled with many different roles or senses of self, which are taken in order for the child to fit in, learn about and rehearse how to fit with varying interpersonal social contexts, for example at home, with grandparents, at toddler groups and other contexts. Similarly, in adolescence there are new roles to be developed. Thus the secure child develops a concept of themselves across different roles carried out in different activities and defined by the social contexts and attachment and learns to differentiate the imaginary from the real.

The child's evolving world is fluid and there can be spontaneous connection and integration of previously incoherent material as they are learning developing models with increasing associations, complexity, differentiation and flexibility. Ultimately this process develops as they enter adulthood into a more crystalline, less flexible, structured brain architecture of sense of self and personality which operates across contexts. The question for us as clinicians is when do these dissociative tendencies become maladaptive or pathological to the child and when do we need to intervene to treat it and how?

10.3. Some models of dissociation in childhood and adolescence

Below is a selection of findings in the child and adolescent dissociation literature that have helped to guide our thinking about childhood underconnectivity and incoherence leading to dissociative behaviours, states and traits. For a more detailed review of this literature we would refer the reader to Silberg and Dallam (2009).

10.3.1. Terr and Kluft

Dissociation in the child and adolescent world seems to have gained an impetus during the late 1970s with the detailed case descriptions of Kluft and others. Kluft (1985) suggested that dissociation may become a protective mechanism that is used over and over again for children who are abused in some way. Terr (1991) suggested that children were forced to use dissociation as a common defence against recurrent chronic abuse, in order to mentally escape what was happening to them, whilst it was happening. By the late 1980's and early 1990s cases series, based on a commonly identified cluster of symptoms, were being reported (Putnam, 1997).

10.3.2. Putnam's model

Putnam (1997) seems to be one of the first to define pathological dissociation in children and adolescents from a developmental-psychopathological model. Whilst clinically dissociation is often conceptualised as a defensive process that protects the individual in the face of overwhelming trauma; Putnam also identified dissociative defences as having three major tasks. The first, he termed automatization of behaviour in the face of psychologically overwhelming circumstances; the second, compartmentalisation of painful memories and affects; and the third, estrangement of the self in the face of potential annihilation.

He developed the Adolescent Dissociative Experiences Scale and the Child Dissociative Check List as ways of measuring the clusters of symptoms associated with dissociation in children and adolescents (see annex). He also identified that whilst PTSD and pathological dissociation were clinically related they were not the same; not all his patients with PTSD developed dissociation and not all pathologically dissociative patients had PTSD. However, there were some that exhibited both dissociation and PTSD. He proposed a model of discrete behavioural states.

He suggested that early in development, a young child's behaviour is organised as a set of separate individual states, for example: being playful, thoughtful, curious and distressed. Healthy cognitive and affective development requires that the child acquire control or modulation over these behavioural states. They are able to move from state to state flexibly with a continuity of sense of self across these. Pathological dissociation reflected a profound disruption of the self-modulation of these states together with failures in the integration of the information and senses of self across these behavioural states, leading to rigidity and incoherence.

10.3.3. Liotti's model

Others have defined dissociation more in terms of attachment styles and relationships. Liotti (2009) says that dissociation is not necessarily always the outcome of violent, abusive or humiliating interactions between an adult and a child. Provided that activation of the attachment system is involved, parental communications that are frightened or confused, but not obviously maltreatment of the infant may set dissociative mental processes into motion if the internal systems are not soothed and re-regulated by a caretaker. He suggested that disordered attachment in infancy increased vulnerability to dissociative tendencies and pathological dissociation. He proposed that disorganised attachment could lead to a primary lack of integration around basic strategies for seeking comfort and protection under stress, in a context of defective care giving.

This would lead to the internalisation of multiple, un-integrated, contradictory, working models of the parent and models of self. These working models generate incompatible behaviour and mental tendencies, which represent and create vulnerability to later dissociative tendencies. He further proposed that there is an additive, cumulative and/or interactive effect between subsequent traumas and the disorganized quality of previous attachments in producing dissociative symptoms.

10.3.4. The work of Lyons-Ruth et al.,

Lyons-Ruth et al., (2006) suggested that in the development of dissociative tendencies that the capacity of attachment figures for modulating fearful arousal in a responsive dialogue with the child would have a major impact over time. Further, that these disturbed parental affective communications are often an enduring day-in-day-out feature of the childhood years. Thus the parent's responses to the child's fundamental needs for comfort and soothing are worked into the fabric of their identity and their biological stress regulation from an early age. These were defined as the hidden traumas of caregiver unavailability and interactive dysregulation.

In their study they found that within their group of children classified as disorganised, there were two polarized types of behavioural profiles for the mothers; those labelled hostile/self-referential and those labelled helpless/fearful. Those in the former sub-group had higher rates of role confusion and negative intrusive behaviour than the latter.

The hostile/self-referential group of mothers also displayed a contradictory mix of rejecting behaviours and behaviours that sought attention from their infants. Their infants were more likely to show a complex mix of disorganised, avoidant and resistant behaviours. In contrast, mothers who were labelled helpless/fearful were more fearful, withdrawing and inhibited. They often failed to take the initiative in greeting or approaching the infant, hesitated, moved away, or tried to deflect the infant's requests for close contact before giving in. Both groups were related to a maternal history of trauma; mothers who had a history of physical abuse or witnessing domestic violence were more likely to display the hostile/self-referential profile; whereas mothers who had a history of sexual abuse or parental loss were more likely to be in the helpless/fearful group.

10.3.5. The perspective of Goldsmith et al.,

A further helpful perspective comes from the work of Goldsmith et al., (2004) who proposed that when a young child is abused by a parent or caregiver, they become conflicted between the relationship and the content of the relationship. They suggest the purpose of dissociation is an adaptive survival strategy and not an escape from pain. The child needs to maintain the attachment relationship, regardless of the content, by dissociating from this content information that would threaten the maintenance of the relationship.

10.3.6. The work of MacFie et al.,

Of particular interest to us is a study done by MacFie et al., (2001). They defined self-integration as a developmental task and achievement. It arises from success at prior developmental stages. It requires a secure pattern of attachment in infancy and it leads to the development of corresponding, coherent, representational models of self in relation to others. It occurs normally with the help of the child's caregivers. The child learns to process and assimilate experiences to create a personal history, a worldview and a sense of who he or she is, separated but connected to others during the toddler and pre-school years.

They studied the development of dissociation in 45 maltreated pre-school children whom they divided into two sub-groups: the abused group consisting of those who had suffered from sexual or physical abuse or both (33 children), from those who had suffered from neglect (12 children). They compared them to 33 non-maltreated controls. The children ranged in age from 3 years 1 month to 5 years 3 months with an average age of 3 years 11 months.

They used a story-stem technique to get a measure of dissociation from the children's narratives. They found that the abused group scored much higher on the measure of dissociation used than the controls, or the neglected group at the outset. They found when re-measuring this a year later that the measures of dissociation increased significantly for the abused group and also increased to a lesser extent for the neglected group. In contrast the measures for the control group indicated a decrease in the level of dissociation over time. The control group was more able to integrate their experiences into a coherent sense of self than the other two groups.

Both the abused and the neglected group were found to be following a different trajectory to the controls with increasing dissociation, particularly for the abused group.

They noted that the sense of self became increasingly fragmented for some in the abused and neglected groups. Whilst this study was just a snapshot in time it indicates that the subsequent neuro developmental trajectory particularly for abused and maltreated children may continue to diverge significantly from their non-maltreated peers from this stage of development onwards.

10.4. Dissociative tendencies

We propose for the purposes of our work with children and adolescents to define dissociative tendencies developmentally as a lack of connectivity, coherence and integration; failures in the child's ability to assimilate or associate information and experience to develop an integrated coherent sense of emergent self. These include lack of coherence in any or between various sensory-motor, emotional and cognitive domains and between events, experiences and contexts. The dissociative responses may develop as a protective adaptive defence mechanism for helping a child survive in conditions where traumatic experience or a flooding of emotion or information; or breaches or ruptures of the attachment relationship threaten the child's survival and integrity.

Symptoms of dissociative tendencies in children can include combinations of the following: fluctuating behaviours and skills, trances, lapses in attention and memory, suicidal thinking and behaviours, self-mutilation, hearing voices, hallucinating, flashbacks, sleepwalking, nightmares, vivid imaginary companions, denial of observed behaviour, multiple physical complaints, promiscuous sexuality and antisocial or assaultive behaviour (Silberg, 1996, Putnam, 1997.)

In our clinical experience the greater the number of symptoms are and the greater the numbers of clusters of these symptoms are and the more frequently they are observed and the more they interfere with healthy daily life functioning the more pathological the dissociative tendencies will be. One child described her experiences of repeatedly being in a dissociative state whilst watching repeated domestic violence as *"like being in a coma."* Another child described herself as standing outside of her body and watching it all happening from a distance.

Thus, from a developmental perspective one may consider that the lack of connectivity or under-connectivity seen in dissociative states/traits in childhood serve a protective functional purpose in the adaptive survival of that child. They need to be recognised as an important part of the child which has helped them survive, by both therapists and parents or caretakers.

Additionally, this lack of connectivity has in the past for the child been stress-relieving and thus rewarding and has been reinforced by this. The child may or may not be ready to relinquish this form of protection even though the original causes may have been removed. Dissociative tendencies need to be very gently approached when considering using EMDR therapy.

This is long term work. It will take a long time to build up the history, map their experiences, stabilize them and then treat them. They will require many additional supports, resources and positive aids before they are ready to start to undertake the desensitization, which will then also need to be titrated carefully and interspersed with other activities to their needs, their current life events and the activities of the systems that surround them, family, peers and school.

In contrast to adult pathological dissociation, the behaviours and boundaries of dissociative tendencies are fluid, often fleeting and permeable in childhood and spontaneous integration can occur. Further, barriers to integration can be more easily overwhelmed in EMDR therapy. There also arises a potential conflict between the use of EMDR, an integrative process; and a child's need to continue to maintain the lack of integration in certain situations where they do not yet feel safe enough in the world.

Thus from the developmental as well as an EMDR therapy perspective, the function of dissociative tendencies may be conceptualized as either a symptom or a resource. In other words when considering EMDR therapy we need to establish whether the dissociative tendencies are still functional and protective to maintain a primary relationship; or whether they have become redundant and are now dysfunctional.

The child may need to learn new coping strategies and defences before they are ready to process material that has been dissociated. They also need to have a normalizing concept developed about why their particular dissociative symptoms and tendencies have come about. They need to know how different feelings, states, voices, etc came to be and how these came to help them in times when things have been hard, frightening, dangerous etc and that all of them are a part of their whole person even if they do not know it yet and they are all equally important. Narratives connecting these are very helpful particularly if the child can't access the sources, which they often can't.

If the dissociative behaviour is still functional for the child, the child is going to become resistant to the EMDR therapy very shortly after it starts. Therapists need to be alerted to this as it may be that they have not realised the extent of the child's fragmentation and dependence on dissociative tendencies to cope. This can be a marker to indicate that further and deeper assessment and stabilisation are necessary and that other aspects of the family system need addressing. The clinician should also be aware that safe place and other similar resources such as Super Mario are forms of controlled positive dissociation that we actively utilize in therapy.

At this point we return to consider the question of timing of the EMDR therapy in the life of the child, their inner world and the inner world and life of the family. To determine this we need again to review the definition of the child's symptom, does it belong to the child alone, or may it rest within the child's family. The question is whether this context is sufficiently containing and protecting and whether the attachment relationships with the child are secure enough. The questions that need to be considered are: is the timing right for integrative work at the child' particular developmental stage; what do we need to do before thinking of trying integrative work in terms of coping strategies, resources and educational information; and do we need to develop internal and external factors to enhance resiliency by working with the parents/caretakers to stabilise the child before considering treating the child's past traumas.

Many clinicians have reported that working, for example, with children with severe attachment disorders who are no longer with their family of origin and are in the state system placed in foster placements, or children's homes, or in refuge asylums or camps, or in war situations, is very problematic and they cannot see how to start it or when they tried it failed. As stated previously, this may be because the child is not yet in the right therapeutic window to begin this work, they need prolonged stabilisation and may not be ready to begin this for a long time until they have mastered survival, have grieved their losses and are starting to make healthier new attachments in their new environments and are developing a sense of achievement in these as described in the Treatment opportunity window in Chapter 3.

10.5. Managing dissociative behaviours and tendencies in therapy

When a child starts to dissociate during EMDR therapy the main duty of the clinician is to help to ground the child back in the present and then to try to find a way of more gently helping the child regain one foot in the present whilst also having one foot in the past. This may be done in many different ways simply wiggling, or even clicking the fingers whilst doing the ABLS may be enough to hook the child's attention back to the present as well as the past.

The clinician may want to try doing much shorter sets with longer breaks in between and get them to look around and notice things in the room, reassure the child that they are not alone but are in the therapy room, with permission perhaps hold their hand during the sets or change the medium of the ABLS from eye movements to taps, or more actively engage the child in the ABLS by getting them to do the tapping in parallel with the therapist. The therapist needs to make their presence during the EMDR more present in the moment when a child starts to dissociate. Other grounding techniques can include asking them if they want a drink of water, a soft toy to hold or even if they need the toilet.

10.6. The contextual view of dissociative tendencies

It is important to realise that we, as therapists, are not outside the therapeutic process, but are a part of the overall therapeutic system and the level of the integrative work will depend also on the vision of the world that we have. The question to be asked is whether we see the child solely as an individual with dissociative tendencies, or whether we can also see the child as a member of a relationship in which dissociative tendencies are a solution. Thus the therapist needs to develop and employ complex integrative thinking when working with dissociative tendencies within children and families. Because dissociation exists in the dynamic of a relationship, the therapeutic relationship plays an even more essential role in the treatment of dissociation than it does in interventions for other problems.

At this point there are greater risks for secondary traumatisation of the therapist themselves because of the intensity of the attunement and nature of the attachment between the therapist and the child and supervision is, as we have often said, very important.

10.7. Summary

Dissociation has been defined in numerous different ways from many theoretical perspectives and is a concept derived mainly from adult psychopathology. There is however a consensus that some dissociative behaviour is normal and that there is a distinction between this and dysfunctional or pathological dissociation. Dissociative tendencies in childhood and adolescence differ in many respects to adults. They are fluid and permeable but have served a functional purpose in the survival of the child by their lack of spontaneous integration. Whether they continue to do so or not is a question of great importance for the therapist in considering EMDR therapy for these fragile children. When considering whether the dissociative tendencies are a symptom or a resource we need to conceptualise the child or adolescent in the context of being a member of a relationship in which the dissociative tendencies may still be a solution. Is the timing right to start any therapy? A careful and detailed consideration of what the child may need to survive and grow must be established. Before any EMDR therapy is started there needs to be considerable work on understanding their attachments and stabilization and work needs to progress slowly and be titrated to the individual needs. The golden rule of thumb with these fragile clients is that "slower is quicker" (Hoffman, 2002).

Chapter 11

Mapping Dissociative Tendencies – Case examples

The blueprint for the under-connectivity and incoherence that leads to dissociative tendencies evolving in any child is a unique individual process which occurs in response to persistent or overwhelming threats to that particular child in its survival at any particular developmental stage and this can include the sense of isolation and abandonment when a parent persistently is emotionally unavailable to the child's emotional and care needs or when they are persistently over-intrusive. The patterns of lack of connectivity is individual-specific, just as individual information processing and associational channels in EMDR therapy are individual-specific.

Thus for each child we treat, we need to learn to understand and trace their own map of these patterns or matrices. These maps tend to be rather hazy at first, but gain clarity with a good understanding of the developmental timeline and also become clearer as the child progresses in time in EMDR therapy, with some hidden aspects only becoming apparent at different stages of therapy, as the connections are made or barriers are dissolved and they become accessible. Sometimes children, when the process of normalizing dissociative tendencies is explained to them are able to identify and draw out their own pictures but often they are not aware of them and then the therapist with the help of the child's surrounding system can start to map the matrices out as in the case of Jason, the Kaleidoscope Kid and Linda, the Cloud Child detailed below.

Also of course remembering that the younger the child is, the more vulnerable they are and the more resilient they will become as the brain differentiates and matures in both structures and neural networks through childhood and into early adulthood. The following three examples of case matrices highlight this movement from a low level of integration to higher levels of coherent integration within the quality of the attachment relationship. We start developmentally from the most vulnerable, fragmented and incoherent child.

11.1. Jason: Multiple caretakers, neglect and multiple traumatisation – The Kaleidoscope Kid

This child is termed the Kaleidoscope Kid as his senses of self were so fragmentary that he presented rapidly and differently at any small change or perceived potential threat just like a kaleidoscope responding to any change in movement. The case of Jason illustrates how incoherent, incohesive and fragmentary self-development was for him with multiple caretakers. He entered the care system aged 6 months because of his mother's inability to care for him appropriately. He was subjected to multiple caretakers and multiple traumatic experiences over the next 10 years of his life.

It is important to recognise that each caretaker defined Jason differently according to their own understanding of his behaviours and their own idiosyncratic view of the world and there were varying degrees of communication between them, with some having none at all and some in conflict, which led to Jason developing eight different fragmentary senses of self. In each of the contexts, Jason experienced some traumatisation and loss. The stars represent the highlights and achievements he experienced and the explosions represent traumatic events. It will also be noted that the sense of self in some cases is distorted by the severity of the traumatisation that he experienced.

At first (self 1) Jason was in the care of his mother who was herself a teenager and not ready emotionally, or mature enough, to be looking after a baby. She was still struggling to look after herself and she neglected him and his basic needs.

Jason's care was taken over by his maternal grandmother at the request of the social services (self 2). She had been present at Jason's birth and had known him throughout his life. Thus she was able to provide some continuity between his mother and herself, giving him some coherence in his emergent sense of self.

However, for example, what the mother had seen as wilful and naughty in Jason's behaviour, the grandmother held a more indulgent and mature view about. He was treated in a more protective, loving and gentler way, so whilst there was some continuity there was also a difference in his two senses of self. This could not be understood in any explicit way by Jason at that age. Then communication between mother and grandmother broke down and Jason lost contact with his birth mother. Grandmother provided Jason with a resilient connective scaffolding attachment.

However, grandmother suffered a severe heart attack and was no longer able to care for Jason and he was taken into foster care (self 3).

Unfortunately the foster home was only a short term placement, whilst longer term caretakers were sought. In the foster home, Jason's behaviour, temperament and sense of self underwent another change, as he was redefined again by the foster caretakers according to their own idiosyncratic understandings. There was little communication with grandmother, as her health was very poor, but there was some transmission of his narrative. Jason who was 2 years old at this time suffered from traumatic bereavement at the sudden inexplicable loss of his grandmother whom he never saw again. He could not understand why his world had changed, or where she had gone.

He became hyper-vigilant, constantly looking at doors opening in the hopes that she would appear. He also became very distressed and threw tantrums when taken to the park and the supermarket as these served as traumatic reminders. His foster caretakers were very experienced and understood his distress and managed him with empathic attunement. In time Jason settled down and lived with them for 2 years, until he was 4 years old, when an adoptive placement for him was found.

Jason moved to his adoptive parents (self 4), who lived some distance from his foster caretakers, after a brief introductory period. They were delighted to be adopting him; he was completely bewildered by his entirely changed world and the loss of his foster parents. He again suffered from grief at their loss and was very difficult to manage. They were bewildered and frightened by some of his behaviours. His adoptive parents persevered but his adoptive mother gradually came to the conclusion that he hated her; and that he had an incurable reactive attachment disorder. The placement broke down before the adoption went through. In the final stages of breakdown, the adoptive mother threw Jason's teddy bear, which he had had since birth into the dustbin in front of him. Jason later retrieved for himself. He had been with them for 8 months.

Jason was moved in crisis to another temporary foster home, there was no time to assess how he would fit into this home (self 5). During his placement the eldest foster son returned to the home and unbeknown to the foster parents, sexually abused Jason then aged just 5 years old. This persisted over some 5 months. Jason's behaviour in this placement was described as very destructive, hyperactive, aggressive and attention seeking. He was referred to a paediatrician for further investigation of this and the sexual abuse was discovered.

Child protection proceedings were undertaken and Jason was again moved into another emergency placement to another set of foster caretakers (self 6) aged 5 years 5 months. There was no contact at all between his former foster caretakers and his emergency foster caretakers. Jason's sense of self was again redefined by his new caretakers, who were very experienced older foster caretakers, but who had given up long term fostering; although they were still being used for short term placements. By now, Jason had also experienced 4 changes in social worker and his narrative was becoming more incoherent, incohesive and indistinct as knowledge of it was lost. Whilst his caretakers were good at containing Jason, they found his hyperactivity and hyper-vigilance exhausting and could not keep up with him.

At the age of 6 years 3 months, Jason was found a long term foster placement with a younger, but experienced pair of foster parents with lots of energy. They had 4 children already, three of their own who were teenagers and a foster daughter aged 10 years. By now Jason had experienced 4 changes in nursery and school and teachers. It must be noted here that changes in school also represent changes in the identity of self in these contexts, as each school has a similar, but different ethos and personality. Jason was not yet able to read or write, but was able to do simple arithmetic.

He was constantly on the go, spoke rarely and his behaviour was very oppositional, aggressive and defiant. He did not understand or respect rules and was constantly disruptive at school, overturning chairs and tables, attacking staff and children and running out of the class unpredictably for no clear reason. A referral was made for psychotherapy for him as he was now in his long term placement. Medication for hyperactivity was not felt to be the best way forward at this time by the paediatrician and the social services. They wanted to wait to see how he settled. This placement broke down 2 years later, when the foster parents were surprised to realise that they were expecting another child. They did not feel that in the long term that they could cope with his needs and those of a new baby.

This time, there was time to plan the changes and it was decided that after all he had been through that Jason needed a specialist foster placement with an independent professional agency, who could provide professional foster parents and also individual psychotherapy and education according to his needs (self 8). Jason was in psychotherapy for over 2 years before it was decided that EMDR therapy might help and that he would be stable enough to participate in this with his psychotherapist present during the EMDR therapy.

The psychotherapist's relationship with him provided the attachment bridge and the safety and the alliance between the two therapists brought the containing structure and context together with the foster parents working as an integrated team. This is an essential point not to overlook before undertaking some individual EMDR work with Jason. The EMDR therapist in this complex case should take to consideration Jason's life context and supporting systems.

Looking at Jason's case, it is clear that Jason's world has been unpredictable, uncontainable, incohesive and incoherent. It was not surprising that he was not able to regulate himself and was incapable of settling to any activity for more than 10 minutes. He constantly had to be on the go physically and was completely unable to use any relaxation techniques. Jason found his respite in constant activity, which required intense concentration and was impulsive and sometimes dangerous. He switched frequently. EMDR therapy needed to be slow and carefully planned and integrated into his daily world.

In Jason's case "slower is faster." The first step into EMDR therapy was optimize his strengths and focusing on what he was already doing, by creating a very active, rhythmic, safe activity instead of trying to think of a safe place. In his case, challenging him to throw soft sponge balls into a bin through a netball basket with either hand alternately and turning this into an active, playful turn-taking competition with the therapist, by seeing how many he could get successively in each turn, was the way in. In this way, Jason was taught to start to regulate his activity by the turn taking and also introduced to ABLS. Other similar activities were used to keep his interest and he began to look forward to the sessions.

Outside of therapy, Jason was being encouraged to develop his sporting skills in many different ways, initially in individual sporting activities and then in team sports, with his foster parents witnessing and supporting this development. By achieving success in these and receiving positive approbation from his caretakers, it was helping him to develop positive resources that could then be built on to develop some sense of success, resilience and self-esteem.

Later on, it was possible to help him to gradually build his different senses of self into short narratives. Given his fragility we started with his most recent events first and gradually and very slowly worked backwards to his early experiences using the Inverted Protocol. His psychotherapy continued and provided a reflective safe place to do this though he no longer needed the psychotherapist present in the EMDR sessions. In time subsequently these short narratives were strung together into more comprehensive, coherent, global narratives, which he was then able to share with his foster parents. They were in turn enabled to help him further integrate this and connect it to his current world of experience, in a dynamic interactional way, relating his emotional expressions and behaviours to his past and connecting them to his present behaviours and grounding him in the present.

In this way, they were able to help him build an emotional vocabulary to reflect on these together and build insight and explanations for his present reactions through contingent communication. Further, through social stories they were able to help him think about modifying his behaviours in the future by repairing past negative experiences. He remained in specialist foster care though he was able to attend a normal secondary school. He received phased but intermittent therapy when new issues relating to his understanding of his past experiences arose in the light of his developing emotional, social and cognitive abilities as he matured in adolescence.

Figure 11.1 is a map matrix the therapist drew of all Jason's life experiences and different senses of self. She was shocked when she drew round it to connect it together to find that the overall image was of a frightening run away ghost of a child which of course is what Jason had appeared to be.

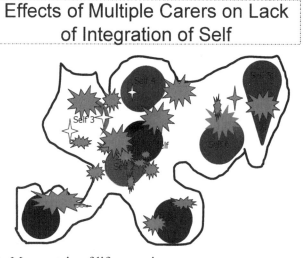

Figure 11.1: Map matrix of life experiences

11.2. Linda and domestic violence – The Cloud Child

This child is called the cloud child as although her primary attachment figure remained consistent, the attachment was damaged by the domestic violence and subsequent events. Thus she had one integral sense of self from which aspects were fogged or not connected. The domestic violence impacted in different ways at different stages of Linda's development. The jigsaw without the clouds represents the aspects of her neuro-developmental achievements at different stages, integrating into what would become in time, when the jigsaw is complete, a coherent adult in-dividual.

Not all the pieces of this jigsaw are yet present as Linda is still only 7 years old. The clouds coming in are the blighting traumas that she experi-enced as a result of what happened in her world and these skewed her developmental achievement capacities at different stages, damaged her attachment to her primary caretaker and created her dissociative tenden-cies) because of their intensity and duration.

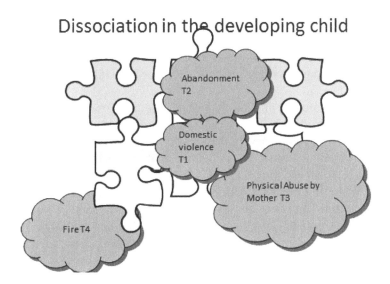

Figure 11.2: Dissociation

The domestic violence occurred prior to her birth and throughout her first year of childhood (T1). This chronic domestic violence threatened the fundamental integrity of her primary caretaker, her mother. Being so young Linda was unable to do anything other than freeze when her mother was threatened. The repeated freezing in turn became her primary defensive mechanism as it was being utilised over and over again to manage the overwhelming threat. It led to the development of a super-highway in her immature neural circuits and in time became her primary coping strategy. Fight and flight were not used and in time became less and less likely to be used, as the neural super-highway was strengthened repeatedly and thus fired first. Developmentally Linda started to suffer as she showed a lack of what should be emergent curiosity in her world and her walking was delayed. She was crawling, but became frightened of walking and disliked standing up, or being stood up.

The domestic violence ceased when Linda was about 18 months old after father had hit mother whilst Linda was in her arms. At this point mother realized the danger to Linda and fled with her to a refuge (T2). They began a new life, but their environment was bleak with few possessions, no permanent home and very little money. The mother developed severe depression as a result of all she had experienced and was less emotionally available to Linda than she had been previously. She also had to attend numerous appointments for housing, financial support, the divorce proceedings and had to leave Linda in the care of strangers in the refuge.

Linda, who was already over-sensitised and dysregulated by her earlier experiences, then experienced a period of feeling abandoned and helpless as a result. She began to walk, but her speech was showing signs of being delayed. She became a clingy, unhappy and needy toddler.

After 6 months, mother and Linda moved into their own new accommodation and set up home. This was a period of greater stability and the mother started receiving psychotherapy for her depression and was able to be more soothing, consistent and emotionally available to Linda. Linda started nursery school and seemed to settle there, but at home she responded to the mother's increased engagement by becoming more and more demanding and throwing prolonged temper tantrums. The mother felt helpless particularly as Linda had the same red hair and blue eyes as her father and when in her rages the mother saw before her the image of her husband and had flashbacks of the violence. Mother retaliated and hit Linda in a forcible way, as though she was defending herself against her husband (T3).This happened periodically over a period of time and Linda withdrew from her and her attachment became avoidant in response to mother's ambivalence. Linda, although she still needed her mother no longer fully trusted her. She became quieter and more withdrawn in general.

The nursery noticed this and in discussion with them, mother realised what she was doing to Linda. With the help of the nursery and her general practitioner Linda was referred to a paediatrician. Linda's delayed development and her behavioural problems were identified and she was referred to speech and language therapy and to the child psychologist.

With careful behavioural management and guidance for the mother about regulating and recognising the child's problems, things settled down. By now Linda's tantrums had ceased and she was a quieter, calmer child who spoke little, tended to live in a world of her own and had found an imaginary friend. The imaginary friend was helpful in her developing language as Linda had to speak for her and this was seen by mother to be harmless if a bit irritating. By the time Linda started school, things were going much better generally for them, mother started to work part-time and their social life improved.

When Linda finished her first year at school, the teacher told mother that whilst Linda was coping and a good girl in class, she was making slow progress, seemed to daydream a lot and was rather isolated from her peers. Her reading and arithmetic were progressing slowly. Her second year at school progressed reasonably, she was starting to make friends and things remained stable at home.

Unfortunately, when Linda was 7 years old there was a fire (T4) in the home caused by faulty electrical wiring and mother and the child had to be rescued by the fire brigade. Their home was destroyed and they lost all their possessions and had to be temporarily re-housed again. Linda was referred to a psychologist again this time because of her recurrent nightmares and fears created by the fire. She dreamt of being alone and unable to reach her mother, of being in a deep hole that she could not get out of. Her imaginary friend was still present and was providing her with some comfort.

EMDR therapy began very slowly for her as she and her mother needed to regain some sense of safety in the world and she needed a long period of stabilisation. There was no attempt to work on her imaginary friend at this stage as she was providing a benign coping mechanism.

Her mother during this period received some EMDR therapy for herself to deal with her past traumas relating to her violent husband.

The first targets for Linda in EMDR therapy were her nightmares and her traumatic memories of the fire. The work followed the reverse protocol, working on the near past before working on earlier traumatisation. She dissociated frequently during the sessions and the process was very slow and gentle. One of the devices used to help her maintain dual attention was that she was given a soft, cuddly toy to hold during the sessions and references to the toy helped to recall her when she started to slip away.

In time she was able to process her more profound traumas of her earlier development, from which she had dissociated using a narrative approach and Mother was able to apologise to her for not having been able to protect her adequately in the past. As the attachment started to repair during the therapy and as Linda gained more confidence in her world her imaginary friend spontaneously evaporated.

The matrix map showed how different traumatic events at different times at different stages in the development of the child led to dissociative functioning in the child, lack of fluidity and an incoherence in the internal system of the child, which undermined her developmental achievements and potential. We learn from this that dissociation is an adaptive response to trauma, firstly the domestic violence from father and ruptures in the attachment, followed by violence behaviour from mother and further attachment disruptions. The therapist has to remember to put Linda's behaviour and psychological make-up into context with her family life experiences and relationships, particularly with her mother and realise/understand that the dissociative tendencies are also providing information about this particular relationship and how to manage it.

11.3. Diana and sexual abuse within the family – The Light Bulb Lass

Diana is known as the light bulb lass because her attachment to her primary caretaker was originally healthy and positive, albeit that her mother was a single parent and she also had a younger ASD child to look after as well as Diana. She was referred aged 16 years old because she had made a number of very serious suicide attempts since her birthday and was suffering from multiple recurrent nightmares, suicidal ideation and very low self-esteem. No apparent cause had been found for these. She was one of 4 children and was the second youngest. It was discovered that she had only started this self-harming behaviour since she had moved into another larger bedroom in the house when her elder sister left home.

Her mother and sister told her what had happened in that room many years ago. Finding out what happened in the bedroom came as a shattering experience, just like a light bulb crashing to the floor and exploding; she lost any sense of who she was.

Her mother and elder sister told her after her nightmares started that when she was 3 years old and her sister 6 years old they had been sexually abused by their 17 year old half-brother while he was baby-sitting them, whilst their mother was at her part time job. She had felt totally bewildered and very angry and in her EMDR processing said that she would rather know than not know. She processed her anger and recalled that when they told her, it had felt like a train had just hit her and passed straight through her. She experienced sadness and despair because they had kept all that knowledge from her all those years.

Later in her session, she processed that she could not remember much of her early childhood. She felt she had missed a lot and it was her mother and sister's fault because they had not told her. She felt as if she had known she would have remembered this. She then processed that she had *"treated him as my brother all these years and now – it's like - he is not who I thought he was- and I am not who I thought I was - and my sister is not who I thought she was..."* She felt she hated him because she did not know exactly what he did, she could not really match up what was said because she did not know. She felt she just could not trust anybody and this made her feel angry because *"...the people I thought I could trust I can't because they lied to me – so - I don't know I..."* When asked if they had lied to her she said that she thought they had because they had just carried on as normal.

After the next set she recalled *"I remember when my mum chucked Mark out and that I felt it was like my fault he had to leave - but I don't really know why I felt like that - because I was the only one who told her what happened..."* She did not seem to recognise what she had just told the therapist but by the end of the next set she said *"...I remember my mum getting the washing machine out and I was coming down the stairs and I said something and I can't remember what I said – but I think that is when I told her because she said it came out in normal conversation – but she told me that I told her in her bedroom but I – maybe I must have told her more than once..."*. She realised that her trust in her mother's relationship had not been broken, but still had identity issues about who she was. After further processing she added *"...I remember my sister telling me that – and my brother saying that I should not tell mum because she said that I just shouldn't tell her..."* After further processing of the reconnecting she said *"I think I must have thought it was normal..."* She required further EMDR sessions but after that first desensitisation session she stopped self-harming. There were other dissociated traumatic experiences in her middle childhood that gradually became uncovered and integrated. She was in therapy for several months.

What we learn from this case is the devastating, destructive impact that dissociated material can have on a child's sense of self and attachments when that dissociated material is re-introduced in a unprotected way by unsuspecting others who have assumed that she has had access to the information throughout her childhood. It illustrates that, although the attachment appeared to be healthy, how fragile Diana's shell was and how her own defence system was still protecting her from accessing this dissociated material prematurely.

The three cases above briefly illustrate different presentations of the lack of integration of dissociative material. They are to be looked through the lens of a developmental process that is guiding and helping us not to define them as a set pattern of a dissociative identity disorder. Further we are keeping this dynamic process by contextualizing these different forms of dissociative tendencies within attachment relationships and how they have affected the development of the sense of self and ability to cope in the world. We have presented here only three individual children and there are as many different dissociative matrices as there are children suffering from dissociative tendencies. Below are drawings made by two 14 years old adolescent girls who have suffered sexual abuse by paedophiles and complex traumatisation that illustrate this further. The full details of their therapy are outside the scope of this book but the drawings depict how un-integrated they are in their own unique ways

11.4. Lily's drawings

The first case is of Lily, who suffered from dissociation and multiple complex traumatisation, which started when her baby brother died when she was just 2 years old. By the time she was seen she was also abusing drugs and alcohol as well as self-harming. She drew the picture in Figure 11.3 when it was suggested to her that sometimes we can feel like we have many different parts to us that relate to things that could have happened to us.

154

Figure 11.3: Lily's drawing - 01

She drew her senses of emotional self and then ascribed different ages to them according to how old they felt to her.

She also drew the picture in Figure 11.4 when she was told that all the parts of her had come to protect her at times when she had been experiencing very horrible things and that they were all equal and good and needed to all be present. It was like they were at the round table that King Arthur had used for his knights, they were all to be equally valued and respected and to have an equal voice.

Figure 11:4: Lily's drawing - 02

The ashamed one was placed in a curtained box so the others did not have to look at it. The little one's hands were being held by the angry one and the sensible one to help it feel safe enough to be there and the sad one hovered behind the angry one. The three pairs of eyes in the top corner represented her psychiatric nurse, her psychiatrist and the therapist who were all present to help contain her and help her feel safe enough to begin the therapeutic EMDR process.

Detailing all of her therapy is outside of the scope of this book but to summarize. It was many months before Lily could tolerate any work on the traumatisations that she had experienced, but these pictures provided the start together with the family's history and it is all there. Lily was in therapy for 4 years during which time she dipped in and out of problems, running away, abusing drug and alcohol, cutting and burning herself and getting involved in very abusive relationships with much older men.

In time she began to become more coherent, to understand some of what was happening to her and what had happened to her and to realize that she was not alone and nor was she entirely helpless. There were many breakthrough moments and heart breaking set-backs.

One of the especially big breakthroughs was when she decided in her 4th year of therapy to talk to the police and child protection services about her experiences of abuse at the hands of the paedophiles, putting on re-cord who had done what. Sadly this could not as in many other similar cases proceed to a successful prosecution but she was consoled by the knowledge that this was now on all their records and the Sexual Offend-ers Register and that it would help protect other young girls in the future. It was a fascinating process to watch as Lily little by little despite the set-backs grew into the lovely, intelligent, caring and empathic teenager she should be with age appropriate and nice boyfriends and moved from school to college and then to a university place.

11.5. Amber's drawings

In the second case, Amber aged 14 years suffered from multiple complex traumatisation and even more severe dissociation and was seriously self-harming by cutting and burning. She was also running away from home. Her condition was more severe and its origins mostly unknown to others and inaccessible to her and her family, but which seems to have started with the death of an important attachment figure. Amber was given simi-lar instructions to those give to Lily to draw herself and about all parts of herself being important and there for very good reasons. Again this case is far too complex to go into detail of therapy in this book. She drew the picture in Figure 11.5 on a piece of notepaper:

Figure 11.5: Amber's drawing 01

The severity of the distortions of her senses of bodily selves is evident as is the dissociation of most of her senses from her body. Asked if she could remember herself in a time before all the troubles started she drew the picture shown in Figure 11.6.

Figure 11.6: Amber's drawing 02

She did not know how old she was but she was very little and had strings attaching her gloves to her coat and was just old enough to jump in puddles which she loved. Notice here that although she drew this as a happy picture she depicted herself in the rain.

Working with Amber in therapy was very long and painful and entailed many breaks and was sadly incomplete as she moved to another part of the country for her own safety. She seemed to be so trapped, like an insect in amber by things around her that did not have any shape or meaning but which kept her trapped inside, wordless. Her family was equally helpless and wordless but determined not to give up and worked as hard as they could to get her to come to therapy. The most devastating traumatisation was clearly pre-verbal.

EMDR therapy started to build resources for her but this could only be done very slowly and she would often end up sabotaging herself in one way or another. Although it was possible to work very slowly on recent traumas the deeper earlier ones remained buried. It was not until near the end of the therapy that is was possible for Amber to start to piece together what might have happened to her and this led to her feeling very unsafe in the area. This then led to her placement in another part of the country where she could start to share with the police and child protection service what had happened. As the therapist was unable to continue to work with her because of her move her longer term therapeutic progress is not known.

11.6. Summary

To conclude this chapter, we want to emphasize again how the therapist needs to be constantly aware of the uniqueness of every individual child, their world and their processing and that the child exists within the context of the family. No models can do justice to the individual unless they are their own or built on their own perspectives as far as these can be ascertained and we always need to follow from the child's developmental perspective and the contextual historical narrative and be guided and led by the child's pace and focus.

Furthermore from the therapist's perspective, screening for dissociative tendencies, identifying them and planning for them, is vitally important to protect the child and keep the therapeutic process as safe as it can be. However, it must also be remembered that EMDR therapy can disrupt previously unknown dissociative barriers during the course of therapy. What needs to happen then is a slowing down of the whole process, firstly grounding the child in the present and then putting as many safety anchors as possible in place, before considering doing any further desensitisation. Secondly and then, titrating to a level and pace that only slowly and gently stretches the child's window of tolerance and thirdly remembering that dissociative tendencies have occurred within the context of interpersonal relationships including perhaps within the therapeutic relationship itself (or at least) and affecting its quality. The therapist needs to seek to understand more about the dynamic of attachment processes and where the ruptures may have occurred and how these can be repaired, remembering at all times the safety of the child is paramount and the safety of the therapist is secondary but also important and necessary to the process.

What we learn from these different examples is that as clinicians, when working within a family system, we need to consider how the above impacts on our daily practise. We need to look at the larger picture, the context; and consider the advantages of the same therapist working with different parts of the system, the parents and the child rather than seeing or working with just a part of it, the child. Conversely can the therapist contain the therapeutic system, or do they enlarge it by asking other professionals to intervene, risking increasing the level of dissociative functioning within the family system. As we hear sometimes *"there are so many people involved, I am losing my bearings"*.

Chapter 12

Autistic Spectrum Disorders

12.1. Introduction

In the previous chapter we discussed the notion of lack of connectivity and incoherence as a function of life experiences and a lack of continuity and breakages in attachment connectivity. In this chapter we look at what may happen with neuro-developmental disorders specifically Autistic Spectrum Disorders (ASD) where lack of connectivity may be hardwired as a part of the disorder or metabolically-mediated. This may also be applicable to other neuro developmental disorders.

Autistic Spectrum Disorders (ASD) children may be traumatised by normal daily living experiences, which they cannot understand and integrate because of their deficits in social communication and understandings. They are often obsessed by what they do not understand, for example the child who hated fireworks obsessively collected used firework cartridges and rocket sticks, and another, Ian, aged 7 years repetitively drew car washes.

One of the author's soon after training in EMDR therapy thought that it may be a way of helping some of these children reduce their distress and confusions about the world because it was largely non-verbal. With permission from his parents they decided to try it with Ian.

12.2. Ian – The car wash obsession

At the time the reason he was obsessed with car washes was unknown. Ian was seen on his own, (now days we would have included the parent in the session) and drew predictably a car wash and this was used as the target. The session was brief he was able to say it was 'bad'. He was told as he was being tapped with his hands on a large fluffy cushion that *"car washes were like showers for cars and the water, soap and brushes were used to clean them and that cars did get dirty with the mud and dust and needed to be cleaned sometimes to get rid of this The hissing noise was the sound of the water squirting out, just like it did from hoses and people's showers only louder and that was because it had to reach all over the car with the brushes and soap to clean it. It needed lots of water and soap to clean it. There were switches to turn it on and off and people pushed these switches to start it and it stopped when the car was clean. Then it dried it with a very big drier like a hair drier and then the car was shiny and clean and it would not be taken back until it was dirty again."*

At the outset his body posture was rigid but changed within a short space of time and eased up. Within 10 minutes, Ian smiled gave direct eye contact and got up to play with the Lego. He did not speak a word and giving eye contact was very unusual for him. The therapist was still unfamiliar with how EMDR could work and felt perplexed and wondered what had happened. However, after just this one session his obsession with car washes completely disappeared to the surprise of all, because it had been there for more than 2 years.

Asked about his obsession with car washes his mother subsequently recalled that when he was around 2-3 years old and still unable to speak more than a few words, he had been in the car with his brother and mother when she took them to the car wash. Ian had had a terrible tantrum and they had had to hold on to him for the duration as he was frantically trying to get out. In those days she recalled he had had frequent tantrums to many things and he did not understand and could not be reasoned with and they rarely went out because of it.

Thinking about it from his perspective and without language to reassure him or give him an explanation of what was going to happen, or warn him something different was happening, one can imagine just how terrifying his experience must have been on confronting the car wash; this huge, red, noisy, spitting, moving monster engulfing the car his mother, brother and himself. Since then the author has used EMDR therapy for resolving many of the fears and confusions that ASD children have had. It does not of course alter their condition, but it does dramatically improve the quality of their lives and those of their families and many things have been learnt in the process.

12.3. ASD definition and neurological perspectives

ASD is an umbrella term for a wide range of as yet, poorly differentiated, pervasive, neuro-developmental disorders affecting social communication, perception, affect regulation, memory, attention, cognition, executive functioning, initiation, language, co-ordination, balance and other areas; and appears to present differently in each individual.

ASDs are thought to have organic aetiology from multiple causes including genetics, environmental toxins, auto-immune deficiencies and others. These are hypothesised to affect how the brain is wired and functions. Initial early differences in brain wiring and functioning in ASD children are thought to continue to affect the brain development as the individual matures through life. Hardan et al., (2009) have found that there is a consistent finding of a smaller corpus callosum and several of its subdivisions when comparing autism to healthy age-matched controls. Hardan et al., (2008) also found an abnormal association between the thalamus and brain size in Asperger's syndrome. Just et al., (2007) found there was functional and anatomical cortical under-connectivity in autism. Recent research in ASD is indicating many things neurologically implicating the frontal lobes, the corpus callosum, the amygdala, the hippocampus and the cerebellum and with disturbances hypothesised in the cerebello-thalamo-cortical pathways.

Interestingly, when considering the impact EMDR therapy may have with ASD are the findings in the field of EMDR research that implicate the pre-frontal cortex, thalamus, amygdala and cerebellum. Further discussion of the brain abnormalities in autism is outside the scope of this book, but the reader is referred for further information to the review of these by Verhoeven et al., (2010).

12.4. ASD and sleep disorders

Sleep disorders are also commonly found in children with ASD and problems with sleep initiation, sleep maintenance and short sleep duration have been reported. Short sleep duration in ASD has also been associated with stereotypic behaviour, the overall autism scores and social skills deficits as well as with repetitive behaviours, (Goldman et al., 2011). An interesting future question for us is how far the sleep disorders may in some way affect the availability of the ASD child's processing in EMDR. Other sleep disorders may also affect EMDR processing in other neurodevelopmental disorders, for example in Aperts Syndrome and Fetal Alcohol Syndrome.

12.5. How EMDR may be working with ASD

The non-verbal attunement that seems to be achieved by the EMDR protocol might also be facilitating in ASD children, a sensitivity to another's affect cues, which may increase emotional awareness, connectivity and motivation to communicate and hence further joint contingent attention. As said previously, one of the hypotheses about how EMDR may be working is that it may be eliciting an orienting response. A failure to orient to social stimuli represents one of the earliest observable and most fundamental of ASD children's impairments. If EMDR does elicit an orienting response, it may even be possible that EMDR could help to promote social orienting and joint attention in some ASD children.

The suggestion is that EMDR might be effectively stimulating some of those pathways that are impaired in ASD. EMDR is a primarily non-verbal process and as such it may also facilitate communicative intent in non-verbal ways, as it appears to be attuning the therapist to the client's non-verbal cues and attuning the client to the therapist's. The processing itself also appears to be providing a scaffold with which some non-verbal and pre-verbal memories become accessible to verbal recall.

General orienting is linked to the cerebellum and social/emotional orienting has been linked to the amygdala, which in some autistic individuals has been found to be enlarged. An aversion to faces has been shown in autistic people to be arousing activity in the amygdala. In EMDR therapy ABLS is administered by the use of physical touch, auditory tones or visual tracking, not by joint facial attention and mutual gaze. If EMDR is eliciting an orienting response, it seems it does this by the use of other socially-linked stimuli rather than faces. (This may be less the case if a mechanical version is used such as a light bar that may not be eliciting a socially linked response.) The question arises as to whether this activity could be helping to by-pass some of the problems associated with facial communication in ASD children. Such stimulation may help to bring a greater social awareness online in children with ASD.

12.6. Clinical observations of using EMDR

One of the authors retrospectively reviewed 10 cases of children seen over a two-year period that had been diagnosed with ASD and had received EMDR therapy at a Child and Adolescent Mental Health Clinic. The cases ranged in age from 8 years and 14 years. There were 9 boys and 1 girl. Of these, 2 of the boys had been diagnosed as autistic and the remaining 8 with Asperger's syndrome by clinical diagnostic interviews. Most had been diagnosed a long time before, but one had only recently been diagnosed.

All the children were well known to the therapist prior to trying EMDR with them and all of them had had more than one session using EMDR and some had had many. Clinical impressions of these ten cases prior to EMDR treatment indicated that the ASD children were not good at connecting memories by association to other memories, they had problems generalising or retaining generalisation over time and they had problems integrating past experiences.

Each of these 10 ASD children had differing arrays of skills and deficits despite all falling into the ASD grouping. Some had pronounced physical difficulties with posture and lax ligaments and in getting things to happen, others a high degree of co-ordination, some had slow whilst others had speeded response rates, some had problems with initiation and planning and other executive function deficits. Many of them had language deficits and all had social communication deficits. All of the ASD children were sensitive in their own idiosyncratic ways to sensory stimulation.

In the cases reviewed, each of the children had received EMDR therapy for specific difficult memories as a part of their treatment in the Clinic. In all cases a parent, usually the mother, had been present during the sessions when EMDR had been administered. This was to provide a 'safe person' during the treatment and they also helped with contextual information prior to and following each session. The length of EMDR sessions varied according to each child's needs and ranged from 3 sessions to 10 sessions. Some children were still receiving treatment at the time of the review. All of the children had received their EMDR therapy from the same therapist.

EMDR therapy was used using a modified protocol for very young children for most of the children, as they could not obtain negative and positive cognitions and could not cope with the VOC. SUDS were usually obtained by showing with their hands how bad it was rather than the 0 – 10 scale.

The protocol also had to be modified to meet with each child's own idiosyncratic needs. One of the hardest things to get right was the timing and the pacing of the ABLS for each child and the speed that worked for different children varied considerably. For example, all the work done with one child, who was a brilliant chess player and who had a time obsession, had to be fitted into the exact hour he had allocated for this. He continually checked the clock and had to finish on time regardless. He was also counting the taps, but fortunately did not insist on a rigorous number each set. He frequently told the therapist how many there had been and exactly how long each took.

At the end of each set, the responses were obtained by just drawings in some cases, drawings and words in others, or by just asking what was happening in others; and by a series of multiple choice questioning for others where there were clear problems in their being able to initiate their responses. On the whole, the therapist had to be generally more proactive in getting responses from the children and more creative in opening up possibilities for responsiveness.

Target selection was a bit problematic given their communicative problems and was done usually by an examination of their parent's observations, the child's fears, rituals and obsessions; and also by intuitive 'best guess' leaps based on clinical experience, judgement and knowledge of the individual child and their current problems. The target would be either drawn or visualised. One child found initiation so difficult that the target "*a boogie*" (mucus) had to be drawn for him.

Targets have included bad experiences at a school, being confronted with a test that required two boxes to be ticked instead of the expected one box only (so it broke the child's rule-bound understanding of testing), having been hurt, hurting others, having to go to school, rejection by a family, death of a parent, parents arguing and other issues including their own past behaviour. For some, as one issue was dealt with using EMDR, the next worrying things on their agendas seem to come up naturally and spontaneously.

In addition to their idiosyncratic fears and experiences, using EMDR with ASD children highlighted that their fears were often no different to other children's in that they were experiencing normal developmental fears. However, they were doing this in a very delayed way, with the presentation of these occurring at later ages and stages, when they were not easily identifiable and they had few means to convey these. These included the fear of strangers, being separated, the fear of losing someone, the fear of death and the fear of growing up and having to look after themselves when they are aware of their limitations.

It is suggested from the work done with these ASD children and others subsequently that EMDR might be more effective if tapping is chosen as the first mode used for ABLS. (From clinical experience this also seems to be the case for other children with developmental delays). In the review it was found that 5 of the children received tapping, 3 others received eye movements initially, but this had to be changed to tapping; and it is of note that in 2 cases where EMDR did not prove effective the ABLS was given using eye movements alone. The tapping was done by placing the child's hands on a large fluffy cushion and then either asking them to tap the cushion with the therapist showing them or by the therapist tapping their hands on the cushion.

12.7. Findings of clinical observations of EMDR with ASD children

EMDR facilitated some associational chaining for the children in ways that words alone did not seem to achieve. EMDR was helpful in achieving this and reaching resolution with specific memories in 8 of the cases. In the remaining 2 cases reported by their parents as not benefitting from EMDR, one was diagnosed with ASD and the other with autism.

Whilst these 2 children did initially appear to be emotionally engaged in the task and gave quite good descriptions of feelings, they were not by the end of the session emotionally engaged and both expressed they were bored. This was in contrast to the other 8 children who had all been either visibly happy or calm. However, when both were asked in the next session if it had helped them with the specific troubling memory, they expressed that it had. This had not carried over into their observable subsequent behaviours. The 2 children who were reported by their parents as not benefiting after EMDR were both children who processed in a very cognitive domain, even though they had said the memories troubled them and initially these seemed to have some emotional valence. It is possible that the targets chosen were not carefully enough selected and did not have enough emotional valence.

EMDR was found by parental report to be helpful to their child's subsequent behaviours and feelings in 8 cases. In addition, gains were reported by some parents in their children's general sociability, confidence, talkativeness and communicative intent and in some in their concentration span. Looking at how the ASD children were processing their memories using EMDR it appeared that they were ranging in their presentation along a memory spectrum, some utilising highly cognitive pathways with low emotion and little sensory awareness; and others utilising high valence emotional and sensory pathways. This seems to fit with the clinical picture of ASD children falling broadly into two groups: those that are very focussed on collecting numbers, facts, events, dates, time but who seem emotionally cold and aloof; and the other group who display agitated, hyper-aroused, hyper-sensitised sensory awareness and anxious, fear-driven obsessional behaviours and who live very much in the now, with their memories not being anchored in time They seem to live by using their experiences and memories rather than by using any logical explanations. In other words they seem to be living largely within their implicit memory system.

12.8. Discussion of clinical observations

The problems ASD children have may partly rest in the functioning, interaction and utilization of the connectivity between both implicit and explicit memory stores along a continuum. One could conceive one end of the continuum as explicit memory narratively processed and in precise detail; and at the other end the processing of memories with emotional and sensory valence stored implicitly and in somato-sensory paths.

The ASD children's capacities and vehicles of communication are impaired and their signals are often not understood, especially as developmentally speaking, they are often out of context for their age and stage and their timing can be unusual. ASD children's non-verbal responses are more evocative of the communications given by very young children, which have become elaborated in time by their continuous use. Cognitive interweaves during the EMDR process that were educational in content were used with most of the children reviewed at some point, to supply information that they did not know yet, or had not yet understood.

Witnessing the EMDR processing seemed to sensitise both their parents and the clinician to what the 8 ASD children were experiencing and conveying emotionally non-verbally. Often their parent could read their children's own idiosyncratic non-verbal messages and were able to signal things to the therapist about these. What they were less in touch with was the memory content of what their children were experiencing. They were also surprised at how well their children did during this treatment and the things that they were able to demonstrate. One child aged 12 years, for the first time outside of school, started to write spontaneously during the processing a thing his mother had never seen. Another was able to show an awareness of role play and others' perspectives. Similar findings have been made when working with children with other neuro-developmental disorders and their families. The non-verbal processing elicits many unreached/unidentified problems.

Through initially targeting 'a boogie' with a child who had pronounced obsessions about germs, it was revealed that the 'boogie' led back to the death of his cat and then to developmental fears of death itself. This led in another session to a fear of growing up because growing older meant that he would be getting nearer to death and he did not want to die. In a further session, a secondary fear arose that he would not be able to look after himself as an adult and fear of his parents dying. Once these issues were known about through the EMDR processing, his parents were able to re-assure him and support him in the context of his daily life. In his own processing of this he recalled that he had watched how to make some food and that he might be able to do this in the future.

Another child processed the terror that he had about getting older. During the processing it was discovered that this had arisen because he thought he had been told by his mother that when children are 18 and grown-up they had to leave home. He took this totally literally. She had no recollection of when this happened and felt it had probably come up some time in a conversation involving her other children talking with her generally. He was overwhelmed by this and feared every day, as that made him older and he hated his birthday. Educational interweaves around this were made for him by his mother and the therapist. During the processing mother hugged him as she told him that he would not have to leave home when he was 18 years old and grown up; and that he could stay with her and his father as long as he wanted to. He later came to realise in processing that he had choices when he was grown up and he might choose to leave home when he was older.

The use of EMDR with ASD children in the presence of a parent seemed to promote better attunement and communications between the parent and the child. Having their signals interpreted helped the ASD children to develop a shared communicative, contingent mode. Following the EMDR therapy many of the parents reported that they were able to build narratives naturally in daily life with their children about their child's traumatic memory as they now understood more about their child's inner world. The EMDR processing and witnessing it seemed to help the parent to map onto their child's somato-sensory and frightening experiences from the child's perspective and understandings. The parents were then naturally able to help their children with developing the themes around these, which in turn seemed to promote greater sociability, eye contact and communication in the children generally.

The parents were more able to notice the environment from their child's perspectives and anticipate things better for them. ASD children seem to live in worlds which are isolating by their communicative problems from others and therefore, are often not available for, or often given, the reassurances and comfort in a way that normal children take for granted in their daily lives. Given that there is also much that they do not understand in daily living, this must make their need for comfort even greater and possibly makes their primary attachments more insecure than other children's in the family. Also because their communication modes are impaired, they remain more dependent upon their primary carers than other children in the family, because their primary carers are more able to interpret them and mediate between them and the wider world. Witnessing the EMDR processing helped to enable their parents to give this more to them and this was rewarding for both the parents and the children, similar findings have been made by the therapist with parents of children with other neuro-developmental disorders.

Since this review was undertaken some 6 years ago and presented in the European EMDR conference in Istanbul, most of the children have been seen again for further EMDR therapy treatment episodes, as different issues arose for them as they continued to develop through childhood and adolescence.

Clinically speaking, EMDR is an effective treatment for some ASD children with troubling memories and it can be used with them and can improve the quality of their lives, although it does not cure their fundamental disorder. The two children, who did not make positive gains observable to others, still reported their specific memories were no longer troubling them and it is unclear what this might have meant for them.

In the 8 children who were reported to make positive gains, the EMDR therapy seemed to promote bottom-up neural kindling. The processing helped to connect feelings and sensations to language thus making them explicit to others (the work of Pagani et al (2012) seems to indicate this). It may be that the 2 children who seemed to function primarily in their cortical memories were not being stimulated in the same way by the ABLS and thus there was no top-down processing possible. It also of note that these were the two children who preferred ABLS eye movements to touch.

12.9. Summary

The review indicates that there is clinical evidence of the effectiveness of EMDR with some ASD children in improving the quality of their lives, but not all. Similar observations have been made with children suffering from other neuro-developmental disorders. This needs detailed research to establish who can benefit and why.

The above is in keeping with other studies of treatments for ASD, where it has been found that there is differential responsiveness to specific treatments. This also indicates the heterogeneity of the ASD spectrum and the need to establish who responds to what and why. ASD children's responses to EMDR therapy could also be used to help in the differential diagnosis of more specific disorders, which are currently poor differentiated and subsumed under the umbrella label Autistic Spectrum Disorders.

Adaptations to the protocol and differing responsiveness for children suffering from other neuro-developmental and metabolic disorders have been observed in some of these disorders and also point to new areas of research and potential therapy, both for the disorders and for EMDR

Finally, some ASD children use rhythmic repetitive movements, for example, pushing of cars backwards and forwards, the rocking backwards and forwards, the flapping and the gaze turning upwards and to the corners of the eyes as self-soothing activities. It may be that EMDR is also tapping into a form of this neural stimulation that the ASD children try to do for themselves naturally and which seems to have a soothing effect.

Chapter 13

EMDR Case Studies

The following are a collection of case studies which we want to share with you to illustrate how it all comes together.

13.1. The Martin Family - Family work with traumatic bereavement

Mrs Martin had asked her general practitioner for advice, following the death of their oldest son of 9 years. He had undergone complicated heart surgery three years previously. Her general practitioner had advised her to get some help for whole family in managing their traumatic bereavement.

13.1.1. The first session

Alex, 5 years old, his brother, Jacque 6 years old, their father, Jules 46 years old and their mother, Carole 37 years old, all attended the first session. After establishing a rapport, father was asked to explain the reason for their visit. He talked about their oldest son Gérard, who had died just two months previously. The family's emotional reactions were observed and in particular Jacque who kept looking his father straight in the eyes. Everybody took turns to explain how he died, alone on the way back from school. Usually one of the parents went to fetch him, but this time he had wanted to come back home by himself like a grown-up child, but he never made it back to the house. When they didn't see him coming back, the parents went to look for him and mother found him dead in a ditch alongside the road.

The narrative of Gérard's death created a lot of emotion and the children looked intensely towards the parents. Jacque told the therapist that his brother was now a little star in the sky and that he thought about him every evening when watching the stars. During his comments, the parents struggled to hold back their tears and their suffering was very evident. It was a very painful situation and it seemed important to be able to see them without the children. They were thinking about only one thing, moving to another house. During this first meeting, nothing dysfunctional in the communication and organisational patterns of the family was observed. There was no mention of major difficulties prior to Gerard's death.

13.1.2.   The next session

The couple were seen alone at the next session. Their suffering prevented them being able to reassure the children. Their relationship was also suffering and they were starting to blame each other. They shared what they felt: what they could understand of what happened, what they would have liked the other one to have done and the feeling of being alone with all this pain. The relationship could not absorb and contain their individual grief. EMDR therapy with each one was proposed and how it could help them to be more at peace was explained.

The clinical treatment planning dilemma was how and with what type of setup: should it be one person after the other, separately, or in front of each other? The notion of preserving the relationship was a key point to consider. Clinical research has shown us that family ties suffer a great deal and can break up in the aftermath of a trauma. It was suggested that EMDR therapy was undertaken with one, whilst the other watched, each taking a turn undergoing EMDR and watching the other. The goal was to relieve some of their individual suffering within the context of their relationship and to help them access and reinforce their common resources to face this shared trauma. It was explained to them that, at the end of each session, there would be a debriefing time to allow the one who listened to share his/her ideas, feelings and personal reactions on what had happened. Father was willing to try EMDR first. His wife stayed in the room and listened.

13.1.3.   Father's EMDR therapy

His target was the image of *"his wife when she found their son's body"*. His negative cognition was "I am lost". His positive cognition was "I would like to be able to think that I can carry on". The VOC was at 4 on the scale. There was lots of sadness and tears, his SUDS level was at 9.

When the desensitisation started, he talked first about how difficult it was to follow the ABLS and then felt more peaceful. Going back to target, he described a sensation of heat, light, emptiness, of things being erased and again of being peaceful, calm and serene. At the end of the session, the SUDS level of disturbance had been reduced to 0 and the VOC level was at 7. He looked more at peace and talked to his wife about how surprised he was with this feeling of peacefulness.

13.1.4. Mother's EMDR therapy

The next session, it was the mother's turn to try EMDR with her husband staying in the room. She chose as her target the moment when "*I found my son with his lips all blue and his eyes rolled up*". Her negative cognition was "*I am a bad mother*", her positive cognition was "I *would like to be able to think I am a good mother*". Her session was also a complete session, during which the desensitization and installation processes were fully completed, SUDS level down to 0 from 10 and the VOC up to 6. She said she could not go all the way up to 7 yet, time had to do its work. They were both surprised to feel so peaceful and were grateful for having been able to share each other's powerful, poignant moments together.

13.1.5. The family session

During the next session, it was decided to work with the children using the narrative technique. One may ask why? In this case the siblings were just 5 and 3 years old and the tragedy had occurred for the whole family. The family did not have a history of other traumas and the attachment patterns were very secure. The use of the narrative technique with the parents would help the children understand what had happened.

Previously, the parents' own traumatic grief and overwhelming pain had prevented them from being able to provide enough emotional stability to ensure a safe surrounding scaffold in which to contain the children's own pain. The whole family would benefit from this, as the parents were able to be more proactive and less helpless, as they were now able to facilitate the children's healing. The children would benefit because in the naturalistic context of the family, it is the natural role of the parents to protect, guide and heal them. With the therapist's guidance in this way, the parents become co-therapists with their children.

Mother told the story of Gerald's death as though she were reading from a book to the children, the children listened attentively and father and the therapist tapped the children on their shoulders. After the story had been told, the therapist checked with each child about what had come up for them. At this point nothing had come up and the children seemed quite calm.

If however, something had come up the therapist would have needed to do some further desensitisation. Then as a way of returning to target to check, father told the story again and mother helped with the tapping. At the end of the story, the therapist again asked the children what had come up. The children were calm, they asked their parents a few questions to help them understand it more clearly and this allowed them to develop a more comprehensive narrative. Throughout the session, the parents remained emotionally containing and reinforced the family cohesiveness that had been jeopardised by their traumatic incident.

Now the family could become again the stable base within which they could all grieve together, heal together and grow together; and the isolation and relationship destruction that is observed too often after a trauma of this kind was averted.

13.1.6. Two years later

Two years later, the mother contacted the therapist again. Many things had happened since their final session. The family had grown, they had another little boy, mother had started to work again, they had moved to a new house and the children's maternal grand-mother was dying of cancer. The mother said the children were sad and that they talked a lot about their deceased brother.

When the whole family came, the therapist sensed tension between the parents. The question arising was whether they were coming back to therapy for the children, the couple, or some other family dysfunction? Were the children's symptoms their own, or the expression of some family suffering? The therapist decided that the children should be seen first together, without the parents, for some EMDR work and then the parents as a couple.

13.1.7. Butterfly hug and drawings for the two boys

The two boys had shared the same traumatic incident and the therapist thought their sibling relationship could be used as a resource and could also be strengthened. Each child was asked to draw their own safe place. It was installed using the butterfly hug whilst they looked at the drawings of the safe place. Jacque, the elder brother, drew the drawing in Figure 13.1 of his safe place: The Beach.

176

Figure 13.1: The beach

Once the safe places were installed, the boys were asked to individually draw what came into their heads when thinking about their brother's death. After completing that drawing they were asked to do the butterfly hug again until a new image came up. They were told that when this happened, they should stop and draw the next one. Each successive drawing replaced the verbal associative process usually observed between the sets of ABLS. We want to emphasise that the therapist needed to be careful not to analyse the drawing and to interfere as little as possible with the processing, similarly to the standard protocol. The drawings below were made by Jacque.

Figure 13.2: Jacque's first drawing

Before making his second drawing, Jacque told the therapist beforehand that he knew that his drawing was something that could never happen. He drew the coffin opening and his brother leaving it.

Figure 13.3: Jacque's second drawing

Jacque said of his third drawing: "We were in the mountains and I am riding my bicycle".

Figure 13.4: Jacque's third drawing

Below is Jacque's fourth drawing. "We are playing with our brother who is inside the sun."

Figure 13.5: Jacque's fourth drawing

After this fourth drawing, it was time to close the session and the boys were instructed to look again at the drawings of their safe places and do the butterfly hug. The children seemed very calm after the session.

13.1.8. The next session

In the following session, when the parents were seen alone, mother's comments were very positive, she had found the children much calmer. However, lots of tension and irritability could be observed between the couple. The mother was very worried for the father, she thought he was working too much, not taking care of himself and not present enough at home. She felt quite alone with the children. Father described himself as being hyperactive, always running away and no longer able to appreciate the present moment. He asked the therapist for help.

13.1.9. Father's Session

The next session with the father alone was a quite straightforward EMDR session on a childhood trauma, when he had been ostracized by his friends when aged 9 years, which had been reactivated following his child's death. The father expressed a lot of emotion and was able to move from a negative cognition *"I am worthless"* to a positive cognition *"I have some value"*. It was a complete session and at the end, the father felt he could let go of the past and appreciate the present.

13.1.10. The couple's session

During the following session with the couple, they both confirmed the changes father had made. He was spending more time with the children and had surprised himself by playing with them.

13.1.11. Three years later

Three years later, the whole family came again. Father had contacted the therapist to help them with Alex, the middle child, who was then 10 years old. During the family session, the therapist was able to evaluate all the changes that the family had gone through over the years. The three children had grown and the family had been moving along nicely, up to the time when Alex started to show sadness about his deceased brother, whom he was talking a lot about. He was isolating himself from the family.

13.1.12. Alex's Session

The therapist decided to see him alone for a few EMDR sessions working on his memories of his brother's death. Alex's sadness lifted and he was then able to work on another memory of being left behind late one evening at school. Of note was the fact that Alex's brother had died on his way home from school and at the time of this most recent referral, Alex was the same age as his deceased brother had been. Alex's response indicated how children need to revisit their traumatic experiences in the light of their developing cognitions and social development.

13.2. The Dupont Family - Complex family work with multiple therapeutic levels of intervention

On the telephone Mrs Dupont, aged 35 years old, explained that her son Axel, aged 5 years old, was badly burned two years previously during a family dinner, by boiling cooking oil that was accidentally poured on his chest by his maternal grandmother. She said that he had been looked after very well during his 2½ months in hospital, but she was worried because for some time he was becoming very difficult at home. She described him as hyperactive, showing uncontrollable fears and withdrawing into himself.

The therapist proposed a family meeting, explaining to her that in order to help her son, a meeting with all the family members would be needed: the child, his mother, his father aged 39 years, his elder sister, 12 years old and his brother, 9 years old. The answer to this proposition was one that we often hear: that it would be fine for the brother and the sister to come but the father would not be able to come. The therapist insisted on how important it was that he be there for this first meeting. The following sessions were held weekly.

13.2.1. The first family meeting

During the session the impact of the traumatisation was discussed and although the incident happened two years previously it was still very much alive. Mother started to cry rapidly as soon as she talked about what happened and became very rapidly overwhelmed. Father sat in the corner of the consultation room, isolated and enclosed in his own world, watching what was going on. He was said to be always on edge. The oldest sister presented very responsibly and was described as a second mother. Axel's brother seemed to be very subdued to the point at which he could almost be forgotten during the session. The siblings both described what had changed since the accident. The parents paid a lot more attention to Axel than to them. *"He does what he wants now"*, they said. The interaction between mother and the children during this session confirmed father's isolation and illustrated a particular family organization, where mother seemed to have a central role in the functioning and the regulation of the family communication, she was at the centre of all the interactions.

13.2.2. The next session

During the second session with the whole family, the therapist observed how the consequences of the trauma on the individual and family levels were becoming more specific and could see how much the family was suffering. The family's organisation was disturbed at all the different subsystem levels, parental, conjugal and siblings. The father was distant, the mother was exhausted and they all expressed a strong need to talk together to exchange cognitive and emotional information about the accident. This sharing of information is the first treatment step, the building of a family narrative. Mother talked about other difficult incidents she went through, the death of a baby when she was 8 months pregnant; a lot of tension between father and his family of origin; and a lot difficulties with his work. Obviously there were numerous individual and relational wounds. At the end of this session, it was decided to see the parents alone for the next appointment. The therapist told the children they would be seen after the parents and they were asked in the meantime to think about drawing a safe place at home.

13.2.3. The couple's session

During the third session, the couple's session, father summarized the situation as follows: *"we are always at loggerheads, I keep everything inside"*. Mother said *"We don't talk any more. I am a piece of furniture"*. The relationship was under a lot of tension. Everything was done around Axel; they were not taking care of their own relationship. During this session, mother was able to share with father her grief about the death of their first baby and loneliness of the three pregnancies where she had to stay in bed because of the medical risks. Father talked about his professional difficulties; his painful relationship with his mother and his brother's accident. His brother had been burnt during his childhood with gasoline. When his brother's accident occurred father said he had felt the same feeling of powerlessness that he had felt for his son.

13.2.4. The next session

The next session was again with the couple. The therapist did an EMDR session with mother in the presence of her husband as it was decided that it would help to heal her past psychological wounds and this could also be reinforcing the couple's relationship. It's an example of integrating work, weaving individual and relational issues. Mother chose as her safe place, "I am *caressing my cat on a chair*". During this session, she took as her target *"the image of seeing my son being burned and jumping everywhere"*. Her negative cognition was: *"I am a bad mother, I did not protect him"*. Her positive cognition was: *"I did what I could"*. The VOC was 1, she was feeling a lot of sadness, her SUDS level was at 10 and the sensation was tearfulness. During this session she expressed a lot of heat sensations, she felt very tired and wrung out with no energy. She went during the desensitisation phase from saying *"nothing would change"* to saying by the end of the session, *"Axel will forgive me."* At the end of the session she was very quiet and calm.

13.2.5. Session five, the siblings' session

The fifth session was for the siblings. At the beginning of the session, the family came in and mother sat on dad's lap whilst the children were finding their seats. Mother said *"It's miraculous I don't know what you did to me."* She was much more at peace and lively. The parents were asked to leave the room as the therapist had decided on seeing the above to work with the children alone using the butterfly hug and drawing technique.

The three children were asked to look at their pictures of their safe places that they had made at home and to do the butterfly hug whilst looking at them. Then the therapist told them to think about Axel's accident and to draw the most difficult/worst memory that they had of this accident. Then they were asked to look at their drawings and do the butterfly hug until a new drawing came into their minds and to do so for five successive drawings. During this session, the children were respectful of each other, sharing the crayons and respecting each other's time needed to process, which indicated the quality of attachment between them.

13.2.6. Session six with the couple

Session six was with the couple again, to finish the EMDR work with mother. She started by saying that she had surprised herself at home, caressing her son's chest, and taking pleasure in doing that and not thinking about the accident. She said she had not been capable of doing that over the past two years.

Mother's EMDR treatment was completed and then father decided to take his turn to work on the memory of the accident, with his wife being present in the room. His safe place was "*being on the terrace, watching the stars*", and the target was "*the image of his son, crying on his bed with the firemen around him*". His negative cognition was: "*I am powerless*". His positive cognition: "*I did what I could*". His VOC 3, he was experiencing a lot of sadness and anger, his SUDS 8 and he was feeling tension in his stomach. During his processing, he reported a strong sensation of heat and made the connection with the old trauma of his brother being burnt in his accident. He processed the heat, his brother, the hospital, the anger, powerlessness, emptiness and then peace. The session was incomplete and safe place was used to close it down. At the end of the session the couple discussed with each other what had happened in the session. He was surprised saying "*It is amazing I have never talked so much, in my family men don't talk.*" She said "*I realise I am taking a lot of space, I don't give him much choice to do things, he never says what he wants, I am just realising that today.*"

13.2.7. Session with the family

The next session was a family session. There was a strong sense of 'joie de vivre' in the family; everybody looked much more at peace. The two boys were closer and collaborating with each other.

The first part of the session was with the family together and then the therapist decided to meet with Axel alone with his mother present at his request, and do some EMDR with him. The target was "*the image of the saucepan tipping the oil on him*". His negative cognition "*I am burning*" (he was unable developmentally to formulate a positive cognition at this point and hence no VOC was obtainable). His emotion was yelling and a burning feeling; his SUDS were 8 and the sensation a burning feeling in his chest.

When the desensitisation process started, he experienced a strong abreaction and he screamed in the therapy room as if he was reliving the traumatic incident. This difficult and painful work was possible because of mother's strong, safe and containing attachment and her emotional availability to support him throughout this reliving and helping him to regulate his affect by her regulation of hers and her resiliency. The mother, through her ability to listen and attune to him, was able to safely contain him and allow him to carry on in safety during the abreaction. She allowed him to go outside his window of tolerance, but by her own calming soothing behaviours, helped him to expand his and recover. Towards the end of the session, Axel yawned a great deal, expressed a feeling of tiredness and then calmed and sat on mother's lap.

13.2.8. The next couple session

The next session was with the couple. This session was to finish father's EMDR processing and to talk to the couple about how things have changed and what they could do for themselves as a couple. The therapist thought that the therapy was probably finished. But then mother said "*My mother, the children's grandmother, wants to come.*" The therapist realised at this point, that he had forgotten about her in the treatment plan. She had been the one who had accidentally poured the burning oil on Axel's chest.

13.2.9. Session with maternal grandmother

The next session was with maternal grandmother alone. She chose as her safe place "*reading a book*". Her target was an image of "*being in the bathroom with Axel looking straight into my eyes and asking me what happened*". Her negative cognition was "*I am guilty*", her positive cognition was "*I am a good grandmother*", VOC was 3, she was feeling very guilty, her SUDS were 8 and she was feeling pressure in her chest and tearful. She experienced a lot of tension and body sensations during the reprocessing and at the end, she was feeling peaceful, calm and happy and her VOC was 7. To close the session, the therapist taught her the butterfly hug as she had seen the children use it and wanted to know what it was.

13.2.10. Two years later

In a telephone follow up session two years later with mother, she reported that the family was doing well and the children were thriving; Axel was a happy young boy.

13.3. Susie -Treating traumatic elements in Anorexia Nervosa

Susie aged 14 years, was referred by the Eating Disorders Team. They had been treating her anorexia nervosa for two years. She was a very good eater during early childhood. Her anorexia started when everyone else at school was saying that they didn't eat anything for breakfast. This made Susie feel 'big'. Also, as she was quite tall she had to buy bigger clothes than them. This became worse after she did a fitness course. A range of stressors contributed to the development of her anorexia including: pressures of adolescence, brother's surgery, demands of her parents and a choking incident that happened to her when she was 10 years old.

13.3.1. The first session

She was referred for EMDR because of her fear of choking once her anorexia had been stabilised and physically she was doing better. A contract to do the EMDR work with Susie was agreed and that this work would continue provided that her BMI was 17 or higher. If it fell below this then the EMDR work would stop until the weight was regained.

The reason for this is that in our experience, those children whose BMI's go below this level are unable to retain material that they process in an EMDR session. Thus although one thinks that progress has been made in one session the next session starts off at the same place as the previous one and this continues to repeat itself. The child is not being able to make any real changes because they are unable to metabolize short term and intermediate term memory into long term storage due to their insufficient intake of adequate and nutritious food.

13.3.2. Next Session

Susie had choked at the dinner table on a piece of potato, but she had no conscious memory of this, although her mother experienced it as traumatic. Mother described how father had to physically intervene and perform the Heimlich manoeuvre. Everyone had been at the dinner table whilst Susie was holding on to the table and going red in the face. Susie was able to tell the therapist that she "*get very tense at the dinner table and I get very hot and I have to be wearing very little clothing*". She started to cry during this conversation and said that standing up to eat was much easier. Susie said the worst bit about eating was sitting at the table. She was asked to concentrate on her image about sitting at the table. She noted that it was the swallowing that was hard. She automatically thinks "*hold on to the table – it will stop you from choking*". Her negative cognition was "*I am going to choke and die*". Her positive cognition was "*It's OK. I can sit down and eat normally*". Her VOC was 2. Her emotions were "*anxious, scared and angry*", her SUDS were 10 and her sensation was in her throat.

Below follows her processing during the session:

<<   *Strange. Made me feel funny. (Her face is red, eyes tearful and body very tense, arms rigid and holding onto the chair).*

<<   *Feel much better*

<<   *Don't feel so tense*

<<   *Not thinking of it. Feeling happy*

<<   *Strange*

<<   *Feel a bit better. I have forgotten it a bit now*

<<   *Doesn't seem as bad as it was before. I would still be a bit anxious in case I did choke*

<<   *Not as bad. I'm not thinking of holding the table when eating*

<<   *Image not as clear as it was. Don't feel I need to think about it as much. Feel better, I don't know why.*

<<   *….. (Her body has relaxed and her face is no longer so red. She was instructed to just notice how her body was feeling)*

<<   *It doesn't seem to be there anymore.*

<<   … (again wordless but relaxed posture colour returned to normal)

Cognitive interweave was made here: "If she was asked to sit at a table and have a biscuit whether she would be able to"?

<<   *Yes*

<<   *Little bit tired   (She was instructed to just notice that tiredness)*

<<   *Feel more alert*

<<   *It's not there. Feel much better. Good feeling. Feel relieved*

<<   *Still a bit tired – feel it in my eyes*

<<   *Tables can't kill you. Something came off in my head. Throat felt a bit weird.*

<<   *It's not there. I'll sit down and have a meal tonight…Because I'm hungry*

<<   *Tables can't kill you. Close the book on it*

<<   *Close the book on it. Ok*

<<   *It's not there. Can't find it*

<<   *It's gone. Feel happy – a lot happy*

The session was then brought to a close as time was up. Susie was looking happy and her mother remarked that it was good to see her relaxed and smiling.

13.3.3.   The next session

The next session was held 2 weeks later. Mother and Susie both said she was now 95% better and that she had been eating her meals sitting at the table since the first session. She did not go red any more, but she wanted to work on what she had noticed following the first session, which was that she was clenching her arms when she swallowed. This was an unprocessed channel of the whole experience of choking and she was asked about the image she got when clenching her arms. She said it was "*I am choking and feeling panicked*". She processed this facet of the target in the session during which it became clear to the therapist as it will to the reader that she had dissociated her head, her thinking self from her body:

<<   *feel it building up*

<<   *weird*

<<   *tired*

<<   *still quite tired*

<<   *still quite tired and a bit blank really – not really feeling panicky – more relaxed than anything*

<<   *I am really tired and like not going to choke*

<<   *sad – I don't know why*

<<   *sad – asked myself why and noticed it here (in throat)*

<<   *it's gone – not as tired still a bit sad*

<<   *very tired and want it all to go away*

<<   *it's like it's OK you can let it go – don't know what that means*

<<   *sort of saying I can let go of my fists and my hands just let go like that without me noticing*

<<   *don't have to hold on to the memory – why can't you be like you used to be...*

<<   *umm – very tired again – not very sad and it's not sore around my throat any more*

<<   *seem more alert and it said wake up and smell the coffee*

<<   *I got tired and then more alert again like on and off sort of thing and then I can't remember*

<<   *Wasn't as tired and fighting against it sort of thing and like don't let it get to you*

<<   *strange – because it's like an image – me sitting at the table eating as a normal person and another of me sitting at the table and like what one would you choose*

<<   *you've got other things to concentrate on like painting your nail varnish perfectly*

<<   *tired but happy at same time – it's weird*

<<   *just saying relax*

<<   *head is starting to hurt and I'm tired*

<<   *it was then I was really alert and all of a sudden my head does not hurt*

<<   *strange – nothing there. Very tired*

<<   *saying again sorry we got mixed messages –we'll look after you more in future*

<<   *saying again – just smile – smiling makes all the difference – I don't know why*

<<   *everything is really tired, legs tired and everything – saying we know you don't want to be like this you want to be fit and healthy and not in danger*

<<   *the muscles in my legs – they started to get stronger when got weak then they started to hurt almost like cramp – then strong again the muscles in my legs*

<<   *saying the panic is completely gone – just tired again*

<<   *I don't know why but it's saying if you get back to normal you'll feel better and I wasn't as tired*

<<   *got more alert all of a sudden*

<<   *Not really thought about it – it's not are you in danger of dying if you swallow*

<<   *No – well – it's really not and you need food to eat to live anyway*

<<   *just saying thank you*

<<   *feel much, much, more alert than I did and really relaxed as well*

<<   *it just said don't let it bother you and you're not going to die when you swallow*

<<   *it was like case closed. I don't want to think about it anymore – my muscles got tired and it just stopped like that*

<<   *you are not going to choke and die just remember that*

<<   *see the sadness and tiredness this was causing and it lifting off – you let it go and you can be happy (she had smiled half way through the set)*

<<   *just be happy*

<<   *Yeah well I'm just smiling because I don't have to think about it anymore – it's not compulsory!*

<<   *It's not bothering me I'd say (posture completely changed sitting back smiling spontaneously*

<<   *where's my piece of cake?*

<<   *um – wasn't much there to be honest (chuckling)*

<<   *just a smile again – I feel happy there is nothing else there – my body is relaxed and doesn't hurt or anything – my eyes are tired but that is it*

<<   *not very tired just happy*

<<   *Blank again – (what thinking now?) that I am not going to be in danger not as though I am going to be run over by a bus*

<<   *stop I want to tell it I hope you feel much better now – now you not going to die when you think and not in danger any more.*

<<   *tired – feeling a bit hungry*

<<   *Fine*

<<   *It was like a conversation in my head!*

13.3.4. The next session

the next session she was doing well and had even been eating in the car. However she was now getting panic attacks. Her negative cognition was *"I am going to die"*. Her positive cognition was *"I'm OK – I'm fine"* her VOC2 and her emotion was *"really uncomfortable and sad"*. Her SUDS 9 and her sensation *"in my back, numb and hot"*

<<   *(tearful) not very nice – sad*

<<   *all hot and bothered – panicky*

<<   *tired*

<<   *feels normal*

<<   *don't feel so hot or not as, not shaky and don't have to gasp – more normal*

<<   *song in my head – song by Shakima – don't bother*

<<   *feels empty there (pointing to her back) feels empty – just got to stand up (does this)*

<<   *tingly, creepy, in one section of my back. If start to feel it slightly twitch legs*

<<   *sit in the car it's better to keep tense and what do – put hand against heart to make sure it is beating...*

<<   *really difficult to cry. Good to cry and feel better*

<<   *tired*

<<   *all alert all of a sudden – I can't feel anything around here*

<<   *not as hot – just want to go to sleep. Hungry as well.*

<<   *feel much better. Much more relaxed and stuff.*

<<   *scared it is going to wear off*

<<   *it's chatting to me again – it's not going to wear off – eat choco-late cake – and not going to bother about this today.*

<<   *singing me a lullaby – 'twinkle, twinkle little star' – it can't be bothered*

<<   *that's enough – Prepare for Starbucks! Case closed. Sounds really aggressive*

<<   *Lilly Allen song – you'll be fine and your brain's here if you need anything and comforts you if you need it.*

<<   *Much better.*

13.3.5. Subsequent Sessions

Susie went on to have further EMDR therapy, but the above illustrates how she had split her physical self from her thinking self and how rigidly she was controlling her body with her thinking and dissociated from the sensory sensations of hunger and the pleasure of eating. The choking was an index event in the development of her anorexia but not the only cause.

Focussing on working with the traumatic event helped to open up the clinical picture of her anorexia which the EMDR therapy was able to do. It was enlightening for her and also helped the therapist to understand in the course of her illness how she had dissociated parts of herself, splitting her head from her body and how these two parts were enabled by the EMDR therapy to have the conversation with each other that was needed for her to integrate her thinking with her physical self and regain her health.

EMDR therapy brought down the dissociative barriers and enabled this to happen. The role of the therapist was to guide her on this journey into developing insight into herself starting from the traumatic event and the subsequent irrational beliefs about the food and the table killing her, to the insights that her body and mind were one and that she needed both to live. She gained the insight to understand her illness.

The therapist's journey with her was a journey of discovery and could not have been predicted. The therapist had no idea that Susie had dissociated in this way as a result of her traumatic experience and other contributing factors until this became evident in the sessions. In our clinical experience it is important that therapists do not go into treatment sessions with preconceptions of what is going to occur during the processing, each therapeutic journey is unique to that individual and we need to remain open minded and receptive to wherever it is going to go. We are just the guides and we accompany our clients on their therapeutic journeys so that they do not remain stuck and alone. We, the therapists, do not know the mind maps or emotional routes or the sensory landscapes we maybe going to pass through and what experiences may have impacted on each individual. Each individual EMDR therapy is a journey into the consciously unknown for the therapist and very often the client.

13.4. Hannah - Inter-generational domestic violence

Hannah was 18 years old when she was referred. Hannah, her mother and older sister were subjected to domestic violence from her father until she was 11 years old. Hannah and her sister were also hit by their father with a slipper on several occasions. When she was 11 years old they fled to a refuge and subsequently had 7 moves, until she was 13 years old when they gained their current home. During this time, Hannah and her sister were put on the social services register as children at risk. Their mother became physically and psychologically unwell and was diagnosed with PTSD.

Hannah's maternal grandmother was murdered by her partner when Hannah was 14 years old. There was a long history of domestic violence and grandmother was stabbed and strangled. The murder had been premeditated and the perpetrator was given a life sentence and was still in prison at the time Hannah was referred. Some six months after the death of her grandmother, Hannah, her mother and sister went on holiday together. Whilst they were there, her sister suffered a severe head injury in a boating accident and it was some time before they knew she would recover.

Hannah suffered further traumatisation when a friend of hers, Michael, died in a car crash when she was 16 years old.

13.4.1. Beginning the work

Hannah was referred in by her general practitioner for help with her feelings of numbness. Hannah knew all these events had happened to her and could relate them, but it felt to her like she was telling a story and she had no emotions attached to them. She felt this was not normal. However, she was waking in the middle of the night with nightmares and felt that she had to make things better in her life. After working with Hannah for some time over quite a few sessions during which the history was gathered and a variety of stabilization techniques used, the therapist and Hannah felt ready to try using some EMDR therapy.

13.4.2. Starting the desensitization

Although Hannah continued to see her father on Saturdays, she described feeling that she loved him, but that she did not like him and that he tended to treat her as a young child or toy. Her earliest memory of her father was of his very angry, threatening face. She had been 2 or 3 years old at the time. Her mother had had an affair with the next door neighbour and her father had beaten her mother up. Father had found out that Hannah and her sister had subsequently spoken to the neighbour and said hello. He had taken a slipper that was more like a shoe and had whacked them with that. It had made marks and was stinging and painful on their bottoms and thighs.

The therapist consulted with Hannah and together they chose to work on this memory as it was the earliest memory that Hannah had of things going wrong. She did not have a cognition about it but was able to say that it made her scared and sad and the feelings were intense and in her heart and stomach.

The reader will remember that when memories are stored at an early age they are stored in the way that age remembers them and thus using the developmental protocol for that age initially is appropriate. As therapy progresses in time it is more possible to use other versions of this until the appropriate age level for the client's current age is achieved. Hannah's memory was partially processed in the session with EMDR therapy and an incomplete session closure was used paying a lot of time to the safety elements in closing it down.

The reader will have realised that of course it could not be completed in the session because it was just one strand in a complex list of bad memories and traumatic experiences extending over some 16 years of her life that she had had, but it was the first one which had damaged her attachment to her father and mother and had skewed her development influencing all her other traumatic memories. The important thing for therapists to remember when working with multiple and complex events over time is that working more gently and very slowly is important and not trying to process everything in one go but breaking it down into more manageable segments and working on each of these and building stabilization in both in the beginning in between and all along the way of therapeutic journey and the toll of just starting this process is likely to be high as is illustrated in this case with Hannah.

13.4.3. The next session

When Hannah was seen for her next session she reported that she had been exhausted after the first EMDR session and also tearful and flat. She had spent the whole of the next day crying and also said that in the past she had tried taking an overdose of pain killers. She had also taken a variety of illegal substances over a 1 year period, but had now stopped. We worked on safe resources, which turned out to be relationships with long standing friends and activities including shopping and going to parties. It is important for the therapist to work at the pace of the child, keeping them safe and lots of time was spent doing this again. Although Hannah had been distressed she felt she had begun something and that she wanted to continue on her journey.

13.4.4. The following session

The next session, Hannah came feeling calmer and said she now understood things a bit better, she had been talking to her mother about her father and her mother had told her that she had felt really bad and guilty about when their father had hit them. Asked how she felt about it now, Hannah thought of him hitting her with the slipper when she was little, and says she feels "*confused and scared and sad*". Her SUDS are 4/5 and she felt it around her heart. She was still not able to offer any cognition and looked puzzled when I asked about these. This was because the memory was still stored and only partially at the age and stage she had been when it occurred.

<<   *I don't really how it makes me feel, like why do that? What's the point?*

<<   *Feel like the love I feel towards Dad feels different when I'm a child*

<<   *He was a bad parent*

<<   *Really sad about the whole situation*

<<   *I don't know I felt really sad and wanted to cry. I cried in that situation.*

<<   *Dad is screwed up. He was savagely abused by his step-father. He plays mind games and would rather pretend it never happened and play happy families.*

<<   *I feel sadder for me in the situation*

<<   *Dad was 30 when he got together with Mum. Mum was just 17 years old and had my sister young.*

<<   *I am more thankful that mum got us out*

<<   *I didn't realise how bad things were – I thought it was normal for parents to fight and argue until I went for a sleep over.*

<<   *Guess I'm shocked by how bad things were compared to others*

<<   *Enough to know a horrible time and I don't know why really*

<<   *I guess I don't really need to know. Mum was abused as a child and dad was abused as a child*

<<   *I'm trying to explain it all. He wanted control over mum and had to have a relationship with us and I am not really sure if he wanted to be a parent. Wanted to think he was normal, but behind closed doors it was not.*

<<   *I have more of a perspective on things really, kind of not happy and not sad. Not glad it happened but glad I can see it in the bigger picture*

<<   *Not feeling as confused*

<<   *Not really feeling anything as I am coming to an understanding. I see him once a week his new partner is there and I get dragged around.*

<<   *I'm not really OK with what has happened*

<<   *I'm very tired*

<<   *I'm thinking about Stuart and he's sort of safety as well. Stuart is my boyfriend*

<<   *Thinking about Stuart again, feeling safe and happy. The relationship with Dad, I am kind of hurt, not so much hurt, I can see it is not right and not fair and the relationship with dad is broken.*

<<   *No so tired any more – it's OK really..... Incomplete session closure.*

As we have found in our clinical experience most children do not know that what happens to them is anything other than normal until they reach an age and when they are able to compare what happened to them with what happens to their peers. As can be seen above, Hannah believed that her life was normal and that was how parents behaved and only discovered on a sleepover that other families did not behave in the same way.

In the above session she is processing an interesting mixture of her young beliefs with her current understandings and this is not uncommon in our experience and represents the integration that is being undertaken in the EMDR therapy. It is also interesting that although Hannah's attachments were damaged that she is being proactive in her own healing process and seeking information and answers about what happened at an appropriate level for her 18 years.

As we have discovered in our clinical work with children and families, the great advantage is that most still have family members who can help reconstruct what happened when they were younger as opposed to many adults who do not. In this way they can help to change the transmission of a trauma to the transmission of a narrative. Mother's apology to Hannah was very important as was her understanding more of her father's history from her mother although father remained avoidant of discussing the past with her.

A note of caution though, during the session Hannah spontaneously refers to her boyfriend Stuart as he currently provides her with a sense of safety and happiness, but this was not developed in any way further by the therapist as of course relationships in this age group are characterized by transitions and changes and she could easily have broken up with him rendering the relationship no longer safe.

13.4.5. The next session

At the next session Hannah came in saying she understood things a bit more and had a more adult perspective. She could say that she felt that her father had treated her mother unfairly. We went back to considering her first image and she reported that it had shifted to another facet of the overall target from when she and her sister had been hit with the slipper to an occasion where father had really beaten her mother up when she was 3 years. It was the first time she had seen her father more like a monster than a human.

She added that she felt grateful that her mother had taken the blame for them and she was also feeling very bad. Her negative cognition was "*I'm helpless and too little*". Her positive cognition was "*It will never happen again, it is over and in the past*". VOC 5 and she was feeling "*sadness and a kind of hurt*". Her SUDS were 5, she commented that she always saw her father as a threat to them and did not really see him as a part of the family and she sees her mother in a stronger light now. The sensation was around the heart area again.

<<   *Don't know at first it felt like, a sensation between my stomach and my heart burning and that angry and frustrated and I could not do anything*

<<   *Not sure what I felt, don't know – more like a threat, a reminder that he is a threat and not what he likes to make himself out to be nowadays.*

<<   *I don't know how to describe what I am feeling it's a bit like having to take it all in and think about it again to realise it.*

<<   *Sad about it*

<<   *Not really sure, feeling a bit like ... don't know*

<<   *Want to protect myself and mum and Beth*

<<   *When we moved out became like the parent of the family – because I hadn't been able to protect them.*

<<   *Think like I am still not OK with Dad, but sort of want to pretend it's OK, but I'll always know what he did to mum and stuff. I feel angry and annoyed that mum was in that situation, she was so young and he was so much older. And he has not said sorry.*

<<   *Seems like too much happened for me to make ...I guess I don't really like my dad for what he's done – he's my dad. One part sees him as a nasty person and I don't want to see him and other part does want to. I do know he is dangerous and that's why my mum and sister don't see him.*

<<   *I'm not responsible for him and shouldn't be. When I was younger I wanted to stop him but I couldn't.*

<<   *Rather be aware of him, I don't trust him with his current partner. He plays a lot of mind games.*

<<   *I guess I have to look from the adult perspective – he's my dad and I should be a good daughter.*

<<   *I sort of have to see that he did wrong to us*

<<   *I still don't trust him*

<<   *He is really messed up in his head, mentally unstable and quite weird – not really a proper father/daughter relationship. I can't really trust him, the whole thing messed up and it shouldn't have been that way and he's broken all my trust because of it.*

<<   *Starting to see everything a bit better whereas before I was feeling a bit sick. I am feeling better about the situation I guess.*

<<   *I think I can see how mum's relationship with dad was like mine. It took her ages to get rid of him.*

<< *I can see things differently rather than a 3 year old. I can see what it was and who he really is.*

<< *it wasn't fair and it shouldn't have happened.*

<< *I was a child he was an adult. He should be like a dad and he's not like a dad and I should have realised it ages ago.*

<< *Always going to care about him, but just because you care it does not mean you are going to have the right relationship.*

<< *Mum and dad are really different. I see her as a parent and dad isn't. She has really cared for us and wanted us to live a good life. She was waiting for the opportunity to leave but was also a bit numbed like me. Something happened and she went a bit mental and realized it and put the best interests of her kids first. Dad does whatever suits him.*

<< *Feel OK about it, come to realise mum and dad are different and Dad is still the same person regardless of how he is acting, he's an adult and he had the decision of whether or not to do that action...*

13.4.6. Next session

When Hannah came to the next session, she reported that she was now much closer to her mother and sister and a lot more open with them about how she feels. She also reported that things were changing with her father; she is seeing him less often and more on her own terms. She said she had been isolating herself from people for a long time and things were changing and she felt really good. She wanted to work on her maternal grandmother's murder. She had realised that she did not want the domestic violence to continue through her generation or to the next generation and work continued though it took a long time and is too long to detail further for the purposes of this book.

This case illustrates how EMDR therapy works over time with complex intergenerational domestic violence and transforming traumas into stories for transmission to the next generation. The work with Hannah took a further 8 EMDR sessions with stabilizing sessions in between and a couple of narrative reflective sessions that she wanted before reaching closure. Her mother was already being given therapy by the Adult Mental Health team and her therapy lasted some four years.

13.5. Rebecca –A girl with Asperger's Syndrome processing her traumatic bereavement of her father

Rebecca has Asperger's syndrome was 8 years old when she was referred because she was having problems at school. Her father had died a year previously from a drugs overdose, his body had been found by her mother when she returned from shopping with Rebecca. Rebecca had not seen her father's body but had attended the funeral though mother said she did not know what Rebecca had understood of this given her Asperger's. Her mother said that Rebecca had not mentioned her father's death since then, nor talked about her feelings at all and she had not cried either. When mother mentioned father she would just go silent and do something else.

13.5.1. Preparation with the parent

She had found in Rebecca's bedroom a letter that Rebecca had written and brought it in because she was uncertain how to approach it with Rebecca. Rebecca addressed it to *"mum and dad"*. She wrote *"...I love you so much and sometimes I feel like I am going to cry because I miss daddy, lots of love Rebecca"*. Below this she had drawn a picture of herself standing at father's grave crying. It was decided that EMDR therapy might help and that the letter could not be used as the target because Rebecca did not know her mother had found it.

13.5.2. Session with Rebecca and mother

Mother sat behind Rebecca in the session to keep Rebecca feeling safe and Rebecca was asked to draw a picture of her father. Asked how she felt about him, she said sad. Using her drawing of father ABLS was started. At the end of each set she was asked to draw another picture. Little language was used and she just drew between the sets and gave the odd comment. Below are her pictures: the first, in Figure 13.7 is her picture of her father.

Figure 13.7: Rebecca's first drawing

Her second picture in Figure 13.8 shows her as very small and the lines down her face depict her crying and her arms are held up.

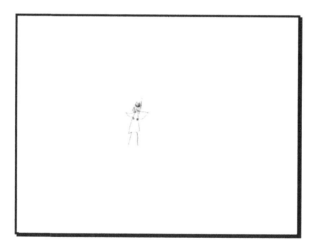

Figure 13.8: Rebecca's second drawing

The next picture in Figure 13.9 she chose to write, indicating that she was feeling a bit better.

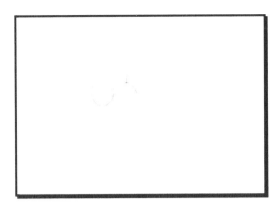

Figure 13.9: Rebecca's third drawing

The next set she seemed to have accessed a treasure trove of happier memories of her father and herself, she divided the paper in two by drawing a line down and put in two memories. In the first drawing in Figure 13.10 they are playing with the cars and in second he is carrying her upstairs. Her mood seemed to have lightened and her body was less rigid.

Figure 13.10: Rebecca's fourth drawing

In Figure 13.11 she drew her father and herself inside the rainbow.

Figure 13.11: Rebecca's fifth drawing

Then, in Figure 13.12 she drew herself and her father and said they were playing in the snow.

Figure 13.12: Rebecca's sixth drawing

There was no explanation for the next picture she drew in Figure 13.13, but mother sitting behind her, signalled that she knew what it was and that it was very important.

Figure 13.13: Rebecca's seventh drawing

Later when Rebecca was not present she told me that she had just realised that it was father who had always comforted Rebecca, he would not let her cry without going to comfort her. Thus, mother had at that moment realised that Rebecca idiosyncratically thought it was only father's role to comfort her. She had not only lost her father, but the person who comforted her when he had died.

After the next set Rebecca was giggling as she drew the picture in Figure 13.14 of herself and her father with very big heads and tiny bodies. It may be that they had visited at some point a hall of mirrors at a fun fair. She seemed very happy after this drawing.

Figure 13.14: Rebecca's eighth drawing

The next picture after the next set had no explanation, but again mother silently indicated that she knew what it was and said later that it was the photograph that they had of father in the lounge.

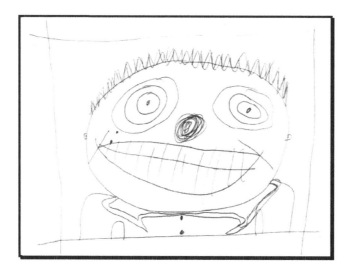

Figure 13.15: Rebecca's ninth drawing

The final picture in Figure 13.16 she drew was of herself, happy, clasping her arms together and smiling.

Figure 13.16: Rebecca's final drawing

After this session mother made a point of cuddling Rebecca and comforting her about father in their daily lives. Rebecca had not had the words to tell her what she was feeling but her processing clearly did. Mother reported that Rebecca was generally happier after the session.

13.6. Miles - An autistic boy processing his fear of his violent father

The reader may recall the picture of the safe place of this 12 year old autistic boy with moderate learning difficulties earlier in the book. It was his game boy. Miles's father suffered from schizophrenia and he witnessed many episodes when his father became very violent and bizarre in his behaviour. Father had eventually been placed in a mental hospital and injunctions were taken out to prevent him coming back to the home, to protect the children and mother.

When he recovered father had gone to live with his own parents a long distance away and the injunctions remained in place. The parents subsequently divorced. Miles was said to be very fearful of his father but as he only had a few words and only gave very brief phrases or one word answers it was hard for his mother to really reassure him.

She became worried when Miles scratched father's face off a photograph of him and showed her. EMDR was done using tapping and drawing with Miles. The photograph was used as the target as Miles had already shared it with his mother. What follows is the sequence of his drawings made spontaneously but very slowly between each set.

After the first set Miles drew father pressing the doorbell. It is interesting to note that Miles drawings are very autistic and idiosyncratic and only show the elements that are relevant to Miles.

Figure 13.17: Mile's first drawing

The second drawing is of father not being allowed in the house and having to go away.

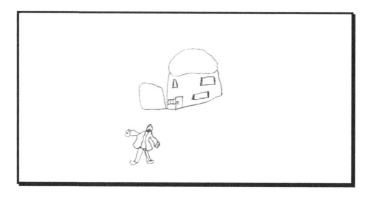

Figure 13.18: Miles' second drawing

In Figure 13.19 Miles drew his father crying because he is not allowed in and has to go back to his own parents' home. What is fascinating about this is that here Miles is clearly expressing his ability to take another's perspective, which no one knew he was capable of doing. Note that father has a beard.

Figure 13.19: Miles' third drawing

The next picture in Figure 13.20 shows his father driving back to his own parents' home.

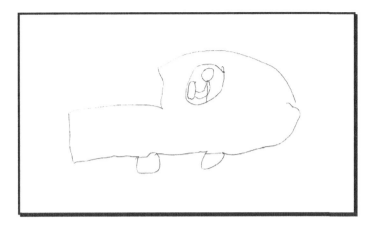

Figure 13.20: Miles' fourth drawing

The next picture in Figure 13.21 depicts father arriving at the paternal grandparents' home. The house looks angry.

Figure 13.21: Miles' fifth drawing

The next picture in Figure 13.22 shows paternal grandmother shouting at father. Miles said she was shouting and when asked what she was saying he said "*You no go to Miles house no more*".

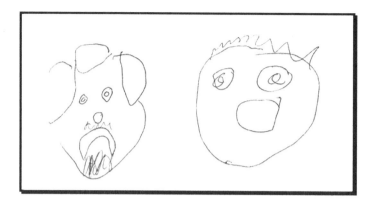

Figure 13.22: Miles' sixth drawing

And the picture in Figure 13.23 shows the paternal grandfather shouting at father. He is shouting *"You no go to Miles' house"*.

Figure 13.23: Miles' seventh drawing

The last picture in Figure 13.24 shows Miles remembering that his father's car is broken and he can't use it any more. His body language indicated he was much less tense and he smiled.

Figure 13.24: Miles' eighth drawing

This was his final picture for that session. He drew his father having to push the car into the garage as it did not work anymore. He was very pleased with himself at this point and his fear had evaporated.

Mother now knew what Miles had been frightened of and was able to reassure him that he did not have to see his father again and that the police would be called if he came to the door. Mother subsequently reported that Miles no longer had to go into mother's bed to sleep at night, but was able to sleep in his own room again.

Miles subsequently went on in other sessions to work on a number of things that had happened to him including a very bad experience of being in a mainstream school in which he had not been able to cope at all and his relief when he processed that he was now at his new school and would never be going back to the other one.

Chapter 14

Conclusion

This book has, we hope, introduced the reader to many wonderful children and their families who have donated their stories so that other therapists can help other children and their families heal, as they have done with EMDR therapy. The spontaneous warmth of their donations towards this book for the well-being of other children is amazing. There is also a sense of pride in which, by their own achievements, they as children can teach us, the grown-ups.

Also there are numerous other children with whom we have worked that have taught us how to develop and refine the EMDR therapy, but of whom we have only talked of in a general way in the book. We owe all these children a very big thank you. It is a privilege to work with our children and their families with EMDR therapy. We never cease to be thrilled by the little miracles when they happen and they can leave the traumas of the past behind and go on to make post-traumatic growth. This book is the collection of their stories of trauma healed to be passed on for the next generation.

One of the most valuable of their contributions has been their willingness to have some of their sessions videotaped, which has allowed us, as therapists, to play and replay them and learn more about the techniques and the mistakes we can avoid in future. They are invaluable as both a therapy review resource and for supervision. When in session, the participation of the therapist often means they do not observe the whole picture at the time. A video allows a review where missed indicators such as posture, body language and other cues can be identified and used in subsequent sessions. It is also for the therapist to see, over a series of sessions how the child has progressed. Further, it enables supervisors to see and review with the therapist their work, and how to develop it.

The videos have been given to the individual therapist trusting in the knowledge that they will only be used for the purposes that they have agreed to with that therapist; and not to be copied or used by others.

Firstly, the permissions of the child and parents are sought to take the videos. The reasons why the video is being made are clearly stated to both the child and the parents. Secondly, it is made clear that only their therapist will use the video and that it will not be accessed or used by anybody else, except in direct conjunction with the therapist themselves. This is one of the reasons why all qualifying to be European Child Trainers have to develop their own tapes as a part of their teaching material.

Videos and DVDs are invaluable teaching resources. When a teaching tape is being made it must be made clear to both the child and the parents that this is the intended purpose for the tape. In addition, it is made clear that control of viewing and use of the tape continues to be theirs, and that the child and/or the parents can retract permission at any time and for any reason. These tapes are a considerable responsibility of the therapist/trainer and cannot be lent to others or used by others and should be protected as other clinical material is, however they are stored, as a part of professional integrity, good practise, clinical governance and data protection.

An on-going responsibility of using EMDR is promoting its use and benefits. Both the authors continue to hold training courses and give papers, in the United Kingdom, Europe and abroad, specifically directed at using EMDR with children and adolescents. In addition, one of the authors holds a monthly teaching session where EMDR is used. During these, with permission from the child and family, qualified professionals, who have applied in advance and had their credentials verified, are able view the sessions through a two-way mirror.

The authors are only two of an expanding group of EMDR C&A accredited trainers in Europe and we also owe a big thank you to them as our peer group. They have humoured, advised, supervised, discussed and developed our body of knowledge by generously sharing theirs with us, in the many hours we have spent together. Meeting together is like a happy, joyful family reunion and the excitement we all share in developing EMDR therapy for children, adolescents and their families is contagious.

The writing of this book has been a metaphor of our work with children and their families. Developing affiliation, trust, sharing, respect of one's life idiosyncrasies, cultural and language differences, confidence between us through our numerous working meetings has allowed this book to be born. Our professional relationship became the container through which the different ideas, thoughts and content could be expressed, argued, discussed and enriched. In a similar way, the therapeutic relationship between the therapist, the child and the family is also a container that provides the vehicle through which the hurt, the pain and the hope is enabled and can be expressed.

As it is common knowledge, we all know that working with someone else will take you longer, but will take you both further to new exciting places. We strongly feel that not only is this book a lot richer than if we had each written it alone, but through this process we have grown.

It is the very same idea when working with children; the therapist will go farther in the treatment working with the child if he works with the parents rather than alone, or against them. Affiliation with the family and attunement to the child are the two strong elements on to which our therapeutic interventions should be built.

We cannot emphasise enough that the work with children is not only about how to do EMDR with them, but also how to integrate EMDR into a contextual dimension.

This is empowering the parents to help to contain the child, to develop or practise nurturing behaviours as attachment rituals, to create resiliency and to heal them.

The challenge for us therapists is to keep this complex vision alive in a time when social and economic pressures can be pushing us to go faster and simpler and try to convince us to think that therapy is like taking a pill.

We all have learned that EMDR is about integrating sensation, emotion, and cognition, but it's also about developing an integrative vision when working with children, their families and the social environment. The presenting symptom can be the target, the manifestation of a past trauma incident for the child and/or the manifestation of a family suffering. Working with children keeps us at the crossing of several fundamental elements where attachment issues, family dynamics, developmental neurobiology and psycho-traumatology meet.

Working with children and their families helps us to develop a richer understanding of life in process, in a dynamic way, not frozen into structure. It teaches us to trust the process, believe in resources outside of us, develop a complementary attitude with our patients and look at life through the glass half full and it opens the doors of hope for future generations.

Conclusion

There is no better way to prepare for the future and as we say in our EMDR culture to work on the future template, to free the present and the future from the painful past. This is an exciting challenge for us all. To the mother of EMDR, Dr. Francine Shapiro and those subsequent pioneers of EMDR therapy with children and adolescents, we and the world owe a huge debt of gratitude.

Appendices

Appendix 1: Acronyms used in this book

ABLS   Alternating Bilateral Stimulation

AIP   Adaptive Information Processing Model

ASD   Autism Spectrum Disorder(s)

CBT   Cognitive Behavioural Therapy

EEG   Electroencephalography

EMDR Eye Movement Desensitisation Reprocessing

PTSD   Post-Traumatic Stress Disorder

SAM   Situationally Accessible Memory

SUDS   Subjective Units of Disturbance Scale

VOC   Validity of Cognition Scale

Appendix 2: Reflections on work by mothers

Hands that Heal

Pitter patter pitter patter, hands to heal the pain

Pitter patter pitter patter, hands to take the strain

Pitter patter pitter patter, opened up the door

Pitter patter pitter patter, found the memory store

Pitter patter pitter patter, help me shed a tear

Pitter patter pitter patter, let me know no fear

Pitter patter pitter patter, mend my broken heart

Pitter patter pitter patter, show me a new start

Pitter patter pitter patter, left the pain upon the shelf

Pitter patter pitter patter, helped me love myself

Pitter patter pitter patter, made me all as one

Pitter patter pitter patter, now I love my mum

Pitter patter pitter patter, took away my strife

Pitter patter pitter patter, gave me back my life

Pitter patter pitter patter, teach me how to be me

Pitter patter pitter patter, the hands that set me free

Pitter patter pitter patter, I don't know what to say

Pitter patter pitter patter, thanks for every sunny day

Trudy L. 2000

Walk With Me

Walk with me, show me the way
I don't know where I am, don't leave me please, please stay

Walk with me, I feel lost and alone
The door has closed behind me, I'm out on my own

Walk with me life doesn't appear real
My life has stopped. I don't know how I feel

216

Walk with me, the tide is very rough
Give me strength as I have none, My body has had enough

Walk with me, I have nothing left to give
Everything is changing, please help me to live

Walk with me, don't let me fall
Help me stand, and cope with it all

Walk with me, hold me tight
Don't let me go, until everything is right

Walk with me, until the hurt is through
Then when its time, I'll walk with you.

Cherie B. 2009

Bibliography

Adler-Tapia, R., Settle, C. (2009). Evidence of the Efficacy of EMDR With Children and Adolescents in Individual Psychotherapy: A Review of the Research Published in Peer-Reviewed Journals. In *Journal of EMDR Practice and Research, Vol 3, No. 4.*

Adler-Tapia, R. & Settle, C. (2008). *EMDR and the Art of Psychotherapy with the Children,* Springer Publishing Company, New York.

Ahmad, A., & Sundelan-Wahlsten,V. (2008). Applying EMDR on children with PTSD, *European journal of child and adolescent psychiatry*, 17:127-132.

Ainsworth, M, S., Bell, S., M. (1970). Attachment, Exploration and Separation illustrated by the behaviour of one year olds in a strange situation. In *Child Development*, vol. 41, No. 11

Anaut, M., Résilience affective in Cyrulink, B., Jorland, G., eds, *Résilience connaissances de base*, (2012). Odile Jacob, Paris.

Bar-Sade, E, (2008). EMDR Europe London conference, U.K.

Bauer, P., J. (1997). Development of memory in early childhood. In N. Cowan (Ed.) *The Development of Memory in Childhood* (pp. 83-111). Sussex, UK: Psychology Press.

Black, D., Newman, M., Harris-Hendriks, J., & Mezey, G. (1996). (Eds) *Psychological Trauma: A Developmental Approach.* London: Gaskell.

Beer, R. and Bronner, M.B. (2010) EMDR in paediatrics and rehabilitation: An effective tool for reduction of stress reactions? In *Developmental Neurorehabilitation* Vol.13 No.5 307-309.

Boris, N.W., Zeanah, C.H., and Work Group on Quality Issues, (November 2005).

Practise Parameter for the Assessment and Treatment of Children and Adolescents with Reactive Attachment Disorder of Infancy and Early Childhood. In *J. Am Acad. Child & Adolescent Psychiatry 44:11.*

Bowlby, J. (1969) *Attachment and Loss: Vol.1. Attachment.* New York: Basic Books.

Bradley, S. J. (2000). *Affect regulation and the development of psychopathology.* The Guilford Press, New York, London.

Brewin, C. R. (2001). A cognitive neuroscience account of posttraumatic stress disorder and its treatment. *Behavior Research and Therapy*, 39, 373-393.

Bronner, M.P., Beer, R., van Zelmvan Eldik, M.J., Grootenhuis, M.A. & Last, B.F. (2009). Reducing acute distress in a 16 year-old girl using trauma-focussed cognitive behavioural therapy and eye movement desenstization and reprocessing. In *Developmental Neuro-rehabilitation, 12:3, 170 – 174.*

Bruni, O., Novelli, L., Savoja, V. & Ferri, R., Psychiatric Disorders and Sleep in Kothare, S. V. & Kotagal, S. (2011) *Sleep in Childhood Neurological Disorders*, Demos Medical Publishing, New York.

Carlson, E., & Dalenberg, C. (2000). A conceptual framework for the impact of traumatic experiences. *Trauma, Violence, and Abuse*, 1, 4-28.

Carter, B., McGoldrick, M. (1980). *The Changing Family Life Cycle*, New York, Gardner Press.

Chemtob, C. M., Nakashima, J., Hamada, R. S., & Carlson, J. G. (2002). Brief-treatment for elementary school children with disaster-related posttraumatic stress disorder: A field study. *Journal of Clinical Psychology, 58*, 99-112.

Chemtob, C. M., Nakashima, J.P., & Hamada, R.S. (2002). Psychosocial intervention for post disaster trauma symptoms in elementary school children: a controlled community field study. *Archives of Pediatrics & Adolescent Medicine*, 156, 211-216.

Christen, M., Heim, C., Silvestre, M., Vasselier-Novelli C. (2004). *Vivre sans violences? Dans les couples, les institutions, les écoles,* collection Relation, édition ERES.

Cohen, J.A., Mannarino, A.P., Berliner, L., & Deblinger, E. (2000). Trauma-focused cognitive behavioural therapy for children and adolescents: An empirical update. *Journal of Interpersonal Violence, 15,* 1202-1223.

Cozolino, L. (2002). The Neuroscience of Psychotherapy: Building and Rebuilding the Human Brain, Norton & Company, New York.

Cummings, E., M., Goeke-Morey, E., M. & Raymond, J. (2004). Fathers in family context: Effects of marital quality and marital conflict. In Lamb, M., editor, *The role of the father in child development*, John Wiley & Sons, New York, pp. 196-221.

Cyrulnik, B. (2002). *Un merveilleux malheur*, Odile Jacob, Paris

Cyrulnik, B. (2006). *De chair et d'âme*, Odile Jacob, Paris

Cyrulnik, B., Jorland, G. (2012). *Résilience connaissances de base*, Odile Jacob, Paris

Damasio, A. R. (1991). *The feeling of what happens*. San Diego, Harcourt,Inc. Trad. française, *Le sentiment même de soi*, (1999). Odile Jacob.

De Bellis, M., Keshavan, M., Clark, D., Casey, B., Giedd, J., Boring, A., Frustaci, K. & Ryan, N. (1999). Developmental traumatology: Part II: Brain Development. *Biological Psychiatry,* 45, 1271 – 1284.

De Casper, A., J., & Spence, M., J. (1991). Auditory mediated behaviour during the prenatal period: A cognitive view. In M. Weiss & P. Zelazo (Eds.*), Newborn attention: Biological constraints and the influence of experience* (pp. 142-176). Norwood, NJ: Ablex.

Dell, P. F., O'Neil, J. A. Eds (2009). *Dissociation and the dissociative disorders: DSM-V and beyond.* Routledge, Taylor & Francis Group, New York.

Delage, M. (2008). *La résilience familiale*, Odile Jacob, Paris.

de Roos, C., Greenwald, R., den Hollander- Gijsman, M., Noorthoorn, E., van Buuren, S.& De Jongh, A. (2011). A randomised comparison of cognitive behavioural therapy (CBT) and eye movement desensitisation and reprocessing (EMDR) in disaster exposed children*, European Journal of Psychotraumatology.2, 5694.*

Eckers, D. (2009). EMDR Europe Hamburg conference, Germany.

Erdman, P. & Caffery, T. (2003). Ed., *Attachment and Family Systems.* Routledge, Taylor & Francis Books, New York, London

Finney, A. (2003). Alcohol and sexual violence: key findings from the research. *Home Office Findings No. 215. London: Home Office.*

Fusco, R. A. & Fantuzzo J.W. (2009). Domestic violence crimes and children: A population-based investigation of direct sensory exposure and the nature of involvement. In *Children & Youth Services Review,* Vol.31, Issue 2. February 2009, pp. 249 – 256.

Gaensbauer T. J. & Hiatt, S. (1984*).* Facial communication in early infancy. In N. Fox & R. J. Davidson*, The psychobiology of affective development* (pp. 207- 229), London: Lawrence Erlbaum.

Giannakoulopoulos, X., Fisk, N., Glover, V., Kourtis, P., & Sepulveda, W. (1994) Fetal plasma cortisol and B-endorphins response to intrauterine deedling*, Lancet,* 344, 77-81

Gleason, M.M., Zeanah, C.H. & Dickstein, S. (2010) Recognising Young Children in Need of Mental Health Assessment: Development and Preliminary Validity of the Early Childhood Screening Assessment. *Infant Mental Health Journal*, Vol. 31(3), 335 – 357.

Gogtay, N., Giedd, J.N., Lusk, L., Hayashi, K.M., Greenstein, D., Vaituzis, A.C., Nugent III, T.F., Herman, D.H., Clasen, L.S., Toga, A.W., Rapoport, J.L., & Thompson, P.M. (2004). Dynamic mapping of human cortical development during childhood through early adulthood. *PNAS*. May 25, 2004. Vol. 101 No. 21, 8174 -8179.

Goldman, S., E. & Malow, B., A., Autism and Other Neurodevelopmental Disorders in Kothare, S. V. & Kotagal S. (2011), *Sleep in Childhood Neurological Disorders*, Demos Medical Publishing, New York.

Goldsmith, R.E., Barlow, M.R., & Freyd, J.J. (2004); Knowing and not knowing about trauma: Implications for therapy. *Psychotherapy: Theory, Research, Practice, Training*, 41, 448-463.

Greenwald, R. (1999). Eye Movement Desensitisation & Reprocessing in Child & Adolescent Psychotherapy. Aronson; Northvale.

Greyber, L.R., Dulmus, C.N. and Cristalli, M.E.(2012). Eye Movement Desensitization Reprocessing, Posttraumatic Stress Disorder, and Trauma: A Review of Randomized Control Trials with Children and Adolescents. In *Journal of Child and Adolescent Social Work Journal* 29.5 (2012): 409-425.

Hardan, A. Y., Girgis, R. R., Adams, J., Gilbert, A. R., Melhem, N. M., Keshavan, M. S., Minshew, N. J. (2008). Brief report: Abnormal Association Between the Thalamus and Brain Size in Asperger's Disorder. *Journal of Autism Developmental Disorders*, 38:390-394.

Hardan, A. Y., Pabalan, M., Gupta, N., Bansal, R., Melhem, N. M., Fedorov, S., Keshavan, M. S. & Minshew, N. J. (2009). Corpus Callosum Volume in Children with Autism. *Psychiatry Research*, 174, 57-61.

Harris-Hendricks, J., Black, D., & Kaplan, T. (first edition: 1993; second edition: 2000). *When Father kills Mother: Guiding Children Through Trauma and Grief*. Routledge. Taylor and Francis Group. London and New York.

Hensel, T. (2009). EMDR with children & adolescent after single incident trauma, *Journal of EMDR Practice & Research*, vol. 3 No. 1, pp. 2-9.

Hofmann, A. (2002), Manual of the EMDR Seminar, Part 2, EMDR-Institute Germany.

Jaberghaderi, N., Greenwald, R., Rubin, A., Zand, S.O, & Dolatabadi, S. (2004), A Comparison of CBT and EMDR for Sexually Abused Iranian Girls. In *Clinical Psychology & Psychotherapy 11, 358 – 368.*

Janet, P. (1889). *L'automatisme psychologique.* Paris: Félix Alcan.

Janet, P. (1907). *The Major Symptoms of Hysteria.* McMilan. London and NewYork.

Jarero, I., Artigas, L., & Hartung, J. (2006). EMDR Integrative Group Treatment Protocol: A Post Disaster Trauma Intervention for Children and Adults. *Traumatology, 12(2), 121-129.*

Just, M. A., Cherkassky, V., Keller, T. A., Kana, R. K., Minshew, N. J. (2007). Functional and Anatomical Cortical Underconnectivity in Autism: Evidence from an fMRI Study of an Executive Function Task and Corpus Callosum Morphometry. *Cerebral Cortex,* 17:951-961

Kemp M., Drummond P., & McDermott B. (2010, January). A wait-list controlled pilot study of eye movement desensitization and reprocessing (EMDR) for children with post-traumatic stress disorder (PTSD) symptoms from motor vehicle accidents. In *Clinical Child Psychology and Psychiatry,* 15(1), 5-25.

Kluft, R.P.(1985).Hypnotherapy of childhood multiple personality disorder. *American Journal of Clinical Hypnosis*, 27, 201-210.

Knipe, J. (2008). The CIPOS method. Paper presented at the annual meeting of the EMDR Europe Association, London, England.

Korkmazlar-Oral, U., & Pamuk, S. (2002). Group EMDR with Child Survivors of the Earthquake in Turkey. In EMDR: Clinical Application with Children, Ed Morris-Smith, J., *Association of Child Psychology and Psychiatry*, Occasional Paper No.19.

Lanius, (2008). EMDR Europe London conference, U.K.

Le Doux, J.E. (1996). The Emotional Brain: The mysterious underpinnings of emotional life. Simon & Schuster. New York.

Lieberman, A.F., Van Horn, P., & Ippen, C.G. (December 2005). Towards Evidence-Based Treatment: Child-Parent Psychotherapy with Preschoolers Exposed to Marital Violence. In *J. Am Acad. Child & Adolescent. Psychiatry 44:12.*

Liotti, G. (1999). Disorganized attachment as a model for the understanding of dissociative psychopathology. In Solomon, J. & George, C. (Eds), *Attachment disorganization, (pp. 291-317).* New York, NY, US: Guilford Press.

Liotti, G. (2009). Attachment and dissociation. In Dell, P.F. & O'Neill, J. (Eds), *Dissociation: DSM-V and Beyond* (pp.53-65). New York: Routledge Press.

Lovett, J. (1999). Small Wonders. Healing childhood trauma with EMDR. The free press: New York.

Lyons-Ruth, K., Dutra, L., Schuder, M. & Bianchi, I. (2006). From Infant Attachment Disorganisation to Adult Dissociation: Relational Adaptations or Traumatic Experiences? In *Psychiatric Clinics of North America. 29 (2006)* 63 – 86.

Maslow, A. (1943). A theory of human motivation. *Psychological Review*, 50, 370-396.

MacFie, J., Cicchetti, D. & Toth, S.L. (2001). The development of dissociation in maltreated preschool-aged children. In *Development and Psychopathology 13 (2002) 233 – 254.*

MacLean, P.D. (1985). Evolutionary psychiatry and the triune brain. *Psychological Medicine.* Vol. 15(2) pp. 219-221.

Main, M. (1993). Metacognitive knowledge, metacognitive monitoring, and singular (coherent) vs multiple (incoherent) model of attachment: Findings and directions for future research, in *Attachment Across the Life Cycle.* Eds: Murray-Parkes, C.M., Stevenson-Hinde, J. & Morris, P., Routledge. London.

Marvin, R.S. (2003). Implications of Attachment Research for the Field of Family Therapy in Erdman, P. & Caffery, T. Ed., *Attachment and Family Systems.* Routledge, Taylor & Francis Books, New York, London.

Maski, K. P., Kotagal, S. & Kothare, S., V. The Science of Sleep: Ontogeny, Phylogeny, and More in Kothare, S. V. & Kotagal, S. (2011) *Sleep in Childhood Neurological Disorders*, Demos Medical Publishing, New York.

Meltzoff, A. N. & Moore, M. K. (1994). Imitation, memory and the representation of persons. *Infant Behaviour and Development*, 17, 83-99.

Meltzoff, A. N. (1995). What infant memory tells us about infantile amnesia: Long term recall and deferred imitation. *Journal of Experimental Child Psychology*, 59, 497-515.

Minuchin, S. (1974). *Families and Family Therapy*. Tavistock Publications Limited, London. Traduction française (1998), *Familles en thérapie*, collection Relations, édition ERES.

Morris-Smith, J. (2002). EMDR: A Case for Pre-Verbal Memory? In EMDR: Clinical Application with Children, Ed Morris-Smith, J., *Association of Child Psychology and Psychiatry*, Occasional Paper No. 19.

Morris-Smith, J. (December 2006). EMDR and Children: Europe Leads the Way. In *Counselling Children and Young People*. BABCP. 24 – 26.

Ogden, P., Minton, K., Pain, C. (2006). *Trauma and the Body, a sensorimotor approach to psychotherapy*. W.W. Norton & Company, New York.

Oras, R., de Ezpeleta, S. C., Ahmad, A. (2004). Treatment of traumatized refugee children with eye movement desensitization and reprocessing in a psychodynamic context. In *Nordic Journal of Psychiatry*, Vol.:58 No 3 199-203.

Ornitz, E.M. & Pynoos, R.S. (1989). Startle modulation in children with post-traumatic stress disorder. *American Journal of Psychiatry*, 146, 866 – 870.

Osofsky, J.D. (2004). *Young Children and Trauma, Intervention and Treatment*. The Guilford Press, New York, London.

Pagani, M., Di Lorenzo, G., Verado, A.R., Nicolais, G., Monaco,L., Lauretti, G., Russo, R., Niolu, C., Ammaniti, M., Fernandez, I. & Siracusano, A. (2012). Neurobiological Correlates of EMDR Monitoring – An EEG Study. PLoS ONE 7(9):e45753. Doi:10.1371/journal.pone.0045753

Perris, E.E., Myers, N.A. & Clifton, R. K. (1990). Long term memory for a single infancy experience. *Child Development*, 61, 1796-1807.

Perry, B., Pollard, R.A., Blakely, T.L., Baker, W.L. & Vigilante, D. (1995). Childhood trauma, the neurobiology of adaptation and use-dependent development of the brain: How states become traits. *Infant Mental Health Journal*, 16, 271 – 291.

Perry, B. (2008). Childhood Maltreatment: A Neurodevelopmental Perspective on the Role of Trauma and Neglect in Psychopathology. In Beauchaine, T.P. & Hinshaw, S. *Child and Adolescent Psychopathology.* John Wiley & Sons Inc. New Jersey.

Piaget J. (1952). *The origins of intelligence in children.* New York: InternationalUniversities Press, Inc.

Pollak, S.D, Cicchetti, D., Klorman, R. & Brumaghim, J. (1997). Cognitive brain event-related potentials and emotion processing in maltreated children. In *Child Development,* 68, 773 – 787.

Putman, F. (1997). Dissociation in Children & Adolescents: A Developmental Perspective. The Guilford Press, New York.

Pynoos, R. S., & Eth, S. (1986). Witness to violence : The child interview. *Journal of American Academy of Child Psychiatry,* 25, 306-319.

Pynoos, R.S. (1995). Traumatic stress and developmental psychopathology in children and adolescents. In Oldham, J.M. (Ed.) *American Psychiatric Press Review of Psychiatry, 12.*

Raffray, T., van Reen, E., Tarokh, L., and Carskadon, M., A., Circadian Rhythm Disorders, in Kothare, S. V. & Kotagal, S. (2011) *Sleep in Childhood Neurological Disorders*, Demos Medical Publishing, New York.

Ribchester, T., Yule, W., and Duncan, A. EMDR for Childhood PTSD After Road Traffic Accidents: Attentional, Memory, and Attributional Processes. In *Journal of EMDR Practise and Research, Volume 4, No 4, 2010.*

Rodenburg, R., Benjamin, A., de Roos, C., Meijer, A.M., & Stams, G.J. (November 2009*)*. Efficacy of EMDR with children: A meta-analysis. In *Clinical Psychology Review,* Issue 7 599 – 606.

Sack, M., Lemps, W., Steinmetz, A., Lamprecht, F. & Hofmann, A. (2008) Alterations in autonomic tone during trauma exposure using eye movement desensitization and reprocessing (EMDR) – Results of a preliminary investigation. In *Journal of Anxiety Disorders,* doi :10.1016/j.janxdis.2008.01.007

Scaer, R. (2005). *The Trauma Spectrum: Hidden Wounds and Human Resiliency.* W W Norton & Co. New York. London.

Scheeringa, M. S. & Zeanah, C. H. (1995a). Symptom expression and trauma variables in children under 48 months of age. In *Infant Mental Health Journal*, pp. 259-270

Scheeringa, M. S., Zeanah, C.H., Drewel, M.J. & Larrieu, J.A. (1995b). Two approaches to the diagnosis of post traumatic stress disorder in infancy and early childhood. *Journal of American Child & Adolescent Psychiatry*, 34:191-200.

Scheeringa M. S., Zeaanah, C.H., Myers, L. & Putnam, F., (2003). Post-traumatic Stress Disorder Semi-Structured Interview and Observational Record for Infants and Young Children. *Journal of the American Academy of Child and Adolescent Psychiatry*, 42(5), 561 – 570.

Schore, A, (1994). Affect Development and the Origin of Self: The Neurobiology of Emotional Development. Lawrence Erlbaum. Hillsdale, New Jersey.

Servan-Schreiber, D. (2003). *Guérir*. Robert Laffont, Paris. Traduction anglaise (2005). *Healing without Freud or Prozac*. Rodale International Ltd, London.

Servan-Schreiber, D. (2007). Paris Conférence EMDR

Shapiro, F. (1989a). Efficacy of the eye movement desensitisation procedure in the treatment of traumatic memories. *Journal of Traumatic Stress*, 2(2), 199-223.

Shapiro, F. (1989b). Eye movement desensitization: A new treatment for post-traumatic stress disorder. *Journal of Behavior Therapy and Experimental Psychiatry*, 20, 211-217.

Shapiro, F. (2001). Eye Movement Desensitization and Reprocessing: Basic Principles, Protocols and Procedures. 2nd edition, New York, Guilford Press.

Shapiro, F., Silk Forrest M. (2005). *Des yeux pour guérir*. Couleurpsy Seuil, Paris.

Shapiro, F. (2009). EMDR Theory Research and Practice, *EMDR Europe Amsterdam Conference.*

Shapiro, F. (2012). Getting past your past: take control of your life with self-help techniques from EMDR therapy. Rodale Inc., New York.

Siegel, D. (1999). *The Developing Mind*. Guilford Press, New York.

Silberg, J.L. Ed (1996). The *Dissociative Child: Diagnosis, Treatment and Management.* Sidran Press, Maryland,USA.

Silberg, J. & Dallam, S. (2009). Dissociation in Children and Adolescents: At the Crossroads. In Dell, P. F. & O'Neil, J. A. *Dissociation &*

the dissociative disorders: DSM-V and beyond. Taylor & Francis Group, New York, NY.

Silvestre, M. La résilience: une histoire de l'intégration des regards inter- et intra-personnels in Delage, M. & Cyrulnik, B. (2010). *Famille et Résilience.* Odile Jacob, Paris. pp.111-126.

Smith, J. & Silvestre, M. L'intérêt de l'EMDR dans la prise en charge des victimes et auteurs de violences intra-familiales in Coutanceau, R. & Smith, J. Eds.(2011). *Famille et Violence.* Dunod, Paris.

Solomon, R. & Shapiro, F. (2008). EMDR and the Adaptive Information Processing Model: Potential mechanisms of change. *Journal of EMDR Practice and Research,* 2, 315-325.

Stickgold, R., (2002). EMDR: A Putative Neurobiological Mechanism, *Journal of Clinical Psychology,* 58:61-75.

Teicher, M. H., Ito, Y., Glod, C.A., Anderson S.L., Dumont, N. & Ackerman, E. (1997) Preliminary evidence for abnormal cortical development in physically and sexually abused children using EEG coherence and MRI. *Annals of the New York Academy of Sciences,* 821, 160 -175.

Teicher, M.H, Samson, J.A., Polcari, A. & McGreenery (June 2006). Sticks Stones and Hurtful Words: Relative Effects of Various Forms of Childhood Maltreatment, *American Journal Psychiatry,* 163:993-1000.

Terr, L. (1988). What happens to early memories of trauma? A study of twenty children under age five at the time of documented traumatic events. *Journal of the American Academy of Child and Adolescent Psychiatry,* 27, 96-104.

Terr, L. (1991). Childhood Traumas: An Outline and Overview. *American Journal of Psychiatry,* 148, 10 – 20.

Tinker, R. & Wilson, S. (1999). *Through the Eyes of a Child: EMDR with Children.* Norton. New York.

van der Hart, O., Nijenhuis E.R. & Steele K. (2006). *The Haunted self: structural dissociation and the treatment of chronic traumatization.* W.W Norton & Company Inc. New York. London.

van der Kolk, B. (May 2005). Developmental Trauma Disorder. In *Psychiatric Annals* 35:5.

van der Kolk, B. (1994). The Body Keeps the Score: Memory and the Evolving Psychobiology of Posttraumatic Stress, *Harward Review of Psychiatry* vol. 1, No. 5, pp: 253-265.

Wadwha, P. (1998). Prenatal stress and life-span development. In *An Encyclopedia of Mental Health*. Ed. Friedman, H.S. San Diego. CA. Academic Press.

Walker L.E. (1979). *The Battered Woman*. New York, NY; Harper & Row.

Verhoeven, J. S., De Cock, P., Lagae, L., & Sunaert, S. (2010). Neuroimaging of Autism. *Neuroradiology*, 52, 3-14.

Wizansky, B. (September 2006). Footsteps through the maze. *The Emdria Newsletter*, 6-11, 17.

Yehuda, R., Schmeidler, J., Giller, E.L., Siever, L.J., Binder-Brynes, K. (1998). Relationship Between Posttraumatic Stress Disorder Characteristics of Holocaust Survivors and Their Adult Offspring. *American Journal Psychiatry*; 155:841-843.

Yehuda, R., Bierer, L.,M. (2008). *Progress in Brain Research*, vol.167, E.R. de Kloet, M.S. Oitzl & E. Vermetten (Eds).

Yule, W. (1999) Post-traumatic stress disorders: Concepts and therapy. Chichester. John Wiley & Sons.

Zaghrout-Hodali, M., Alissa F., & Dodgson, P. W. (2008). Building resilience and dismantling fear: EMDR group protocol with children in an area of ongoing trauma. In *Journal of EMDR Practise & Research*, Vol. 2.

Zarowski M., Kotagal, S., and Kothare, S., V., Narcolepsy, in Kothare, S. V. & Kotagal, S. (2011) *Sleep in Childhood Neurological Disorders*, Demos Medical Publishing, New York.

Annex

Child Dissociative Checklist (CDC), version 3, Putnam, 1997
Adolescent Dissociative Experiences Scale (A-DES), version 2 from
https://secure.ce-credit.com/articles/102019/Session_2_Provided-Articles-1of2.pdf

The European Parliamentary Assembly (2004). Campagne pour lutter contre la violence domestique à l'encontre des femmes en Europe. The Parliamentary Assembly, Doc. 10273. Strasbourg, France.
http://website-pace.net/documents/19879/24569/200906_EGA_AT.pdf/dd356afb-50ab-4ac1-911e-a966d593ed0d

Flyers for Children, Adolescents and Parents: www.emdrkindenjeugd.nl

The Guidelines for the Evaluation of Dissociative Symptoms in Children and Adolescents, published by The International Society for the Study of Dissociation. In the Journal of Trauma and Dissociation (2004), 5,3.
http://www.isst-d.org/downloads/childguidelines – ISSTD-2003.pdf .

NCTSN, (2003). National Child Traumatic Stress Network,
www.nctsn.org

PTSD Semi-Structured Interview and Observation Record for Infants and Young Children. Department of Psychiatry and Neurology, Tulane University Health Sciences Center, New Orleans. Sheeringa, M.S., Zeanah, C.H. (1994).
Obtainable from Professor Sheeringa email: mscheer@tulane.edu

Children Revised Impact Events Scale, Depression Self Rating Scale for children and children Post Traumatic Cognition Inventory.
www.childrenandwar.org

Index

Lightning Source UK Ltd.
Milton Keynes UK
UKOW07f0337130115

244356UK00011B/104/P